George (I mean Rorich)

Hope you enjoy this! Thought
of you and can use it as proof
to your children that they didn't
wear leather helmets when
you played

John & Rob Mem

TURKEY DAY
GAME CENTENNIAL
1907 - 2007

SHAWN BUCHANAN GREENE

G. Bradley Publishing, Inc., St. Louis, Missouri • www.gbradleypublishing.com

HOW THE BOOK CAME TO BE

In the fall of 2006, the historical societies of Webster Groves and Kirkwood joined to sponsor the first annual "Adult Friendship Dance." That dance was the idea of Bob Feldmann of Webster Groves and was a blast!

In the second planning meeting for the 2007 Friendship Dance on January 24th, I was stressing the fact that this dance is sponsored by the historical societies and at each place setting there should be a booklet that describes the history of the game that is now in its Centennial year. The booklet should be substantial and it should be something the attendees will be pleased to receive and take home to read and treasure. Sarah Ernsky replied, "It could even be a coffee table book." That remark was like a diamond bullet. Of course it should be a book and what other year would be better than the Centennial year?

That started a round of inquiries to Wally Schramm and Jim Hall, both key figures in the production of the highly successful *Kirkwood: A Pictorial History*. This led us to Brad Baraks, the publisher of that book. I asked Brad but two questions; could he deliver a book like the *Kirkwood: A Pictorial History* by November and how does a book like this come together financially? Brad said that he could, but the numbers suggested that we needed some seed money.

Three individuals came together to provide the seed money, George Krieger, Charles Schneider and Michael Kearney. We formed the Turkey Day Game LLC to develope, market and preserve the history of this great tradition. George later dropped out due to time constraints, so now we are eight that are making this happen: Charles Schneider, Founder; Michael Kearney, Founder; Brad Baraks, publisher; Shawn Greene, principal author; Marilynne Bradley, artist for the cover; Mark Arnold, designer of the logo; Candice Gwin and Erin Schafers, marketing.

By Michael C. Kearney
Founder of Turkey Day Game, LLC
Kirkwood Alumnus 1956

DEDICATION

This book is dedicated to the memory of our Pioneer and Statesmen classmates, who, with an uparalleled spirit and sense of history, have created and continued the greatest football tradition in our country.

It is with overwhelming pride and a sense of honor that we are able to tell the greatest story of our two communities, thereby helping to insure that this history will never be forgotten. It is our fondest hope that this grand tradition continue for many generations to come.

PUBLICATION STAFF

Author........ Shawn Buchanan Greene

Turkey Day Game, LLC

   Founder .... Charles A. Schneider

   Founder .... Michael C. Kearney

Book Design .... Diane Kramer

Dust Jacket Artist .. Marilynne G. Bradley

Logo Design .... Mark Arnold

Photo Editor .... Michael Bruner

Dust Jacket Design ...... Michael Bruner

Publisher ..... G. Bradley Publishing, Inc.

ISBN 978-0-9774512-4-1
Printed in the U.S.A.

TABLE OF CONTENTS

Shawn Buchanan Greene
Principal Author
Webster Grove Sports Hall
of Fame Committee
Webster Alumnus 1987

Michael C. Kearney
Founder, Turkey Day
Game, LLC
President, Kirkwood
Historical Society
Kirkwood Alumnus 1956

Charles A. Schneider
Founder
Turkey Day Game, LLC
Webster Groves Sports Hall
of Fame Committee

Marilynne G. Bradley
Art Teacher
Webster High School
1969-1998

Jon Clark, Ed. D.
Principal
Webster High School

Alan Coggan
Kirkwood Alumnus 1956

Kenneth M. Coggeshall
Webster Alumnus 1911

Dale L. Collier
Head Coach
Kirkwood Football
1980-1993

Jerry Collins
Activities Director
Webster High School
Webster Groves Sports Hall
of Fame Committee

Patricia Corrigan
Reporter
St. Louis Post-Dispatch
Webster Alumna 1966

David Damerall, Ed. D.
Superintendent
Kirkwood School District

Gregory Filley
Member
Kirkwood Chain Gang
1973-Present

Photo
not
available
Commodore Flint
Webster Alumnus 1926

Lawrence P. Frost
Head Coach
Kirkwood Football
2003-Present

Charles D. Fuszner, D.M.D.
President
Kirkwood Football Alumni
Association
Kirkwood Alumnus 1973

Don Melvin Gaines
Webster Alumnus 1945

Harlan Gould
Kirkwood Alumnus 1920
Jane Pollard Gould
Kirkwood Alumna 1923

Robert G. J. Hoester
Kirkwood Alumnus 1942

Tom Holley
Kirkwood Alumnus 1965

J. David Holley
Principal
Kirkwood High School
Kirkwood Alumnus 1967

Mike Holley
Teacher
Kirkwood School District
Kirkwood Alumnus 1975

Sherwood Hughes
Kirkwood Alumnus 1937

Clifford W. Ice
Head Coach
Webster Football 1999-Present

David Lee Jones, Junior
Captain
Kirkwood Football 1948
Kirkwood Alumnus 1949

Cindy Jones Coombs
Captain
Kirkwood Cheerleaders 1973
Kirkwood Alumna 1974

Jack M. Jones
Head Coach
Webster Football 1965-1989

Lee M. Keefer
Webster Alumnus 1950

Henry Kuhlman
Assistant Coach
Arizona Cardinals
Webster Alumnus 1955

Brad Lechner
Producer CCIN Turkey Day
Game Broadcast
Kirkwood Alumnus 1990

John Lenich
Kirkwood Alumnus 1973

William T. Leonard
Captain
Kirkwood Football 1940
Kirkwood Alumnus 1941

Carole Lintzenich Buck

Audrey Lyoos Marti
Kirkwood Alumna 1950
& Dane Marti

 Kenneth W. Manwarring
Head Coach
Webster Football 1990-1998

 Greg Marecek
Founder
Webster Groves Sports
  Hall of Fame
Webster Alumnus 1967

 Nina Starbuck McArtor
Commercial Subjects Teacher
Webster High School 1935

 Eugene S. McArtor
Webster Alumnus 1958

 T. Allan McArtor
Webster Alumnus 1960

 John W. McArtor
Webster Alumnus 1961

 Ninalee McArtor Galleher
Webster Alumna 1966

 Franklin McCallie
Principal
Kirkwood High School 1979-
  2001

 Alvin Miller
Kirkwood Alumnus 1983

 Mark Moody
Principal
Webster High School
  1902-1904
Webster Alumnus 1893

 Murl R. Moore
Principal
Kirkwood High School 1947-
  1963

 Genry Moss Moellenhoff
Webster Alumna 1963

 William Woodson Moss
Webster Alumnus 1965

 Candice R. Moss
Webster Alumna 1967

 Kim Moss Kirsch
Webster Alumna 1971

 Kevin Murphy
Staff Columnist
Webster-Kirkwood Times

 Andre K. Nelson
Webster Alumnus 1980

 Tom Poshak
Director
Kirkwood High School

 Charles A. Roberts
Head Coach
Webster Football 1907-1931

 Susan Selbert Kain Burkett
Collections Manager
Kirkwood Historical Society
Webster Alumna 1958

 W. Scott Smith
Webster Freshman 1907

Photo
not
available

 Frances E. Spaulding
Webster Alumna 1911

 Penny Stein
Director, Coach
Kirkwood Pom-Pon 1972-1995

Photo
not
available
John W. Taussig
Kirkwood Alumnus 1903

 Harrison Trask
Kirkwood Alumnus 1956

Photo
not
available
Guy Edwin Trulock
Kirkwood Alumnus 1916

 Brent Underwood, Ed. D.
Superintendent
Webster School District

 Michael D. Wade
Assistant Principal
Kirkwood High School
Head Coach Kirkwood Football
  1994-2003

 Sally Winters McNeill
Webster Alumna 1971

 Dorothy Worley Frier
Webster Football Queen 1945
Webster Alumna 1946

Ever since I was a child I had always sworn that I would never miss a Thanksgiving in Webster Groves or Kirkwood and likewise the Turkey Day Game. Despite this sworn statement, I did miss Thanksgiving and the Turkey Day Game in 2002 while I was living in Nihon (Japan). Sure, living in a foreign country, half a world away, may seem like a good excuse for missing a high school football game, but this game is much more than a "high school game."

Living abroad is an eye opening experience and just as many residents in the Saint Louis metropolitan area take the Saint Louis Arch for granted, so do many residents of Webster Groves and Kirkwood take the Turkey Day Game for granted. I, along with many school officials, have been frequently asked since the declaration of the Centennial Game, what the facts are concerning the game and the rivalry. How long have teams existed for the schools? Was 1907 the first year that the two schools played against each other?

These questions and many more are answered in this first book ever written about the rivalry and the Turkey Day Game; however you must understand some basics before you begin reading. First, this book actually documents two events between the schools; the football rivalry and the Turkey Day Game. While many consider them the same, the reality is that they are two separate traditions which frequently intersect. Second, although the early teams that bore the schools' names had some players that were not students of the schools, this was the only way to find enough players for the teams and it was likewise the way that all teams at this time were organized. This statement is being made to dispel any notion that these were not high school teams. To further make the point, while faculty members and community members played on the teams, they were of ages that were sometimes the same or not that far removed from the high

school students, so it was not as though twenty-eight year old adults were pummeling sixteen-year old adolescents. Fourth, some early scores were not recorded on the Turkey Day Game record because the games were not actually held on Thanksgiving. It was not until 1916 that the first game not played on Thanksgiving was entered onto the record. Because some uproar is anticipated as to the changing of the long accepted record between the schools, which games were played on Thanksgiving and which games were not becomes particularly relevant. This book therefore considers a Turkey Day Game one in which the game was played on Thanksgiving, despite postponements. The book considers all other games to be a part of the record for the football rivalry.

As to my writing style, my brain processes English spelling as an Englishman. When I was at Webster Groves High School many papers were returned to me with red circled words with the note "British spelling – OK." It took me a while to understand that I was spelling my words with United Kingdom English, which at the time I did not even know that there was a difference between that and American English. Other than my old English teachers, no one else seemed to notice until the advent of word-processing software that detects and highlights such things. I consider authors a type of artist and I therefore have left my spellings unchanged to American English. In this regard, you will have to permit me my eccentricities. Likewise, I have always found it odd that Americans would reject British spelling but be the last nation in the world to hold to the old English Imperial form of measurement. I believe that especially now, the United States is quickly and subtly moving to the metric system and in order to help posterity, something that I learned while trying to read and understand documents written from 1930 and earlier, I have provided measurements in both Imperial and metric form. Again, you will have to permit me my eccentricities. Also, although my thinking is so clinical as to use the metric system, when I discuss decades in the book, I regard them as 0-9, as opposed to 1-10, as is chronologically correct. In a book, the 1960s is a more difficult decade to discuss if you are discussing the years 1961-1970, as opposed to 1960-1969. Mathematicians, please forgive me. Finally, records in all athletics are expressed as (wins-losses-ties), so that a record of (8-0-1) would mean that the team won eight games, lost none and tied one and a record of (8-1) would mean eight wins, one loss and no ties.

I apologize to all of you whose names or accomplishments did not make it into the book. There is so much to tell and so little room to do it. Although I secretly giggle when someone spends thirty minutes to an hour to tell me about the game that was played in a foot of snow (30 centimetres) or in freezing weather, that does not mean that each and every story is not a good one. Actually, it is the game that is played on a sunny day that is the exception to the rule, which makes including all of these types of stories impossible to do. Likewise, there are so many All-Conference, All-District, All-Metro and All-State players from both schools that it would take an entire book just to discuss them. Given the space, the best that could be done to document the rivalry has been done, with particular focus going towards the earliest years whose documentation is scattered in disintegrating old papers and on hard to read microfilm.

This book is being printed in a 500 limited edition that is numbered and embossed. All books are being printed on 100 pound gloss paper and the font is Garamond. Additionally, there were six Founders Editions released to those instrumental in the book's creation. Marilynne Bradley is responsible for the watercolour

that appears on the book cover and the logo was designed by Mark Arnold.

Without providing details as to what they did and in no particular order, I would like to thank Mike Kearney, Charles Schneider, Brad Lechner, Brad Baraks, Pat Voss, Sue Burkett, Heather Price, Brent Underwood, David Damerall, Jerry Collins, Flo Ryan, Dave Holley, Jon Clark, Mitch Eden, Cathy Vespereny, Ginger Fletcher, Candice Gwin, Erin Schafers, Mary Ann Schafer, Jack Jones, Dale Collier, Ken Manwarring, Mike Wade, Cliff Ice, Larry Frost, Chuck Fuszner, Dave Jones, George Buchanan, Scott Kemper, Bob Moody, Terry Coggan, Alan Coggan, Harrison Trask, Jack Frier, Dottie Worley Frier, Vic Miller, Marilynne Bradley, Mark Arnold, Grant Brady, Steve Woodard, Tom Holley, Phil Greene, Dean Hoag, Walt Smallwood, Bob Wagner, Andre Nelson, Joe Marting, John Buhl, Willy Winters, Sally Winters McNeill, Mike McNeill, Kevin Lemmie, Keith Jones, Lee Keafer, Cid Keane, Greg Marecek, John Reed, Carole Lintzenich Buck, Julie Fletcher, Mike Holley, James Bielefeldt, Molly Barrett, Sandy Dunkel Elfrink, Erv Dunkel, Sherwood Hughes, Gentry Moss Moellenhoff, Woody Moss, Candice Moss, Kim Moss Kirsch, Bill Lenich Junior, John Lenich, Audie Lyons Marti, Dane Marti, Nina Starbuck McArtor, Gene McArtor, Allan McArtor, John McArtor, Ninalee McArtor Galleher, Kelly Marler Francis, Bud Leonard, John Drexler, Matt Lechner, Hank Kuhlman, Charley James, Bob Krone, Alvin Miller, Randy Kriewall, Lisa Nordmann, Mark Moody, Commodore Flint, John Taussig, Scott Smith, Ken Coggeshall, Frances Spaulding, Guy Trulock, Murl Moore, James Hixon, Uncle Charley, Chikako Hori and my inspiration and forgotten hero of the game, Gang Greene. May this book serve as a testament to your greatness.

Sincerely,
Shaawn Buchanan Greene

This Thanksgiving represents an important milestone for Webster Groves High School, Kirkwood High School and their school communities. On November 22, 2007 we commemorate 100 years of the Turkey Day football competition, the oldest rivalry west of the Mississippi River. Here are two outstanding school districts – academic leaders recognized for excellence by the State of Missouri – that also exemplify the highest standards of sportsmanship.

Both school communities can take pride in this storied tradition, which has united our citizens and produced many, many treasured memories. That these two high schools have come together for 100 years to celebrate their rivalry demonstrates the tremendous spirit and pride that define our schools and cities. The Turkey Day football tradition reaches across generations, reflecting what is best about students, parents and residents of the Webster Groves and Kirkwood school districts. I am honored and delighted to be part of this wonderful tradition.

Go Statesmen!

Brent Underwood, Ed. D.
Superintendent
Webster Groves School District

Turkey Day week is an exciting time to be at Webster Groves High School. The friendly Turkey Day rivalry between WGHS and Kirkwood High School has become the pulse of these two close-knit school communities. For the past 100 years, students, staff, and the community have come together to make their mark in the rich history of the Turkey Day Game tradition. The tradition isn't so much about winning the game or beating Kirkwood; rather, it's all about bragging rights and bringing home the Frisco Bell. When asked what former students remember most about their years at WGHS, they'll always recall the Turkey Day Game and whether they brought home the Bell.

Over the past century, this rich tradition has continued to foster the school spirit and academic success at WGHS that is second to none. Turkey Day activities give students a sense of pride in their school and community, and the excitement each year leaves students motivated to excel in academics, extra-curricular activities, and in the area of community service.

I am honored that our students, staff, and school community experience such an event year after year. Without a doubt, the relationship that these two school communities have developed over the years is a result of a simple football game that is now revered across the entire nation.

Go Statesmen!

Jon Clark, Ed. D.
Principal
Webster Groves High School

There are many aspects of the Turkey Day Game that make it special to me, but the one that sticks out the most is the sense of community that is displayed among our current students, as well as our alumni and community, and even to our neighbors in Kirkwood. In today's society, the thought of a true friendly rivalry has become a myth. However, that is not the case here. It is truly an awesome sight to see so many people from our two communities come together and celebrate a tradition that has lasted for generations. The game and its history seem to have taken on a life of their own and that life is very healthy right now.

Looking forward to and preparing for the Turkey Day Game is something that has become a year round task. It is one of the most enjoyable, yet also most stressful parts of my job. Knowing that for so long so many people have worked so hard to develop and maintain such a strong positive tradition is something that I try to keep in mind whenever decisions are to be made about the game. It is my hope that the Turkey Day Game will continue to bond the Webster Groves and Kirkwood communities for many more generations.

Jerry Collins
Activities Director
Webster Groves High School

Thanksgiving Day in the Kirkwood and Webster Groves school districts is more than a time for family celebrations: it is a time for both communities to celebrate their history. They gather each Thanksgiving not just for the turkey, but also for the "Turkey Day" game, one of the oldest high school football rivalries in the country. The melding of football and Thanksgiving in these two Midwest communities is a tradition that dates back to 1907 and the first recorded football game between Kirkwood and Webster Groves high schools.

Since then the teams have played not only for their schools, but for their communities as well. Turkey Day has come to symbolize community spirit and pride through activities that involve students and residents. Students and alumni join in pep rallies and bonfires, local businesses participate in chili cook-off fundraisers, and hundreds of families and community members postpone their Thanksgiving turkey dinners to attend the annual Turkey Day Game.

Congratulations to the Kirkwood Pioneers and the Webster Groves Statesmen for providing 100 years of joy and celebration through a football game tradition that is an integral part of both communities.

David Damerall, Ed. D.
Superintendent
Kirkwood School District R-7

The annual Turkey Day football game between the Kirkwood High School Pioneers and the Webster Groves Statesmen is said to be bigger than life itself by some. I'm not sure if that is true, but I am sure that there aren't many events in a student's senior year at either high school that are more meaningful than Turkey Day.

For those of us who live in the Kirkwood and Webster Groves school districts, Turkey Day is more than a just a game. It is tradition. It is history. It is an exciting time for both schools and communities to come together and celebrate youth and the exhilaration of a friendly, yet intense football competition that dates back 100 years. The decorations, the pep rallies, the bonfires, the chili cook-offs and the friendship dance attended by students from both schools are a few of the events which help to bring our two communities together during the weeks and days leading to the Turkey Day Game.

Like many lifetime residents of Kirkwood and Webster Groves, the Turkey Day game has become part of our family's Thanksgiving celebration. Turkey Day victories for the Kirkwood Pioneers make for extremely joyous celebrations in our home. Unfortunately, we've had more than a few quiet Thanksgivings, too.

Kirkwood and Webster Groves are very special places to live. The friendly spirit of competition of Turkey Day only enhances what is unique to each community. Both communities take pride in their schools and both are great places for families and children. I look forward to welcoming Pioneer and Statesmen fans dressed in their appropriate school colors to Lyons Field in Kirkwood on Turkey Day 2007.
Go Pioneers!

Dave Holley, Ed. D.
Principal
Kirkwood High School

A TALE OF TWO RAILROAD CITIES

Although many separate details and people independently surround the creation of both of the communities of Webster Groves and Kirkwood, Missouri, they have regardless been bound fundamentally with the building of a railroad and the man tasked as its chief engineer. James Pugh Kirkwood was born in Edinburgh, Scotland on March 27, 1807 and later moved to New England, where he gained attention for his building of the Starrucca Viaduct, near Lanesboro, Pennsylvania, considered to be the largest stone viaduct at its time, and being the first and most expensive American bridge to employ the use of concrete.

In 1850, James Kirkwood came to the City of Saint Louis, Missouri as the chief engineer of the Pacific Railroad, who was made responsible for the construction of the railroad from Saint Louis to Pacific, Missouri. Just a year prior to his arrival, the Missouri legislature had granted a charter to the Pacific Railroad, responding to local and national proponents desiring national railroad expansion. Two individuals, Hiram W. Leffingwell and Richard S. Elliott, formed a real estate company with the purpose of forming the first planned community in Saint Louis County, which they planned to do along the new Pacific Railroad route. On October 20, 1851 an association was formed with 40 members who elected to call themselves The Kirkwood Association. In 1852, the association purchased 120 acres of land from Owen and Catherine Collins, 80 acres from Abram and Mary Mitchell and 40 acres from Thomas and Rachel Walsh for a total of $19,200. In February 1853, the Missouri legislature passed an "Act to Incorporate the Kirkwood Association," resulting in it becoming a city.

Along the train route from Saint Louis to Kirkwood, was an odd shaped area of woods, subdivided into areas of several different names. Several prominent residents living in the area, led by a man named Artemus Bullard, founded a school that would open a year later than the new Pacific Railroad route, only a few hundred metres from its path on Church Street, which is now named Gore Avenue. The school, Webster College for Boys, whose buildings are now occupied by Edgewood Children's Center, was named in honour of Daniel Webster, an American lawyer, United States Senator and Secretary of State of the United States by Artemus Bullard, who being originally from Massachusetts, greatly admired the well known statesman who had lived in the same state.

The area surrounding the college, therefore, became known as Webster Park, which along with several other neighbourhood areas, Webster, Old Orchard, Tuxedo Park and Selma, in 1896, incorporated as the City of Webster Groves in order to implement public services and to provide for one common city government. The name of the city was originally intended to be the City of Webster, but there was already a postal stop named Webster in the State of Missouri at that time, so the name of the City of Webster Groves was decided as an alternative, with the "Groves" portion of the name deriving from a grove of trees located in the area.

Daniel Webster

Artemus Bullard

James Kirkwood

Original Webster College

Hiram Leffingwell

Richard Elliot

Football that is played in America began as an incident started in 1823 in Rugby, England, during an interclass game of football. In the game, one of the players became frustrated by his lack of skill in kicking the ball and, picking it up, ran with it. Despite it being against the rules, the advantages of carrying the ball led to the adoption of this type of play at Rugby in 1841 and became known as Rugby football. In America, Rugby football began to use a system of lines and zones that resembled a gridiron. For this reason, the game in America and Canada later became known as gridiron football and in America and Canada was later shortened to the term "football," while the name that did not permit the use of hands became known as soccer, taken from the term "association football." In the United Kingdom and most other countries of the world, the name of Rugby and gridiron, or in many cases it is referred to as American football, apply to the games that utilize hands, where the original form of the game that does not utilize hands retains the name of football. Oddly, in English speaking former colonies of England, each country uses the term "football" for whichever version of the game is the most popular. For example, Canadians and Americans refer to gridiron football as football, and call association football soccer. Australians and New Zealanders also refer to association football as soccer. However, in Australia, both the games of Rugby football and a derivative game called Australian Rules football are played. In Australia, Australian Rules football is called football and the other two games are called Rugby and soccer.

The first football game in the United States was played in November, 1869, in which Rutgers defeated Princeton playing the game under the rules that did not involve the use of hands. In 1874, McGill University of Canada played Harvard University, the first half of the game being played under the original rules, and the second half played under the rules innovated in Rugby. The following year was a Rugby rule game between Yale and Harvard, which appealed greatly to the Yale players. As a result, an association of five colleges was formed in 1876 to play Rugby rule football. As time evolved with the game of football in America and Canada, before the beginning of each contest the players would agree upon which of the various rules known for play would be used, which is how the game of gridiron football evolved differently from that of Rugby Association Football.

The earliest known teams for Kirkwood and Webster Groves are 1894 and 1899, respectively for each school. The first news publication for Kirkwood High School was aptly named *High School Journal*, which was first printed in October, 1902. In the November, 1902 edition it reports under the heading "LOCAL NOTES" simply that "The high school has adopted red and blue as its colors." In the June edition of the same school year, it again reports in the "Society" section, "On the evening of June 5, Prof. and Mrs. Kinkead gave a reception to the senior and the junior classes and the Faculty of the Kirkwood Schools… The house was tastefully decorated in crimson and white, the newly adopted colors for the school." There are no stated reasons for the adoption of blue and red and later blue's replacement with white. The only conjectured reason for the change from blue to white is that the rivalry between the University of Missouri and the University of Kansas was as hot as the games would later be between Kirkwood and Webster and in the context of that relationship, what Missouri school would want to play wearing the colours of the villainous Kansas, especially since Webster already had nearer the colours of Missouri?

It is possible that nothing would be known about Webster's initial forays into the game of football, had three individuals who had played on Webster's first teams not written letters documenting their remembrances. The first two individuals, Mark Moody and Commodore Flint wrote letters to the Webster Groves High School's annuals in the 1920s, the *Echo*, and Scott Smith was interviewed in 1975 for a Webster Groves High School writing project which was published under the name *IN RETROSPECT: Webster Groves, Missouri*. Together, their letters give the greatest insight into not only who played on the teams and coached, but also who else in the area had teams, where the teams played and what the playing conditions were like.

According to Mark Moody, Webster football was inaugurated in 1903, with other forms of athletics among the boys. Although he states that this was the year that football was "inaugurated" at the school, he must have meant that the team became officially school sponsored, as a motion was made and seconded at a Webster School Board meeting on April 16, 1903; "…that the Dept. of Physical culture now ably conducted be rendered as prominent as possible and so extended as to include the High School." It can be inferred from this statement that "now ably conducted" means that sports were already being played on behalf of the school, which is further confirmed in a *Kirkwood High School Journal* article from fall, 1902, in which "M. Moody" is shown to have played right guard for a "Web-

ster" team and also that a "Webster" team played in 1899 against the Kirkwood Military Academy, according to its school journal. According to Moody's letter "there were not enough boys in the school to make a team, much less furnish substitutes, the actual number of high school students being not more than six, including the principal of the school who occasionally played as guard." The principal that he refers to as playing guard is a reference to himself. Mark Moody was the head teacher and principal of Webster High School from fall 1902 and left for the Saint Louis School District in fall, 1904. It should be known that it was because the team respected Mark Moody so much that Webster adopted the colours of orange and black. Moody was undoubtedly admired both as an administrator and player on the team and because of that admiration, when the players on the team were charged with deciding team colours, they voted to adopt orange and black in honour of Mark Moody's college alma mater, Princeton University.

Because of Mark Moody's letter, it is also known that the first recorded coach of the Webster football team in 1903 was Tom L. Gibson, of Rolla School of Mines, now University of Missouri-Rolla. Gibson was born October 20, 1882 in Webster Groves and had a brother on the team who played right tackle. Gibson may have commuted to Webster Groves from Rolla for the games and he is also known to have written a series of newspaper articles for the Webster News-Times that were later bound into a book, *Memories of Old Home Town*, in December, 1946 by the Webster Groves Chamber of Commerce, documenting some of the earliest history of the settlement and growth of the Webster Groves community. In one of those articles he cites having only coached for the Webster Groves football team for one year.

According to Commodore Flint, who graduated from Webster High School in 1906, in the years from 1903 to 1905, there was no County League in existence at that time, and the Central High School was the only high school in the City of Saint Louis. The Kirkwood, Webster Groves and Ferguson high schools were the only county high schools having teams, and the only other preparatory school teams in Saint Louis were those of Smith Academy and the Manual Training School. It was therefore customary for the Webster High School team to play games with independent teams or with almost anyone with whom they could get a game. The letter from Scott Smith gives additional details to these two letters, but adds a new piece of information in documenting the second known coach for the Webster team as Coach A. W. McCollough, who he states was also the athletic director for the school.

The first dedicated Webster Groves High School building was begun construction in 1906 and completed in 1907, with the previous "at home" Webster football games being played on the field that would soon be adjacent to the new high school that was being built. The athletic field at that time was not properly graded and was also not enclosed in any fashion. According to Commodore Flint, it was customary for the boys on the team to hire someone to cut the weeds in the fall, and then the prospective team members would rake the field, burn the weeds, buy the lumber, erect the goal posts and also buy their own uniforms. In effect, the members of the team carried all expenses of the team and were responsible for all field maintenance. For service on the team, players were not awarded sweaters, which would later become customary, but those who made the team were permitted to wear a "W," provided that they paid for it themselves.

Until 1905, at the national and collegiate level, play had become increasingly rough and dangerous, with 18 deaths occurring in that year alone, creating a popular demand for rule changes. President Teddy Roosevelt got involved and invited representatives of the big three schools, Harvard, Yale and Princeton, to the White House to convince them of the need for rule changes. As a result, the national Football Rules Committee was formed and acted with the creation of a set of rules that would allow for more action and scoring, while also achieving a greater degree of safety for the players. Of the changes, three were the most important; the introduction of the forward pass, the change from five yards to ten yards to achieve a first down and the banning of mass formations and group tackling. The formalization of the rules at the collegiate level caused some lesser formalization of the rules at the high school level, including at Webster and Kirkwood.

The next year in 1906, Eddie Cochems, the head coach of Saint Louis University, not only had his team throw the first forward pass in football on September 5, 1906, but he also innovated the pass by having players throw it in direct lines with rapid speed to the receivers. Although Cochems is considered to be the man who had innovated how a modern pass is thrown, at the time his innovation was not widely understood so that other teams who utilized the pass often did so by lobbing the ball to the intended recipients. Also, in the early years of use, the pass did have certain limitations from where it could be thrown, but it would later become legalized from anywhere behind the line of scrimmage on February 25, 1933. The first use of the pass for Webster or Kirkwood is documented in a newspaper article written in 1906 regarding the November 10 game between Kirkwood and the Smith Academy Scrubs, which notes; "The Smith second eleven defeated the Kirkwood High School yesterday afternoon by a score of 23 to 5. The feature of the game was the demonstration of the forward pass by the Smith players and their interference." As mentioned, Webster Groves High School was completed in 1907 and in the same year, the Centennial birthday of James Pugh Kirkwood would be celebrated and the oldest high school Thanksgiving Day football rivalry west of the Mississippi River would inaugurate.

1894 Kirkwood Football Row 1: Brian McGeary, Charles Harper, Harry Allen, Allen Maule, Leonard Wolff Row 2: George Lycett, Delaplaine, Frank White, John Morris, Burt Wolff, Arthur Brent, Arthur Kimball.

THE FIRST YEAR OF FOOTBALL AT WEBSTER HIGH

In 1903, Webster inaugurated football and other forms of athletics among the boys and little did we dream that it was the beginning of such a marvelous record as has since been made by Webster teams.

The football team would make our present athletes howl in scornful glee. There were not enough boys in the school to make a team, much less to furnish substitutes. I think there were not more than a half-dozen players who were members of the school, even including the principal of the school who filled in at guard. In agreement with the other county schools, we completed the teams with outsiders.

As I recall, we played two games with Ferguson High School, one game with Kirkwood High, one with Marion-Sims College second team, and one with Smith Academy second team. Marion-Sims beat us, but not the others.

At this time the present colors, Orange and Black, were formally adopted by Webster High.

By Mark Moody, Webster Alumnus 1893,
Webster High School Principal 1902-1904
An Excerpt of a Letter Written in 1926

1903 Webster
Photo taken in front of original Bristol School.
Row 1: Jake Suber, Fran Salisbury, Bob Thompson, Mark Moody, Harrison Clarkson Row 2: Unknown, Howard Ripley, Justin Kendrick, Tom Gibson, Unknown, Percey Wilcox, George Retenhouse (front), Jack Gibson (back), Leonard Martin, Morgan Coggeshell, Herbert Fidler, Charlie Anderson

THE 1902 WEBSTER AND K. H. S. GAME

On October 11th, the Webster and K. H. S. teams met in combat on the gridiron at Kirkwood. The game was called at 3 p. m. with a good attendance. A special array of Kirkwood girls were on hand, but nevertheless the Webster boys proved themselves the better team in the hard fought battle which ensued.

In the first half the ball was pushed backward until it was finally sent over the K. H. S. goal line. In the second half the ball had changed hands several times, but it was evident that the Websters were gaining. Although they had to squeeze to make their five yards, they usually did it. At last Coggeshall, behind a splendid interference, got out of the crowd and ran for a touch down. However, Webster failed to kick a goal. When the scrimmage began again the ball was held almost in the same place until within one minute of the end of the half, but luck was against us as was certainly shown when Coggeshall again got away for a touchdown. This goal was also missed, leaving a final score of 16 to 0 in favor of Webster.

By John W. Taussig
Kirkwood Alumnus 1903
Written for the High School Journal November 1902

FOOTBALL AT WEBSTER HIGH SCHOOL - TWENTY YEARS AGO

Although the picture reproduced in this issue of the "Echo" is of the football team for 1905, several of the boys in this group played on the high school team in the years, 1903 and 1904. There was no team made up strictly of high school students previous to the fall of 1903, although teams playing under the name of Webster Groves High were in existence possibly two years earlier than that time. These teams, however, permitted boys to play who were not students at the high school, simply because there were not enough boys in the school with the necessary physical qualifications to make up a strictly student team.

The County League was not in existence at this time, and the Central High School was the only high school in St. Louis. The Kirkwood High School and the Ferguson High School were the only county schools having teams at that time, and the only other preparatory school teams in St. Louis were those of the old Smith Academy and the Manual Training School. It was, therefore, customary to play games with independent teams or with almost anyone with whom one could get a game.

The greatest achievement of the team shown in the picture was to hold the Smith Academy team to a score of 6 to 0 in the fall of 1905, when they were the Preparatory School Champions of St. Louis and vicinity. Incidentally, this is the largest score by which this team was defeated in both the years 1904 and 1905.

All "at home" games were played on the present high school athletic field, which at that time was not improved as it is at present. The field was not properly graded, and also was not enclosed. It was customary for the boys on the team to hire someone to cut the weeds in the fall, and then the prospective team members would rake off the field, burn the weeds, buy the lumber, erect the goal posts and also buy their own uniforms. This accounts for the somewhat non-descript appearance of the team. In other words, the members of the team not only were not furnished with uniforms, but themselves carried all the expense of the football team, even including the football.

Such a thing as a dressing room or a shower bath was unheard of, and it was necessary for the players to don their uniforms at home before going to the field. There were no school buildings of any kind about the field, so that the team could not leave between halves. Visiting teams usually dressed in the tall weeds near Lockwood Avenue.

The players were not awarded any sweaters, but those who made the team were permitted to wear a "W," provided they paid for it themselves. As a matter of fact, the writer was on the football team three years, the track team two years, and the basketball team one year, and during all of that time was awarded one track shirt.

The basketball team mentioned above was the very first basketball team that ever represented Webster High School and was organized in the fall of 1905. The line-up of the football team as shown in the picture would be as follows: R.E., Buchanan; R.T., Gibson; R.G., Flint; C., Kaufman; L.G., Todd; L.T., Kraft; L.E., Merrill; Q.B., Shepardson; R.H.B., Skinner; L.H.B., Ludlow; F.B., Tudor. Of these boys only four are now residents of Webster Groves.

By Commodore Flint
Webster Alumnus 1906
Written for the 1925 Echo Yearbook

"I Tried to Duck Him..."

I had the privilege of helping break in the new Selma School. It had an athletic field in back of the school, but I can't recall it having any seats, just an athletic field. We didn't have a gym. We had a room in the basement where we'd go and put on our uniforms, and get ready for practice.

The game was played like it is now. We had four quarters of fifteen minutes, but it wasn't nearly as exciting as it is now. The people today get all buoyed up and get out there and, of course, Webster always did have a good team. In those days, the people just didn't get as excited about it as they do now. They enjoyed the football. We had a big crowd that day. It was different than it is today. To my recollection, we had only one team. We had reserves, but no offensive and defensive team. I was a freshman.

We had football gear, but they were not nearly as heavy as they are today. I don't know how, for the life of me, a person can break an arm or a shoulder in a game today with all that padding they've got on them. Our motto was, "Hit them hard and tell them nothing."

My recollection is that the cheerleaders were all male. It was before the girls really got active. My recollection is that we had the fellas [fellows] do the cheerleading. Now, they have the girls.

I had an accident in the first game which was between Webster and Kirkwood. I still have the mark. I caught the ball on the kickoff. Kirkwood had a big team and there I was, same size as I am now (5' 7") [172 centimetres] a little under that, but I caught the ball and I was a good runner. I started tearing down the field when I saw a man, who looked to me like a giant, one of the Kirkwood fellas, who weighed every bit of 225 pounds [102 kilograms], come charging at me. I tried to duck him. The ground was frozen hard and that fella hit me below the knees. Before I realized what had happened, my nose hit the hard frozen ground. See, it's broken. That's my mark of high school. They

took me in the place where we dressed for the game and knocked me out. When I came to, somebody was working over me. That was the last football game I played at Webster High, and I only played three minutes of that game.

Well, to be frank about it, my recollection is that Webster won the game, 6-0, I think it was. But I wouldn't make an affidavit to it, because it's been so far back.

There weren't any activities before or after the game; it was a cold-blooded game. We put on our clothes and left. Now, they have their big celebrations. Mr. McKellow [A. W. McCollough] was the man in charge of the team. I know it was a hard fought game, though.

Tension? They're bitter as they are today, on the field, before and during the game. I can tell you right now there'd be sarcastic remarks, things of that sort; several times there'd be a fight, but that spirit has always existed between Kirkwood and Webster.

The game was played on the field in back of Webster, the first time it was ever used. I still remember several of the fellas, but you get back to 1906, that's 69 years ago. That's a long time for a fella to keep that stuff in his mind: [Charlie] McArthur, Bonny Lewis, Harold Todd, Charelton Todd, that's about all the fellas I can remember now.

By W. Scott Smith
Webster High School Freshman 1906-1907
Written in 1975 for IN RETROSPECT: Webster Groves, Missouri

Laying of the cornerstone for
Webster High School, 1906.

KIRKWOOD HIGH WINS COUNTY CHAMPIONSHIP
DEFEAT WEBSTER BY 17-12 SCORE

Win Game by Uphill Playing –
Kirkwood Team Showed Excellent Organization.

Coming from behind and playing some uphill football all the way, Kirkwood High School won the county football championship from the Webster High team at the Stadium Saturday afternoon in the preliminary to the Washington-Milliken contest by a score of 17-12. Webster opened the game with a dash that carried all before them and earned a touchdown by fast playing. Smith kicked the goal. Shortly after, Kirkwood made its first score, but Simmons missed goal and Webster was ahead at the beginning of the second half.

Kirkwood kicked off to Webster and held them for two downs when Thielecke, the husky right tackle of the Webster team was sent around the end for a sixty-yard run, and Smith again kicked goal. It looked as if Webster had the game won and sewed up right then, but Kirkwood came back with a vengeance and pushed over their second touchdown and Simmons made the goal, but Webster was still ahead. In the final moments of play Kirkwood showed excellent organization and made a double-quick march all the way down the field until they scored the winning touchdown and Simmons kicked goal, leaving the count Kirkwood, 17; Webster, 12.

Lineup:

Kirkwood		Webster
Crutsinger	L. E	Lewis
Chamberlain	L. T.	Collins
Knowlton	L. G.	C. Heath
Jenness	C.	Todd
Dohr	R. G.	Duffy
Hawkins	R. T.	Thielecke (c.)
Clayton.	R. E.	Dewey
Hawkins.	Q. B.	Hitler
Sim[m]ons (c.)	L. H. B.	Smith
Mudd	F. B.	Cogsaw [Coggeshall]
Lowe	R. H. B.	F. Heath

Referee – Stone
Umpire – Krause
Touchdowns F. Heath, Sim[m]ons, Thielecke, Mudd, Lowe
Length of halves 25 minutes

The 1908 County Football Championship
By The Kirkwood Tablet
Printed Saturday, November 14, 1908

TURKEY DAY 1907

In the 1900s, the era of America's pioneer days began to fade as a new one came into existence. In 1900, a ragtime piano player named Scott Joplin moved to the City of Saint Louis and in three years time composed some of his best known works; *The Entertainer, Elite Syncopations, March Majestic* and *Ragtime Dance*. Also, in addition to riding on horses or in horse-drawn buggies, Americans were now driving a modern invention known as an automobile. By 1908, Henry Ford introduced his Ford Motor Company Model T to the public, which started the popular usage of the machine.

Unfortunately, no documents from 1907 have been found explaining the reasons and circumstances behind why the first Turkey Day Game was organized between Webster Groves and Kirkwood. In game programs, starting in the early 1950s, some articles began appearing that attempted to provide some background or narrative to the tradition but the best information comes from three sources; Kirkwood High School's first school publication, *High School Journal* and a similar publication by neighbouring school, Kirkwood Military Academy, named *The Bugler*. The final source is an old Kirkwood High School composition book, owned by Elizabeth G. Thomas. Within that composition book, Thomas had pasted many newspaper articles regarding Kirkwood and Webster's high school sports, clubs and other general news, in addition to keeping some hand-written notes.

The December, 1902 *High School Journal* has written, "The final game in Kirkwood was the High School-Athletic game on Thanksgiving afternoon. Several members of the regular team were prevented from playing by that fatal disease called 'Parental Objection' and other causes. Their places were taken by alumni of this school. The business men were composed of the Kirkwood boys who work in town together with some that go to the city schools. A big crowd finished their dinners in time to get out to the game." Kirkwood had three football teams at that time, one belonging to Kirkwood High School, a second named the Kirkwood Athletic Association and a third belonging to Kirkwood Military Academy. The Kirkwood High School and Kirkwood Military Academy teams were composed mostly of students, faculty and alumni of the respective schools, but there were probably no strict rules about who could join the teams or who might play in any particular game. As previously noted, a Webster team is mentioned in *The Bugler* as early as 1899 and this and other early teams, while representing the high school, were composed of any community members who knew how or had an interest in playing the game of football. The Kirkwood Athletic Association, as written in the *High School Journal*, was composed of other Kirkwood area players not associated with either Kirkwood

High School or Kirkwood Military Academy. According to the December 1902 *High School Journal* entry, it appears that the Turkey Day Game may have started as a contest between the high school and the Athletic Association teams. As time progressed, there emerged one team in Kirkwood, that being Kirkwood High School. Because the Athletic Association was a looser association of players, it probably dissolved by 1907, causing Kirkwood High School to find a new Turkey Day Game opponent. Webster was an ideal rival because Kirkwood and Webster were two of the three original high school teams playing football in Saint Louis County at the time and they were within close proximity to each other and therefore did not require a great deal of travel time to play the game. Also, as it related to the holiday of Thanksgiving, it corresponded roughly to what might be considered the end of the football season and it served as an opportunity for the two schools to determine which of the two was truly the best Saint Louis County team. It should also be noted that in the United States, other school rivals were playing similar year-end football matches on Thanksgiving. The first Webster-Kirkwood Turkey Day Game was played at the Kirkwood High School Athletic Field, which was located behind Kirkwood's first high school building, now the location of Nipher Middle School, at 700 South Kirkwood Road.

Remembering that in 1907 the automobile was still a new invention and striving towards mainstream use, travel in the Saint Louis area was therefore done mostly by horse and railcar, which made traveling in the area time-consuming affairs. Also, the rules regarding the game, although probably adhered to more at the collegiate level, were not so closely followed at the high school or club level of play. It is rumoured that at least one game at this time may have started at one or two o'clock in the afternoon and played continuously into the evening until both teams had tired of playing, with little regard being given to rules and, consequently, to penalties being assessed against players or teams. Scoring was also different at this time, a touchdown being awarded five points for crossing into the end zone and one point being awarded as an extra point for drop-kicking the ball through the uprights of the goal posts after a touchdown. It may be the case that the extra point kick had to be done from three yards back from where the ball actually crossed into the end zone, as done in Rugby football, making extra point kicks extremely difficult if the touchdown was not done near the front of the goal posts. Also, the extra point kicks were not held balls, but rather "drop-kicks," which was done by dropping the ball to the ground and kicking it as it bounced off of the turf on its first hop, through the goal posts, also a Rugby style of play.

Kirkwood Football 1907

In Elizabeth Thomas' composition book, she has hand written notes that indicate that there were three football games between Kirkwood and Webster in the fall of 1907. The first game was a County League game held on Saturday, October 5 at The Stadium, by which Kirkwood won 5-0. The Stadium was the earliest name for the stadium built for the 1904 Summer Olympics, later given to Washington University and now named Francis Field. The second game between the two schools that year was held on Monday, November 4 at the Webster High School Athletic Field, by which Kirkwood won the game 6 to 0. Finally, as would be appropriate, a third game was held between the two schools at Kirkwood on Thanksgiving, by which Kirkwood won again, 5 to 0.

Further evidence provided in an article written for Webster High School's first annual in 1911, *The Senior*, suggests that the first Turkey Day Game may have been organized as part of an annual series of contests between the two schools to win a cup purchased by both. The winner of three of five contests between the two schools in football, declamation, debate, essay and track would win possession of the cup for the next school year. Any school that won the cup for three years in a row would win the cup permanently. In 1907, the contest might have originated as the best of three football games.

In 1908, the teams played two games against each other, one for the County League Championship, the other being the Turkey Day Game. Kirkwood won the County League Championship against Webster 17-12 and again won the second Turkey Day Game, this year held at Webster, by the score of 5 to 0. In 1909, there was a game played between the two schools, but it was not

played on Thanksgiving. Instead, the County League had a series of games played at The Stadium, in which Kirkwood and Webster played on October 29 for what was labeled a "preliminary game." For many years there has been only mention of this game and its score was unknown, until Elizabeth Thomas' composition book was found and purchased by 1975 Kirkwood alumnus, Mike Holley. The inside cover of the notebook not only has a summary of the game, but the only known 1909 team photograph, proclaiming Webster Groves football the Champions of Saint Louis County with a 7-1 record and having defeated Kirkwood 23-0. Of note is that the manager of the team is listed as "Loberts," but is clearly a young Charley Roberts, who had been hired to teach mathematics.

Charles Arthur Roberts was born on November 13, 1880 in a small Missouri town named Revere. He graduated college from First District Normal School, which later changed names several times to various versions of Northeast Missouri State College and most recently in 1996, to Truman State University, where he received a degree in Pedagogy in 1904. Roberts was an able athlete and scholar belonging to his university's baseball and football teams, where he played the position of quarterback and was President and Treasurer of the Twentieth Century Debating Club. Roberts was quite a character on campus and on the field, as the 1904 First District Normal School *Echo* yearbook quips, "This is Roberts, our midget second baseman, who is noted for his generosity of language during the game and who continually loses his supporter and threatens to send a 'loss announcement' to chapel." In August of 1907, the Webster School Board, as part of an emergency measure, offered contracts to James T. Hixon, to be hired as the school principal and to C. A. Roberts to be a math teacher. Usually the teaching staff was hired the previous May, but because of unknown circumstances, the new principal that was hired resigned before the school year began. From 1907 to 1931, Charley Roberts, "Uncle Charley" to students and players, served as Webster's football, basketball and track coach, as well as athletic director and would obtain Webster's most storied and victorious record as a coach. In the early years of football at Webster, it is unknown how much supervision there was for the teams at a faculty level, but according to an article written regarding his death in the October 10, 1946 edition of *The Echo* newspaper; "In September, 1907, Coach became Webster's coaching staff, guiding the destinies of early football, basketball, baseball, and track teams, and occasionally playing on them himself."

ELIZABETH G. THOMAS

She probably sat in the front row, Miss Elizabeth G. Thomas, but don't hold that against her.

Though I taught for twenty years in the Kirkwood School District and therefore faced over 2,000 students, I never taught Miss Elizabeth G. Thomas. But I would have liked to have had her in class. I met Miss Thomas through eBay, and no, it's not what you think. I bid on and won her 1911 Kirkwood High School Composition Book.

Miss Elizabeth G. Thomas lived in Webster Groves and went to school from 1907 to 1911 or so, but it isn't clear where she went to high school. Although she lived in Webster, she owned and filled up a Kirkwood High School composition book that offers an interesting glimpse into her personal life and to the universal concerns of high school students.

Why do I think she sat in the front row? Her World History notes are meticulous and thorough, and her penmanship bespeaks a young woman quite concerned with neatness and order. Even 100 years later, it is clear that she was interested in "getting it all down." There are even insertions and marginal notes that indicated that she went back over her notes and corrected them as needed. I surely didn't see much of that from 1984 to 2004 when I taught. She also compiled numerous lists, including the entire junior class attending Kirkwood High in December 1908 – all 24 of them. She even noted those students who quit school before graduating, (including O. J. Mudd, Jr., perhaps of Mudd's Grove fame?)

But Miss Elizabeth G. Thomas was not simply a drudge. Miss Elizabeth G. Thomas was quite interested in sports, the arts, and dare I say, the young men of her time. It may be hard to believe, but she pasted a picture of the four-mile relay team over her class notes pertaining to 15th century Bohemia. Her 26 page notebook is divided roughly in half between curricular and extra-curricular items, which is about the right balance, in my opinion. Not only is her book filled with scraps from the local newspapers regarding track meets and football contests, but she duly reports the results from the debate and declamatory contests in 1909.

Finally, Miss Elizabeth G. Thomas had an eye for the absurd. Tucked unobtrusively into her notebook is an item from the local newspaper, with a headline that reads "Diploma Withheld From Loud Hosiery Crusader." It seems as though Kirkwood student Monroe Hoffman shocked the standards of decency at the time by not only smoking cigarettes on campus, but for wearing "loud hosiery." He was suspended, and the indignant senior boys threatened to strike if Mr. Hoffman was not allowed back. "A compromise was effected, however," reads the article, "and while the rest of the class received their diplomas last night, Hoffman will wait and receive his in September."

Thanks Miss Thomas, for a glimpse into the world of a high school student 100 years ago.

By Mike Holley
Kirkwood Alumnus 1975
Written June 4, 2007

1909 Webster Football (7-1) - Head Coach Charles A. Roberts
County League Champions
Row 1: Bill McCartney, Cy Merrell, Miller, Sam McCartney Row 2: Coach Charley
Roberts, Fred Heath, Lewis, Ken Coggeshall, Todd Row 3: Mackey, Jim Howze, Bill
Heath, Marshall Dewey, Grant Wyatt, Simmons

WEBSTER EARLIEST KNOWN SCHEDULE

WEDNESDAY, OCTOBER 11, 1899
Kirkwood Military Academy @ Kirkwood; 6-0 Win

SATURDAY, OCTOBER 12, 1901
Kirkwood @ Unknown; 22-0 Win

SATURDAY, 3 P.M., OCTOBER 11, 1902
Kirkwood @ Jack Sturdy's field; 16-0 Win

1903
Ferguson Win

1903
Ferguson Win

1903
Kirkwood @ cow pasture; 25-14 Win

1903
Marion-Sims College Seconds; Loss

1903
Smith Academy Win

1906
Kirkwood @ WHS Athletic Field; 6-0 Win

SATURDAY, OCTOBER 5, 1907
Kirkwood @ The Stadium; 0-5 Loss

MONDAY, NOVEMBER 4, 1907
Kirkwood @ WHS Athletic Field; 0-6 Loss

THURSDAY, NOVEMBER 28, 1907
Kirkwood @ KHS Athletic Field; 0-5 Loss

WEDNESDAY, OCTOBER 28, 1908
St. Louis Central Seconds; 6-5 Win

SATURDAY, NOVEMBER 7, 1908
Kirkwood @ The Stadium; 12-17 Loss

THURSDAY, NOVEMBER 26, 1908
Kirkwood @ WHS Athletic Field; 0-5 Loss

1909
Alton; Loss

SATURDAY, OCTOBER 30, 1909
Kirkwood @ The Stadium; 23-0 Win

SATURDAY, OCTOBER 16, 1909
St. Charles @ The Stadium; 13-3 Win

SATURDAY, OCTOBER 30, 1909
Kirkwood @ The Stadium; 23-0 Win

TUESDAY, OCTOBER 19, 1910
Soldan @ Francis Field; 0-26 Loss

THURSDAY, NOVEMBER 24, 1910
Kirkwood @ WHS Athletic Field; 13-10 Win

FRIDAY, NOVEMBER 29, 1911
Kirkwood @ Francis Field; 14-12 Win

SATURDAY, NOVEMBER 28, 1912
Smith Academy @ Francis Field; 0-67

1916
St. Charles 14-0; Win

1916
East St. Louis; 0-13 Loss

1916
St. Louis Central; 31-6 Win

1916
Ranken; 13-0 Win

1916
Washington University Freshmen; 6-0 Win

SATURDAY, NOVEMBER 3, 1916
Kirkwood; 6-0 Win

SATURDAY, NOVEMBER 17, 1916
McKinley; 14-7 Win

KIRKWOOD 1907 LINEUP

LE	W. Hart
LT	E. Hawken
LG	G. Heege
C	Richard Jenness
RG	E. Dohr
RT	L. Stanley
RE	Paul C. Simmons
	J. S. Wilson
QB	O. C. McCullough
LHB	Oscar J. Mudd, Jr.
RHB	Urban S. Mudd
FB	E. MacBeth

Substitutes: J. Schweizer, Fred Chamberlain, R. McDonnell

KIRKWOOD EARLIEST KNOWN SCHEDULE

SATURDAY, NOVEMBER 9, 1895
Kirkwood Military Academy @ Kirkwood Baseball Grounds; score unknown

WEDNESDAY, NOVEMBER 14, 1900
Kirkwood Military Academy @ Spring Park; 5-5 Tie

WEDNESDAY, OCTOBER 3, 1901
Kirkwood Military Academy @ KHS Athletic Field; 0-6 Loss

SATURDAY, OCTOBER 12, 1901
Webster @ Unknown; 0-22 Loss

THURSDAY, NOVEMBER 28, 1901
Kirkwood Athletic Association, @ KHS Athletic Field; 0-0 Tie

SATURDAY, 3 P.M., OCTOBER 11, 1902
Webster @ Jack Sturdy's field; 0-16 Loss

THURSDAY, NOVEMBER 27, 1902
Kirkwood Athletic Association @ Jack Sturdy's field; 5-0 Win

UNKNOWN, 1903
Webster @ cow pasture; 14-25 Loss

UNKNOWN, 1906
Webster @ WHS Athletic Field; 0-6 Loss

SATURDAY, NOVEMBER 10, 1906
Smith Academy Scrubs @ The Stadium; 5-23 Loss

SATURDAY, OCTOBER 5, 1907
Webster @ The Stadium; 5-0 Win

FRIDAY, OCTOBER 11, 1907
Keans @ Steel's Grove; 12-0 Win

MONDAY, NOVEMBER 4, 1907
Webster @ WHS Athletic Field; 6-0 Win

SATURDAY, NOVEMBER 9, 1907
St. Charles Military Academy @ SCMA Athletic Field; 41-0 Win

THURSDAY, NOVEMBER 28, 1907
Webster @ KHS Athletic Field; 5-0 Win

FRIDAY, SEPTEMBER 25, 1908
Yeatman @ KHS Athletic Field; 0-5 Loss

SATURDAY, OCTOBER 3, 1908
McKinley Seconds @ KHS Athletic Field; 0-15 Loss

SATURDAY, NOVEMBER 7, 1908
Webster @ The Stadium; 17-12 Win

THURSDAY, NOVEMBER 26, 1908
Webster @ WHS Athletic Field; 5-0 Win

SATURDAY, OCTOBER 30, 1909
Webster @ The Stadium; 0-23 Loss

THURSDAY, NOVEMBER 24, 1910
Webster @ WHS Athletic Field; 10-13 Loss

FRIDAY, NOVEMBER 29, 1911
Webster @ Francis Field; 12-14 Loss

As music transitioned to jazz and then blues, the pursuit and application of science gave way to the modern era. An amateur mathematician named Albert Einstein published his General Theory of Relativity during this decade, but by the decade's end the nations of the world would plunge into war as a result of European militarism.

The establishment of the first rules governing the game of football between Kirkwood and Webster would prove disastrous for Kirkwood in the next twenty years, as in all of that time they would only win one Turkey Day Game. This is not to say that the record became 21-3, because several games were not played or counted for different reasons during this time. Also in 1910, the Kirkwood Military Academy burned and a decision was made to not rebuild it, leaving Kirkwood High School as the last remaining football team in the City of Kirkwood.

During the period between 1910 and 1919, it has been reported that there were three Turkey Day Games that were not played. This statement is false for several reasons. The record overlooks a game played between the schools in 1911, which occurred a week later than Thanksgiving under similar circumstances of the 1909 game. Also, while in 1914 and 1918 no football games were played between the schools, the games that are counted for Thanksgiving in 1916 and 1919 were not actually held on Thanksgiving, the 1916 game being held on November 3 and the 1919 game actually being held the Friday before Thanksgiving. In all of the years recording the rivalry, there has been an issue as to whether you count all of the games played between the two schools or only those played on Thanksgiving Day. This issue is murkier in the early years because, in the example of 1911, there was only one game between the two schools, but it was held on Friday, November 29 as the County League Championship Game. Webster won the game 14-12, but because Thanksgiving Day was celebrated on November 23, the score and win were never counted as a Turkey Day Game victory. In future years, scores between the schools have counted if the game was postponed by one or two days and other games have counted, such as in 1919, when Kirkwood and Webster played the Friday before Thanksgiving so that Webster could play Maplewood on Thanksgiving for the County League Championship.

With the establishment of the formal rules for the game of football in 1910, came the solidifying of the County League, of which Webster Groves and Kirkwood were both members. The Saint Louis County League, which might have come into existence in 1906 or 1907, was on its way to becoming an influential organization in the State of Missouri. The League offered championship games in each of its sports and also had a year-end cup that was presented to the high school that accumulated the most points in athletics through its league play. The championship game in football often came down to an end of the year game, which may have frequently been held near or on Thanksgiving, between the County League's two strongest football teams. The winner of this contest was considered the County League Football Champion, won the County League Football Championship Cup and 20 points towards the year-end, more illustrious, County League Athletics Cup.

This decade's history of Kirkwood's football program are known because of the documentation taken by the Kirkwood Historical Society from Guy Edwin Trulock, who graduated from Kirkwood High School in 1916, and whose family had moved to the community in 1903. Fortunately, Trulock had saved a notebook that he had written, titled "My Diary 1914-1916." In it, Trulock recorded a great amount of detail of the Turkey Day Games of those years. In it he describes how a young eighth-grader named Maitland McKee joined the Kirkwood football team. "Mait, ...with his size and excellent football ability, had caught the eye of Coach Ashley who, incidentally, needed a fullback for his high school team. Whereupon Mait's educational processes were speeded up to a point where he suddenly found himself in the freshman class of 1913. It was wholly coincidental that he right away became the regular fullback." As it was previously mentioned, Kirkwood only won one football game in this decade and it was the magical year of 1913. Trulock tells a great tale of this game from the Kirkwood perspective, but there are always two sides to a tale and in this game Webster tells a different story. On the morning of the Turkey Day Game, in 1913, the star fullback for Webster Groves, while hitching his family's horse to a buggy, was shot in the arm by a careless hunter. Undeterred, this player still went to the Turkey Day Game and played with his arm bandaged and taped to his side. As though this misfortune was not enough, in the middle of the game the star halfback then broke his ankle. Whether Kirkwood could have won this game despite the horrible accidents befalling these players is a debate for the ages if asked amongst a group of Kirkwood and Webster alumni and it further illustrates how no side will concede that they were bettered in a Turkey Day Game when it comes to the issue of pride.

Guy Trulock also disclosed in his diary the reason for the Turkey Day Game cancellation of 1914. In that year Kirkwood won the County League Championship in a game against Ferguson High School. According to Trulock, "The two schools didn't play in 1914, some sort of argument. Kirkwood was unhappy. They had most of their veterans back and had polished off Fer-

THE BEGINNING OF THE MODERN ERA

guson 40-0 for the County Championship." George Alter, who also played on the team, was quoted as saying "We beat everybody we played that year. Webster Groves was afraid of us. At least they refused to play." If Alter's statement is true, then the 1914 Kirkwood team would be Kirkwood's first undefeated and untied team in the school's history. The next year in 1915, Kirkwood had lost many of its members from the 1913 and 1914 teams and subsequently lost that year's Turkey Day Game by the score of 19-6.

The year 1917 proved to be an incredible year for Webster Groves football and its prospects in the Turkey Day Game, due to Webster's first All-Star athlete, Allen George Lincoln. In this, his junior year of school, "Linc" and the Webster Groves team soundly defeated Kirkwood, to the tune of 76-0. Linc was noted for scoring 46 of the points single-handedly, which may have been the national high school single-game scoring record at that time and was confirmed to be the single-game scoring record that year. According to Lincoln's nephew, J. D. Nolan, Linc was such a dominating force in the game that the Kirkwood players on defense began chanting "Get Lincoln! Get Lincoln!" for motivation and the assault that he received in the game as the focus of the Kirkwood team caused him to have to be carried off of the field at the game's end due to his injuries, much to the dismay of his grandmother who was in attendance. Many newspapers during Linc's senior year of high school in 1918 proclaimed him to be the best high school athlete in a decade in the Saint Louis area. In football in 1917 and 1918, Linc was known to have scored more than half of his team's points in each of the games in which he played. His senior year, Linc also served as team captain of all top three sports, football, basketball and track. In track, Lincoln scored enough points on his own to have won many of the track tournaments in which his team competed. Again, in basketball, Lincoln was able to score half of his team's points for the entire season, although playing the position of center, which at that time was not considered the highest scoring position on the court, but doing so because there was no other adequate player on the team to play the position. Finally, while playing for the University of Missouri in the Turkey Day Game against the University of Kansas, Lincoln kicked a 49-yard field goal, also scoring all of his team's points, to win the game 9-7. In the words of Charley Roberts, "Lincoln was a team in himself."

In 1918, Lincoln's senior year, the final Turkey Day Game cancellation occurred in this decade of the series. One might as-

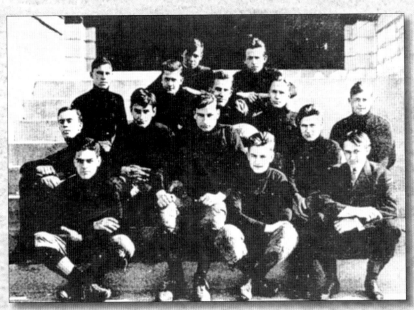

**1910 Webster Football
Head Coach Charles A. Roberts
County League Champions
Thursday, November 24, 3:00 p.m.
at WHS Athletic Field
Kirkwood 10 Webster 13**

Tudor, Chauncey Heath, Smith, Baker, Bryant, Sam McCartney, Grant Wyatt, Simmons, Cy Merrell, Spradling, Simmons, Clayton, Ken Coggeshall, Clayton, Jones, Dameron

sume that the cancellation occurred because of the sound thrashing that Kirkwood received in the previous year, but in fact it was due to the cancellation of school for several weeks during the latter half of the football season, and along with it the Turkey Day Game, due to an influenza scare that was a part of the great pandemic affecting Europe and America at the close of the Great War. Also, as a result of the war, another tragedy would beset Webster Groves High School. A beloved student, Richard Kopplin, would be killed in action on July 15, 1918. Because of this, the Webster Groves Senior class of 1919 would dedicate the *Echo* annual to him and also have the Webster Groves High School Athletic Field dedicated Kopplin Field.

In the Webster Groves 1919 *Echo* yearbook, the same year of the Turkey Day Game cancellation and Kopplin Field dedication, there is a cartoon depicting Webster Groves' football team as a tiger, stomping upon its prey. It is being mentioned here, because until 2006 there was much speculation that Webster Groves' selection of orange and black as its school colours had to do with it using the tiger as a mascot. No other yearbook or written reference is made regarding this thought, and it was not until the grandchildren of Mark Moody, Bob and David Moody, had come forward with the information, that the true reason for the adoption of these colours was known.

Kirkwood Football
Head Coach J. F. Engerson
Row 1: Deacon, Crutzinger, Conway Row 2: Sencheon, Oscar Doerr, Kraft, mascot Compton, Charley French, Bill Heidorn, George Alter, mngr. John Geppert Row 3: Don Ewing, Whitmore, Bates Compton, Enno ?, Donald Mabrey, Unknown

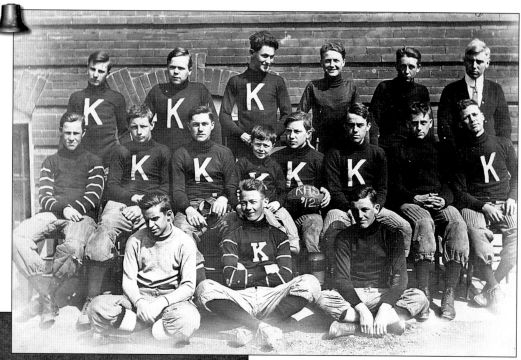

Webster Football
Head Coach Charles A. Roberts
County League Champions

The Turkey Day Game 1912

**1914 Kirkwood Football
Head Coach W. C. Ashley
County League Champions**
Row 1: Prentice Henderson, Unknown, Bud Hoester, Johnny Crutsinger, Unknown, Fred Good Row 2: Bob Dohr, Unknown, Unknown Row 3: Robert Runge, Maitland McKee, Unknown, Unknown, George Alter, Coach W. C. Ashley (Red Soengen is unknown in photo)

1914
— GAME CANCELLED —

**1914 Webster Football (3-4)
Head Coach: Charles A. Roberts**
Row 1: Hamann, Floreich, Booth, Gaines, Salveter, Edward Stevenson Row 2: Northrup Avis, Gibson, Alvah Clayton, Ridgeway, Roy Sheldon, Dick Kremer Row 3: Gibson, Beard, Edward Cushing, Ellis, Miller, Redfearn, Schall, Coach Roberts

**1915 Webster Football (6-1)
Head Coach Charles A. Roberts**
Row 1: Doddridge Gibbons, Kessler, Carl Stadelhofer, Salveter, Halman, Gaines, Kremer, Avis Row 2: Meyer, Becker, Haman, Richard Kopplin, Coach Charley Roberts, Schall, Fisher, Gibson, Irland Row 3: Aristotle Jannopoulo, Allen Lincoln, Horton, Buser, Mortinson

**Kirkwood Football
Head Coach: Ed Beumer**
Row 1: Stewart Vickers, Ray Kinsella, Granville Hawkins, Preuliss M. Henderson, George L. Edwards, Fred Kinyon, Walter Spinner Row 2: Coach Ed Beumer, Averill Huckins, Bud Hoester, Terry Hageman, Elmer Behrens, Oscar Klemme, Art Johnson, Harry Vance, Coach Frank Tillman

The 1916 Turkey Day Game

**Webster Football (5-2)
Head Coach: Charles A. Roberts
County League Champions**
Row 1: Coach Roberts, Salveter, Stuart Gaines, Frank Irland, A. Gaines, Bill Howze, Avis, Coach Duff Row 2: Richard Kopplin, Allen Lincoln, Aristotle Jannopoulo, Horton, Fischer, Henry Buser Row 3: Carl Stadlehofer, Spencer, Doddridge Gibson, James Haswell

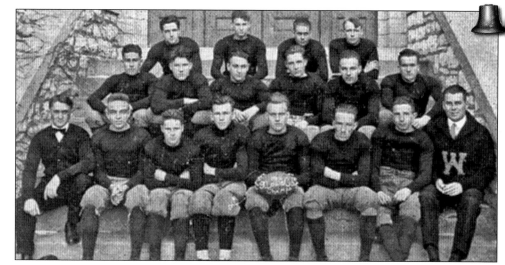

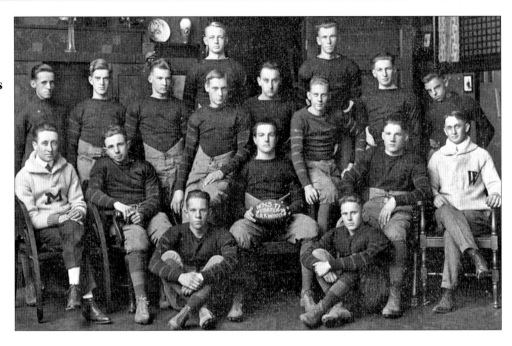

1917 Webster Football (5-2)
Head Coach: Charles A. Roberts
County League Champions
Stuart Gaines, Percy Phillips, Wright, Doddridge Gibson, Northrup Avis, Farrand Booth, Baughn, Robertson, Al Lincoln, E. Spencer, Frank Irland, James Haswell, Alvin Spencer, Jannoupoulo, Carl Stadelhofer, Alfred Cantwell, Chauncey Vaughn, Coach W. W. Browne, Coach Charley Roberts

Al Lincoln in the 1917 Turkey Day Game

The only documented Webster-tiger connection

1918
- GAME CANCELLED -

1918 Webster Football (3-1)
Head Coach: Charles A. Roberts
County League Champions
Allen G. Lincoln, Chauncey Vaughn, E. Spencer, Alfred Cantwell, Kenneth Gaines, J. Morris, P. Wright, R. Eckert, Sanford Avis, Allen McMath, Alfred Cantwell, Percy Phillips, Steve Thornton

A WORD FROM ... OUR COACH

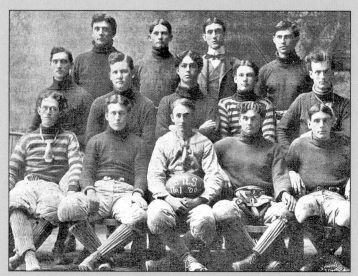

Normal Football 1900 (Roberts, holding the ball)

Normal 20th Century Debate 1901 (Roberts, first row, far left)

Normal Baseball 1904 (Roberts, holding the bat)

The object of all athletics is not so much that we win, but the enjoyment derived and the development of intellect and body into useful citizens. A well balanced mind is always in a healthy body. There may be a few exceptions, but the world is not ruled by weaklings. Take one glance at our Presidents, Governors, Senators, etc.

The condition of athletics in Webster High is far above that of the average High School. We are not hampered by any Athletic League or hostile School Board. This leaves Webster free to choose her opponents, which is the only way to have pure athletics. The good will that each boy has for the other (no favoritism being shown) is another excellent feature. All of these things bring excellent results.

In football we have lost the championship of St. Louis County but once since straight High School teams have been played. The track team has not been defeated for the highest honors of the county for seven years. The basketball and baseball teams have always been able to hold their own. The swimming team has had to go out of its class to even get any competition. Y. M. C. A.'s [Young Men's Christian Associations] and A. C.'s [Athletic Conferences] have been beaten with ease.

This success would be impossible if it were not for the interest shown by the Athletic Association, which gives the proper financial basis without which athletics would be a failure. Loyalty to your school should prompt you to join the Athletic Association. The idea that I won't join because I can't play should not exist. The very reason that you can't play should spur you to join the Association, and in this way help, since you can't in any other. If each boy in school were to look at it in this light, the number in the Athletic Association would be doubled and our financial standing much better.

By Charles A. Roberts
Webster Football Head Coach 1907-1931
Written for the 1911 The Senior *Yearbook*

1919 Kirkwood Football (5-2-1)
Head Coach Albert "Hap" Bernard
Row 1: Chester Sokowsk, Eddie Mack, Chester Brown, Deacon with mascot, Fletcher, Mutt Martin Row 2: George Signor, Billy Biggs, Raymond Brown, Julian Payne, Grunts Hawkins, Robert Hucksby, Ed White, Billy Groeschen Row 3: (also on the team: Bernard, C. Kentnor, C. Burdick, R. Runge, R. Kinsella, , C. Burdick, H. Newell

Webster
Football
1919

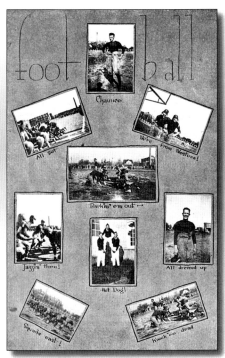

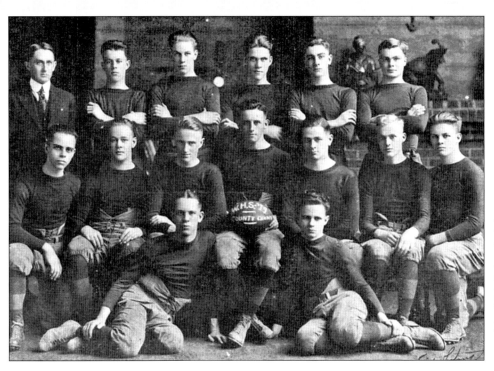

1919 Webster Football (8-1)
Head Coach Charles A. Roberts
County League Champions
Allen McMath, Sanford Avis, Alfred Cantwell, Chauncey Vaughn, Percy Phillips, Kenneth Gaines, Senne, Elam, Thornton, Woods, Fritz, Baldwin, F. Cantwell, Steve Thornton

Perhaps no interscholastic contest is looked forward to with such great interest as the Webster-Kirkwood football game. For that reason, therefore, this game will be described in detail. In order that the description may be more interesting, I shall tell it, not as seen from the grandstand, but as witnessed by one of the players.

"Ready, Webster? Ready, Kirkwood?" The Captains cast a final look behind them and nodded. The Referee's whistle sounded. Merrell, who kicked off for Webster, sent the ball in a long, low curve to the Kirkwood fullback, who dropped it, but before he could recover it, we had broken through the Kirkwood line and were about him. In an instant the ball was covered under a heap of bodies, which were still squirming when the Referee's whistle called a peremptory stop. Little by little the tangle loosened. At the bottom lay a defender of the Orange and Black and under him the ball. Thus started the greatest football game in the history of Webster High School.

From my position as fullback, I glanced over the two teams as they lined up. There was a great Kirkwood team, strong, heavy and confident of victory. In contrast to this was the much lighter Webster line, yet the very manner in which they crouched on the line of scrimmage showed their determination and grit. A few heavy line plunges brought us within five yards of the goal and our quarterback, "Cy," glanced over us as we prepared for our final struggle. Then began the signals 24-54-29-48. Our muscles grew tense as we watched the ball. Suddenly it was passed and Bryant and McCartny, followed by Heath on one of his famous tackle through tackle plays, crashed through the Red and White line. For a moment all was chaos, then, as I extracted myself from the struggling mass of humanity, I heard the cheers and shouts of the Webster rooters and knew it was a touchdown. It had only taken us three minutes to get it.

The second quarter witnessed many great tackles made by Smith and Heath. It was during this quarter that Kirkwood made her first touchdown. It was in the last few minutes of play when this accident happened. A Kirkwood player broke through our line, but was tackled as usual. The force of the blow, however, knocked the ball from his grasp, and Chamberlain, Kirkwood's star player, recovered it and made a touchdown.

We went into the game the second half with a "do or die" spirit. There was a great deal of open play this quarter, which gave Tudor and Wyatt a chance to show their ability at handling forward passes and punts. Here also came the greatest event of the game-"Cy" Merrell's drop-kick from the 30-yard line. It was the points thus gained that eventually won the game for us.

The last quarter proved to be the hardest struggle of the game as we were all almost exhausted. Spradling, however, continued to make his long distance gains, even though hindered somewhat by an injured leg. Simmons, through his accuracy and quickness, saved many a forward pass from the hands of the foe, while Baker, the foundation of our line prevented the heavy Kirkwood backs from breaking down our defense. It was in this quarter that Kirkwood made her second touchdown. Twice we heard them for "downs" and on the third down they crossed over the line for a fraction of a foot, but were soon pushed back by Webster. The Referee called it a touchdown on the argument that he had heard the man say "down" when he crossed the line, yet none of the players next to him heard him. Therefore, the question arises-could the Referee have heard him at the distance he was from the player and with the five hundred or more rooters cheering and shouting as they were? "Tell it to the Danes."

With this touchdown the game ended, giving us the victory. There were no "grandstand" plays during the game, as every one was playing for Webster and not for himself. While we were all bruised and scratched, yet there had been no serious injuries. Wyatt, who seemed to take delight in butting his head into every opponent, paid for it by a slight cut which put him out of the game for sometime. Clayton very ably filled the position of right half, while Simmons went to right end until Wyatt recovered. All who saw this game will no doubt agree that it was the greatest our team has ever played. Too much credit cannot be given to our Coach, who spent evening after evening in training us for the contest. Webster is indeed fortunate in securing the services of Mr. Roberts as Athletic Director.

By Kenneth M. Coggeshall
Webster Alumnus 1911
Written for the 1911 The Senior *Yearbook*

Ken Coggeshall

THE KIRKWOOD - WEBSTER CONTEST

The Kirkwood-Webster Contest is not one contest as the name implies, but a series in which Webster and Kirkwood High Schools match their strength in brain and brawn. They are without doubt the star events of the year in both schools. But why are they so important – do Kirkwood and Webster oppose each other for the mere love of strife? No indeed! The cause of this rivalry is a cup three terms in succession, it becomes a permanent trophy of the winner. So if Webster wins the contest for the next two years, as we expect her to do, the trophy will then be her's and Kirkwood in no manner can take it from her.

But why, you ask, do we expect Webster and not Kirkwood to gain this acquisition? Because, gentle reader, Webster has shown her superior strength by the work she did last year. The contest started with a football game, which the Webster team won, not by their strength and weight, but by cleverness and quick plays. Kirkwood howled with rage when beaten and swore vengeance on Webster – yea, even threatened to defeat her so badly in the rest of the contests that she would cry out for mercy. Next came the declamatory contest, in which Webster matched two girls, Joy Hutton and Helena Wolfram, against Kirkwood's two boys. The young men declaimed their pieces so dramatically that they were received with

Alfred Booth,
author of the
Webster Alma
Mater

Frances Spalding

gales of laughter instead of tempests of weeping, while the two girls' declamations were recited with so much pathos that tears gleamed even in the eyes of hard-hearted Kirkwood. Of course, it is unnecessary to say that Webster won. The essay contest, of which the subject was, "the Future of the Mississippi River," drew apace and passed, leaving the laurels to Webster's two writers, Kenneth Coggeshall and Alfred Booth. Then about a month later came the debate, in which Webster's team, Kenneth Larkey and Dorothy Cutter, argued so well that they quite convinced the judges that the question should be decided in their favor. And last, but not least, Kirkwood and Webster again met – this time to try their strength on the field. Kirkwood was desperate. She put forth her mightiest effort to win, but without avail, for Webster out did her at every turn and left the field victor. Full loath did Kirkwood give up the cup which she had held for two years and was so confident of keeping. But now Webster has the trophy, won by the score of 5-0, and hopes to keep it; when in later years the Seniors of '11 enter the old school house and peer into the trophy case, they will see a small cup reposing among numerous other ones and will point to it with pride and say the Class of 1911 helped to win it.

By Frances E. Spaulding
Webster Alumna 1911
Written for the 1911 The Senior *Yearbook*

. . . .

MY TIME IN KIRKWOOD

My time in Kirkwood begins in '01 when we lived next to our cousins, the George F. Brunners, out on, I think, West Madison Street. Memory is a bit dim for that era because I was sill on the bottle, Horlick's that is, although faded pictures of admiring relatives gazing at the newcomer are still extant. There followed a period in St. Louis with return to my grandparents' house at 426 S. Webster Ave. (Kirkwood Rd. - I never could figure out why they called it "Webster" Avenue in the first place) in 1908. That's when the action began, as far as I was concerned, and continued until 1916 when I was bundled off to the Park College Academy, following in the footsteps of Gordon Ricker and Smiley White. Fortunately for memory, while researching this memorabilia, I

ran across a notebook in faded handwriting inscribed "My Diary 1914-1916." The great events of that day seemed to be centered in high school athletics. So, that's where we will begin.

Football then, as I suppose now, was the big season of the year and the game with Webster was looked upon as a junior Armageddon. Thanksgiving Day 1913 was a day to remember as we eighth graders boarded the Kirkwood-Ferguson cars and, with red and white streamers floating from every window, took off for the neutral ground of the Washington University stadium.

Kirkwood seldom defeated Webster in those days but hope sprang annually. One stout basis for that hope in the fall of '13 was Maitland McKee who lived next door to Eddie Mack. Mait was a giant for his age. Eddie was my size, slightly below normal, physically, that is. They were an original Mutt and Jeff combination. Mait, however, with his size and excellent football ability, had caught the eye of Coach Ashley who, incidentally, needed a fullback for his high school team. Whereupon Mait's educational processes were speeded up to a point where he suddenly found himself in the freshman class of 1913. It was wholly coincidental that he right away became the regular fullback.

To get back to the morning of Thanksgiving Day, Webster scored early, as predicted, but failed to kick goal. The score stood 6-0 until well in the second quarter. Then Big Mait, the freshman fullback, took over. Over the goal he plunged but the kick was wide and the score at half-time read Webster 6 Kirkwood 6. But the Kirkwood rooters, who were both numerous and vocal, including two leather-lunged uncles of mine who had come along to work up a Thanksgiving dinner appetite, were beginning to feel that a "moral victory" was impending, even if KHS could tie mighty Webster, the durable county champions. This feeling grew stronger as the two teams struggled through the third quarter without a score. Then, came the great moment.

Midway through the final quarter Kirkwood had the ball on Webster's 45-yard line, three downs and no gain. With fourth down coming up a kick was in order. Back went halfback Donald Ewing, whose fine spiral punts had kept Webster deep in their own territory. But, what's this? Johnny Crutsinger, our great quarterback of those days, was kneeling. A prayer? No, Ewing was going to try a placekick from midfield. Ridiculous! The ball was snapped, Johnny held it. Ewing swung a might foot. The ball sailed true and far, fifty yards in the air, and right smack over the middle of the crossbar. Kirkwood led 9-6. What an uproar from the stands. But the game wasn't over. Webster received and rushed the ball to midfield. Less than two minutes to play and Webster was forced to kick. Back stepped Lacey their fullback and a drop kicker of note. (Drop kicks were legal in those days.) He kicked. The ball rose high and far and just missed goal posts by inches. Kirkwood had won. McKee's bulk and Ewing's foot had combined to make a Thanksgiving Day in more ways than one for Kirkwood High.

The two schools didn't play in 1914, some sort of argument. Kirkwood was unhappy. They had most of their veterans back and had polished off Ferguson 40-0 for the County Championship. Came the 1915 season and KHS hadn't done too well. Consequently, when Thanksgiving came around and the game with Webster had been restored, there was little prospect of thanks on the part of Kirkwood followers. Mait McKee had left town. Donald Ewing had graduated, likewise Johnny Crutsinger, Red Soengen was about the only veteran left from the 1913 champions. In McKee's place was Donald Alter, now a distinguished retired professor, but in those days a formidable muscleman who could, and did, pick up us freshmen, one in each hand, and toss us out the locker room if we became too pesty. Donald had played in the line, but when McKee went off to St. Paul, Coach Ashley brought him back to fullback.

Things happened fast in that game. An underdog and undersized (except Alter) but fired-up Kirkwood squad took the kick-off and in a few plays were on the Webster 12-yard line. The stands were jubilant. It had been thought that Kirkwood would be lucky to find eleven whole bodies to put on the field, let alone achieve a first down or two. But they reckoned without strongman Alter. Webster dug in to show those smart-alecs that the preliminaries were over. KHS would be made to pay for this unseemly exhibition of rashness. Howard Sprague called Don's number, fullback over tackle. Right at the heart of the big Webster line. I can still see Don, head down, legs pumping, both arms around the ball... Blam! You could almost hear the impact all over the stadium when he hit that line. Black and gold shirted bodies flew every which way. Don was over the goal standing up. The scoreboard read Kirkwood 6 Webster 0. Was another upset in the making?

The point after touchdown was missed and the score still stood 6-0 until well in the third quarter. But bulk and experience were beginning to tell. Webster went on to win 19-6, sackcloth and ashes. "Avenge that 19-6 defeat" is scrawled all over my diary for the month of November 1915, but the picture of fullback Alter blasting through the Webster line is still pleasant to recall after more than half a century. Ah, sweet memories of yesteryear.

By Guy Edwin Trulock
Kirkwood Alumnus 1916
Written for the Kirkwood Historical Society Review,
September 1968

THAT OLD GUARD WAS OUT OF LINE

Harlan: Let me tell you this, I started following Kirkwood High School football in 1913 and I saw Kirkwood beat Webster in 1913 by a field goal, drop kick I think it was... in 1913. The next time they won was in 1930... 17 years. I think I went to every one of those darn games.

Jane: We lost by one point over and over. We beat everybody in the county but Webster beat us.

Harlan: That was 17 years. I'll tell you how one of the games was won. The new high school was built and there was quite a valley, you know, where Nipher is now. They used to run the football field east and west and that meant on the west side you were down in a hole. We had Webster and we had six points ahead of them and the fourth quarter they were down in the valley and had to go 80 or 90 yards to get a touchdown, almost the end of the game, and the guy threw a pass, a short pass over the line, and a great big lumbering guy, who was playing guard, he grabs the ball, he was the biggest guy of the bunch, he grabs it and nobody paid much attention. He started running and they finally woke up that maybe the guy had the right to have that ball, illegal pass, and they start chasing him but he is too far along, so he made a touchdown and they got the point after. You know what happened? Old Coach Roberts said that was a designed play, that old guard was out of the line. He pulled back and the other guys got in the line, so there was the proper number in the line. It was a designed play and that touchdown, by Joe, they beat us 7 to 6. That was the worst game you ever saw. It was from 1913 to 1930 before they finally beat Webster. In 1932, they were County Champions. Kirkwood had good teams in those days, a guy named Malcolm Patrick and Jack Patterson were the stars of the big guys playing in the line. I saw most all the Kirkwood-Webster games. I missed only a couple since 1913 on. I liked them.

Jane: You attend most of the other games during the season too.

Harlan: I attend almost everything that is athletic. So far as my playing, I play a lot of sand lot football, but I didn't play any high school teams, except as a sand lot substitute. I would drop in to sub for them, but I didn't play a game of football. But, I did play basketball and we did play tennis and we won the County Tennis Championship. I was finalist and Betty and I won the tournament. My brother Spencer, he played five years in football and I believe he played five years in basketball. They thought they were ghouls. I got five years of them. He started playing while he was still in high school and he was good.

Jane: With the football, they stopped it. I think they have not played it for two years, once during the war and the other time the rivalry between them.

Harlan: Well, it got pretty hot and heavy back in the '20s. We had good teams that got licked all the time. The time this guy ran this 80 yards that was a guard, catches the football and catches a pass. When they got a little mad they used to have a fight afterward. We lived across the street at the time. We lived in what was known as the George Locket. There were three down there, George Lane, Albert Gallerton and George Locket. We were living across the street from George Locket at Idlewild and Kirkwood Road. That kinda irritated the people and I got so dern mad that they stopped playing and even changed the name of Webster Avenue to Kirkwood Road. Of course, Webster had been named after Daniel Webster. Webster Groves was called Webster to start with, but they had to call it Webster Groves, because there was another Webster in southwest Missouri. But, we got tired of the word Webster.

Jane: All because of the guard?

Harlan: That was very irritating. We had a good team that year. The kids were your high school group. George Edwards, most of them... they were a good team.

By Harlan Gould, Kirkwood Alumnus 1920
Jane Pollard Gould, Kirkwood Alumna 1923
Excerpt of a transcription by the Kirkwood Historical Society, June 5, 1989

WEBSTER DEFEATS KIRKWOOD, 6-0

On Saturday, November 3rd, our team defeated Kirkwood's in a hard fought game, 6 to 0. The teams were more evenly matched that the Websterites had been led to believe; and many of them were surprised to learn, before the game, that the Kirkwood supporters had no doubt but that their team would win.

At three o'clock over 500 people were in the stands of which somewhat more than 300 wore the Webster colours. Before 3:30 there were probably 750 persons watching the game. The game was called at 3:10. Webster took the east field and kicked off. In the first minute of play Kinyon of Kirkwood was injured and replaced by Hagerman. Kirkwood was forced to kick and Webster held the ball on her own 30 yard line. Lincoln gained 5 yards on an end run, but Webster failed to make her distance, and kicked.

The Red and White ran the ball back to Webster's 40 yard line, where Webster was penalized 10 yards. An attempted forward pass failed and Kirkwood tried a field goal. The kick was well placed and missed the goal by a very small margin. Indeed it was so close that everyone in the stands thought it was good and the Kirkwood rooters went wild for a few moments.

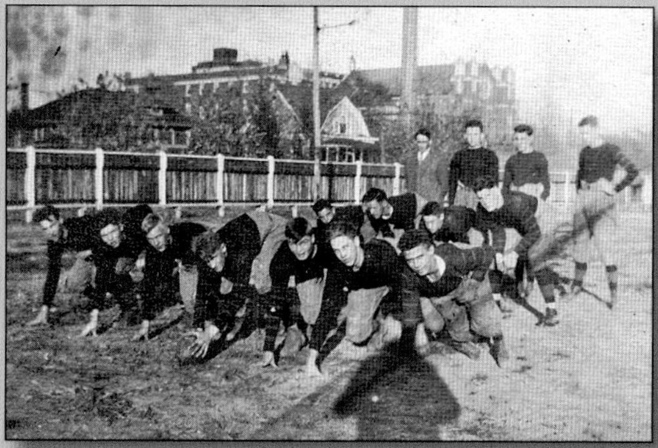

The 1916 Webster team posing at the WHS Athletic Field

The ball was brought out to the 20 yard line and Webster was forced to kick. Kirkwood got the ball in the middle of the field and tried a couple of line bucks without much success. A fake kick failed and the Orange and Black held the ball on their 40 yard line. From here Gaines made 10 yards by some good dodging. Here the first quarter ended. **Score, Webster 0, Kirkwood 0.**

The teams changed goals and Webster carried the ball some distance down the field. An end run gained 5 yards. Two line plunges added 5 yards. A forward pass succeeded and Webster gained 10 yards more. On an end run Henderson, one of Kirkwood's backs, was injured slightly, but continued the game. Kirkwood finally got possession of the ball on her 20 yard line.

Three line plunges gained a few yards. On the last one Irland received a bad cut over the eye, and was forced to leave the game. Fischer was substituted.

A beautiful forward pass gained 20 yards and an end run brought Kirkwood 10 more. Stadlehofer did some pretty tackling which stopped Kirkwood's rush down the field for a few moments. Then two more forward passes were tried and each gained 10 yards. Here Webster's line strengthened, as it always did when her goal was threatened and a couple of line plunges gained little or nothing, but the ball was rather close to Webster's goal when the whistle blew, ending the quarter. **Score, Webster 0, Kirkwood 0.**

The second half began at 4:04. Kirkwood kicked off. Webster was unable to gain and was forced to punt and Kirkwood held the ball on her 20 yard line. From here she carried the ball to the middle of the field when it was fumbled and "Punk" Howze, who lived up to his reputation and played a wonderful game, broke through and carried the ball 30 yards before he was forced out of bounds. Kirkwood suffered a 15 yard penalty for tackling him out of bounds and the ball was taken almost under the Kirkwood goal. From here Lincoln carried the ball across. Avis failed to kick goal.

Webster kicked off. Kirkwood, after several ineffectual attempts to gain, was forced to kick. The kick was a poor one and Webster got the ball on Kirkwood's 35 yard line. A forward pass was blocked and the ball became Kirkwood's on downs. Two plunges were stopped by Howze and Kirkwood kicked. Avis got the ball on the 20 yard line. The third quarter ended here. **Webster 6, Kirkwood 0.**

Webster carried the ball as far as her 40 yard line, where it was lost on downs Kirkwood drove the ball back to the 15 yard line, a forward pass was attempted, which, had it been successful, would have given Kirkwood a goal. But the Kirkwood back was forced to throw high and the ball passed over their left-end's head, when he was already behind Webster's goal line.

Webster was given the ball on her 20 yard line and carried it to the middle of the field, where it was lost on downs. Kirkwood brought it within 20 yards of our goal, where our team got possession of it again. It was carried to the middle of the field and stayed there until the game ended. **Final Score Webster 6, Kirkwood 0.**

The High School Echo
Webster Groves, MO
Thursday, November 22, 1916

ALLEN LINCOLN
WEBSTER'S ALL-EVERYTHING

Thousands have played the game over a hundred years and every game produces a star, but on the Webster side Allen Lincoln still stands out as our greatest athlete.

Allen was a bigger kid than his classmates when he entered Webster High in the fall of 1915, eventually exceeding 6 feet [183 centimetres] and 200 pounds [90 kilograms], an impressive size for those times. Webster was at the start of its glory years when it seemed that the Orange & Black won everything. But even in the face of this competitive field he would become, in the opinion of legendary coach and Athletic Director, Charles Roberts, our greatest athlete. So impressed by this athlete, Coach Roberts would regale his students with Lincoln tales 30 years after the fact, according to Dottie (Worley) Frier '46.

Coach Roberts' opinion was based on facts. In the historic 1917 game, Lincoln ran the ball, threw it and kicked it racking up nearly 400 yards, six touchdowns and making good on 10 of 11 extra-point kicks, earning 46 of the 76 points scored in the shutout of Kirkwood. Although there are no records from this era to confirm it, it was thought to be the highest amount of points scored by a single player in one game. Lincoln had big touchdown runs of 80 and 45 yards. In a time when passing was still in its infancy, he went airborne for 160 yards and when Kirkwood had the ball, he played defense.

Other sports came just as easily as football. He was the starting center on the basketball team, often scoring more points than the other team combined and accounting for half of the Statesmen points for the season. Coach Roberts was fond of telling the press that "Lincoln was a team by himself."

At track meets he medaled in the 100 yard [91.5 metres] and 220 yard [201 metres] sprints and then would medal in the javelin, shot-put, discus and broad-jump, usually for meet records. In the spring of 1917, Coach Roberts took Lincoln and four other Statesmen to Columbia where they captured Webster's second Track and Field Championship and repeated it again for their third in 1918.

But our All-Everything was more than a great athlete. He was liked by his classmates who called him "Linc," he founded the W Club that awarded varsity letters, was a student leader and a writer of poetry.

After being recruited by a number of universities he entered Mizzou in the fall of 1919, quickly becoming the freshman football team's captain. Usually playing halfback, he took over as quarterback his junior year to upset arch rival Kansas and win honorable mention as All-American that year. Later he followed in the footsteps of his friend Coach Roberts in becoming a college coach, most notably at the University of the South, in Suwannee, Tennessee.

Ninety years after he last played for the Statesmen, old alums from both Kirkwood and Webster Groves talk with awe of the inherited memories of Allen Lincoln, our greatest athlete… our All-Everything.

By Charles A. Schneider
Webster Alumnus 1967
Written August 1, 2007

LINCOLN STARS AS WEBSTER CRUSHES KIRKWOOD 76 TO 0

Husky 17-Year-Old Player Scores 46 Points in County Championship Football Struggle at Francis Field.
SCORES TOUCHDOWN AFTER 80-YARD DASH
Receiving Ball on Kickoff, in Third Period, 186-Pound Youth Stiff-Arms His Way Through Entire Team.

One big high school boy, 17-year-old Allen Lincoln, changed what might have been a tooth–and-nail battle for the St. Louis County Scholastic football championship into a cataclysmic rout, at Francis Field, yesterday afternoon. It was the unusual ability of this youth that enabled Webster High School to decisively retain its county supremacy by mercilessly trouncing the plucky players of Kirkwood High School, 76 to 0.

It would certainly be an injustice to state that some 15 youths who at times aided Lincoln during the contest were negligible factors in the victory, inasmuch as several showed unusual gridiron precocity. But besides the material havoc wrought by this 186-pound super-youth, which is in figures represented by 46 points, it was he who broke the Kirkwood morale and disheartened the defeated team in its efforts.

Allen Lincoln was placed in the quarter-back position in the lineup. But this was only to add the calling of signals to his duties. He ran from fullback position, kicked and passed from fullback position, formed in the interference, and was the effulgent member of the secondary defense. He was the center of Webster's entire attack and the moving spirit in the defense. He acted like a varsity man in a "prep" school game. Some might say that it was due to his teammates' clever interference, that Lincoln gained. This is untrue, because he ran ahead of his interference, and advanced by mean of his own brawn and sprinting ability.

Lincoln Kicked 10 Goals.

Here is what he did: He scored six touchdowns and kicked 10 out of 11 goals from touchdown. The one that he missed, his first attempt, struck one of the side posts. Included in his invasions of Kirkwood's sacred precincts was one 80-yard ramble from his 20-yard mark through the entire Kirkwood team, after he had caught the initial kick of the second half. That gallop down the gridiron was worth going a distance to see. He stiff-armed away the two Kirkwood ends who were down on his end with the wind, he dodged two more of the fleeter opponents, and then ran into a whole assembly of the enemy, but pounded over or through the mass like a "tank" through the Hindenburg line.

Late in the game he caught a punt on the alien 45-yard line, while on the run, and tore around the left wing of the opposition for the entire distance and a touchdown. The final Webster score of the day came when he brushed off left tackle and then cut in through end for the 20 yards which separated him from the goal line. It is useless to mention his frequent gallops in the midfield, as almost every Webster score was directly due to one of these runs.

Webster Uses Forward Pass.

Outside of Lincoln's prowess, Webster also had several other means for carrying on a successful offensive. The forward pass was exploited efficiently on 11 occasions and netted about 160 yards of Kirkwood territory. The passes were successful generally through the able co-operation of Halfback Wright, who was acquired the knack of grabbing Lincoln tosses while in almost any position.

Then the vigilance of left tackle Irland was asserted on several occasions, when this youth took advantage of Kirkwood errors by rushing through the barrier, picking up the bounding pigskin and rushing for touchdowns in true Sammy White fashion. Irland's first success resulted in Webster's second score in the second period. Kirkwood was sponsoring an offense on its 42-yard line. A pass from the center went wild and rolled back to the Crimson's 27-yard line, whence Irland tore through like a panther, snatched the ball, and was behind the goal post before Kirkwood had fairly given pursuit.

On another occasion, Webster had missed an attempted placement kick and Kirkwood played from its 20-yard line. After three line buck failures, a punt was attempted, but Stadelhofer broke through and blocked the ball. Again Irland was behind the Kirkwood line, picked up the ball, and raced for a touchdown.

Kirkwood Strong at Start.

The first period of the game was as close and as sparkling as could be hoped for in a high school contest. The Kirkwood chaps, outweighed, as they were, put up a plucky scrap and turned away two threatened attacks on their goal-line. Webster could not score in this period.

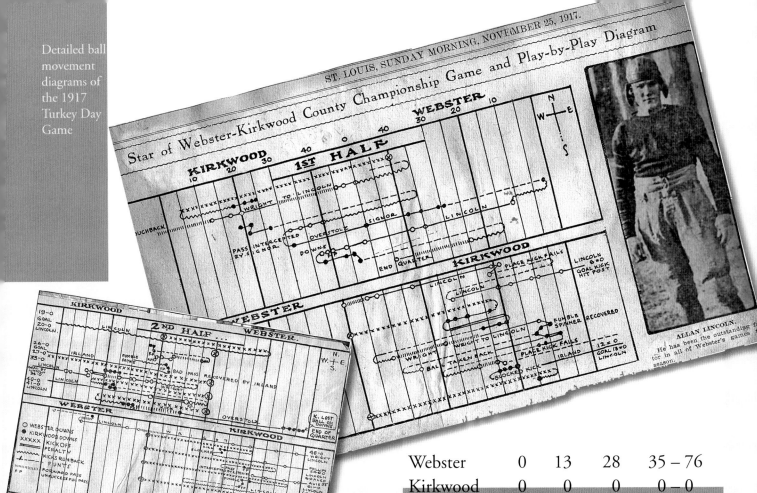

Detailed ball movement diagrams of the 1917 Turkey Day Game

ST. LOUIS, SUNDAY MORNING, NOVEMBER 25, 1917.

Star of Webster-Kirkwood County Championship Game and Play-by-Play Diagram

ALLAN LINCOLN.
He has been the outstanding factor in all of Webster's games this season.

Webster	0	13	28	35 – 76
Kirkwood	0	0	0	0 – 0

LINEUP

WEBSTER		KIRKWOOD
E. Spencer	Left end	Dice
Irland	Left tackle	Vance (c)
Haswell	Left guard	Spinner
A. Spencer	Center	Kenyon
Jannopoulo	Right guard	Keck
Stadelhofer (c)	Right tackle	Newell
Gaines	Right end	Huckins
Lincoln	Quarterback	Lackey
Phillips	Left halfback	Payne
Wright	Right halfback	Signor
Gibson	Fullback	Overstoltz

REFEREE: Krause. Washington.

UMPIRE: McClung. Occidental.

HEAD LINESMAN: Pratt. Alabama.

WEBSTER SUBSTITUTES: Booth for Gibson, Gibson for Booth, Avis for Gibson, Vaughn for Phillips, Robertson for Irland. Kirkwood substitutions – Mock for Keck, Gros-chan for Signor, Johnson for Kenyon, Van Dam for Dice.

WEBSTER SCORING: Touchdowns – Lincoln (6), Irland (2), Wright, Phillips, Avis, Goals after touchdown Lincoln (10).

For a time even Kirkwood outplayed the ultimate victors. Overstoltz and Signor, without interference, rushed through the wide holes that had been opened by the line and made telling gains, advancing the ball 40 yards on its most decisive march. Not until the ball was in its own territory could Webster hold. But with that stiffening of defense, Webster took over the aggressive and held it throughout the remainder of the contest, except on one occasion.

Late in the third period, Kirkwood carried the offense into the gold and black's territory for a nonce: but was held when only a few yards from the promised land. The advance was mainly due to a prettily executed 18-yard forward pass and a 40-yard broken field run by Overstoltz. Only six yards were gained in the four succeeding downs, and the ball was turned over to Webster.

Kirkwood used the direct pass system throughout the game, with the box formation of backs. This is generally considered a sound system, when the line holds long enough to give the backs time to form some sort of defense, but in this case the Kirkwood line did not have that required strength.

By St. Louis, Sunday Morning, Printed November 25, 1917

THE WEBSTER HIGH SCHOOL ATHLETIC FIELD AND KOPPLIN FIELD

At the turn of the century, Webster school leaders recognized the need for a separate high school building, apart from the one that their current two-year high school occupied with its other grades at the Bristol building located on Gray Avenue. The location that they found was the newly plated Webster Place subdivision owned by the Webster family on Selma Avenue. The cornerstone for the new high school was laid in 1906, the building being completed in 1907.

The developer for Webster Place selected the Pilgrim's settlement at Plymouth, Massachusetts, for the subdivision theme, subsequently naming the bordering streets Plymouth, Bradford, Samoset and Standish. The original Webster High School faced Bradford Street, with the athletic field just behind it facing North and South.

The first playing field for the high school was simply named "Webster High School Athletic Field." Before and during the construction of the high school, the field was used by the Webster football team, with the players paying for the cost of the field maintenance and equipment. Later, after the construction of the high school, the field became enclosed, stands were erected and spectators entered through a Hellenic columned entrance. An odd part of the stadium's design is that it was built behind the high school, facing in an East-West direction, where most fields face North-South, so that the sun does not favor one team over another.

In 1919, after 1917 Webster alumnus Richard Kopplin was killed in action in the Gerardmer sector of Alsace, France, the senior class of Webster High School had the field dedicated "Kopplin Field." From its dedication in 1918 until construction started on Roberts Gymnasium in 1946, the football field behind Webster High School bore Kopplin's name.

During its use as a football field, it was continually written and said that the grass on the field was sparse; causing it on hot days to be baked hard or on wet days resulted in games being played in "ankle deep mud." Opposing teams loathed playing on the field in these conditions as the 1927 Clayton High School yearbook, the *CLA-MO* notes, "The Webster game was postponed as is the annual custom and then was played in a sea of mud as per usual."

Today, Kopplin Field has been divided for use in three parts; a baseball field, a parking lot and a portion of Roberts Gymnasium. During the time that Roberts Gymnasium was being built, Webster home games were played at Maplewood High School, with the exception that the 1946 Turkey Day Game was held at Kirkwood. Today, there still stands a stone monument with a plaque honouring Richard Kopplin at what was the southeast corner of the field, near the corner of Big Bend Boulevard and East Bradford Avenue.

By Charles A. Schneider
Webster Alumnus 1967
Written August 9, 2007

Webster High School and
Kopplin Field in 1925

Kopplin Field's columned
gates are seen to the right
of The Armory

RICHARD C. KOPPLIN, JR.

EBSTER ALUMNUS 1917,
NITED STATES 138TH INFANTRY
LLED IN ACTION, JULY 15, 1918

Richard was born in 1899, growing up on Ridge Avenue in the Selma neighborhood that had recently been annexed by the new City of Webster Groves. After attending the Selma School, which later became Goodall Elementary, he went to the still new Webster High School where he earned a starting backfield position on Coach Roberts' team. There, he shared ball-carrying duties with an up-and-coming underclassman by the name of Allen Lincoln. In the 1916 team photograph, they are seated together.

Richard embodied the character of the times. He was known to his fellow students for his modesty, gravity and excellent behavior. He was a regular attendant of Emmanuel Episcopal Church and Sunday school, even making a point to attend services while he was stationed with the Missouri National Guard, 35th Division, in St. Louis.

At one time when he was stationed nearby, the mother of another Webster boy in his division expressed some anxiety as to the welfare of her son, as the camp was situated near "a very evil neighborhood" and the mother feared that her son would be corrupted. Upon hearing her say this, a person who knew both boys responded "there is no danger; he bunks with Richard Kopplin."

Maybe it was natural for him to be like this, since he came from good stock. Richard's mother was a leader in her church and a pillar of the Monday Club, on South Maple, that operated the public library for the community. During the war, Mrs. Kopplin was a leader of the Monday Club project to knit socks for the soldiers serving overseas.

When the soldiers of the 138th Regiment were being transferred from their base in Oklahoma to Long Island, New York, for transport to France in the spring of 1918, the troop trains came along the old Frisco line, passing the old South Webster station on Selma Avenue. Somehow, the word got out that the boys were coming through Webster Groves and many of his classmates joined Richard's mom to show their support for the 18 year-old Statesmen as he went off to "make the world safe for democracy."

Richard Kopplin lost his life fighting at the front in the Gerardmer Sector of Alsace, France, being almost the only man from Webster High School who was killed in action. Years later, *The Echo* newspaper wrote of his heroic life and death and how he should be an inspiration to all of them. They were proud to claim him as a classmate and especially so to name the athletic field that he played on as a fitting memorial to his memory. *The Echo* challenged a new generation of students to retain the memory of Richard Kopplin in their hearts and minds forever as a life inspiration.

Ninety-one years after Richard Kopplin last ran the ball in a Turkey Day Game, we honor his memory along with the many other players of the game who later served their community and nation.

By Charles A. Schneider
Webster Alumnus 1967
Written August 9, 2007

THE 1920S ....

The "Roaring Twenties" definitely roared in Webster Groves and Kirkwood. With the passing of the Volstead Act, the United States became "dry." In Saint Louis, Anheuser-Busch Brewery began selling beverages without alcohol, while people across the country inebriated themselves at clandestine locations called a "speakeasy." A new style of music was being played called "swing" at many of these speakeasies and the communist ideology was firmly in place in Russia and other member states of the Union of Soviet Socialist Republics, which had come into existence during the Great War.

In the years 1919, 1920, 1921 and 1922, Webster Groves won the County League Championship in football in consecutive years in addition to beating Kirkwood. The 1922 game was particularly close in that it ended 7-6, the game being won by a blocked extra point kick. Most of the games with Kirkwood were played on Thanksgiving, with the exceptions of the 1919 and 1921 games, which were held on the Friday before Thanksgiving. In 1919, Webster played Maplewood for the County League Championship on Thanksgiving and in 1921 Webster elected to play Alton High School, in Illinois, who had its own longstanding Turkey Day football rivalry with neighbouring Alton school, Western Military Academy. Why Webster and Alton High School chose to forsake their longstanding Turkey Day Game rivals is unknown, however, Kirkwood did play Maplewood High School instead of Webster in its own Turkey Day Game that year. Webster tied Alton in its game 0-0 and Kirkwood beat Maplewood handily 21-0. The record in 1922 from the inauguration of the Webster-Kirkwood Turkey Day Game was now 11-4 in favour of Webster, Kirkwood not having won the game in nine years.

So the stage was set in 1923 for something very big to happen. In this year, both Webster and Kirkwood had each lost one game in the County League, meaning that the winner of the 1923 Turkey Day Game would share the County League Championship that year with University City High School, split the twenty points with them that went towards the year-end County League Athletics Cup and also be allowed to have the County League Football Championship Cup for half of the year in their school. Needless to say, both communities were charged about that year's Turkey Day Game, but especially Kirkwood who, in addition to having the game held at their own Kirkwood High School Athletic Field, thought that the time had come for them to avenge themselves for years past. Unfortunately for Kirkwood, although the 7-0 victory for Webster may seem close, the record does not reflect that the officials in that game recalled three Kirkwood touchdowns due to penalties and by the end of the game caused Kirkwood fans to riot at the field. Apparently, tensions were so high that vandalism, skirmishes and pranks continued throughout the night between the two communities and continually for a period of time after that. Walter Vesper, who played for Webster in the 1923 game, was quoted by his daughter in the 1964 Turkey Day Program as saying, "There was a hot time in the old town that night." Webster had once again won the County League Championship, but the riot was so unsettling to Webster High School Principal James T. Hixon, that he consulted with Coach Charley Roberts and together they decided that the game with Kirkwood would be suspended for two years to ease tensions. Hixon met with Kirkwood Principal Frank Tillman and informed him of the suspension, but Kirkwood would also avoid play with Webster and other County League teams because of its withdrawal from the league in October, 1924.

During the football season of 1924, both Kirkwood and another County League school, Normandy, had withdrawn from the County League. Kirkwood's and Normandy's withdrawal had to do with a new

Alton Football 1921

WEBSTER GROVES' GOLDEN YEARS

County League rule that had been passed requiring a student to attend a school for one semester before they were eligible to play on an athletic team. Normandy had opened a new school in 1924 and had absorbed many former Clayton High School players. One player, Clay Van Reen, was Clayton's former quarterback and team captain and he was not about to forfeit his senior season due to this rule. In a game against Webster, Van Reen was ejected from the game for hitting Webster's team captain, Roger Slater. Van Reen was soon after suspended for the entire season because of his contested eligibility. Kirkwood, being a school that was attended by many students from outside the city, was found to have several ineligible players due to this new rule and they also resigned from the County League due to what they felt was an unjust rule.

Kirkwood's and Normandy's withdrawal from the County League caused a scheduling problem for the league in 1924, as well as for the two departed schools. The County League was now left with University City, Maplewood, Webster, Clayton, Ritenour and Ferguson. Each of these schools desired to play seven or eight opponents in a season in football and they were now challenged with the task of finding other teams to play. Kirkwood and Normandy faired lesser than they did when they were in the league, because they had to act as independent agents in finding games to play. Regardless, Kirkwood did manage to end their season playing five or six opponents. In an editorial titled "Let's Get Together," *The Echo* newspaper lamented in December, 1924, "[Kirkwood] had no championship to struggle for, no historic cup to win. Games played with nothing to work for amount to little more than exercise. If they lost, they lost; and if they won, they won nothing."

To enforce the game suspension with Kirkwood, Webster entered into a two-year agreement to play on Thanksgiving with their newest rival Clayton High School, with whom they were now competing on

Someone You Can Count On ...

Back in 1926

as Quarterback
for the Webster Statesmen,
nicknamed John "Gang" Greene

Or Today

John R. Greene Realtor

Two Convenient Offices
"Buying or Selling"

KIRKWOOD
128 East Jefferson
YOrktown 5-1212

WEBSTER
17 East Lockwood
WOodland 2-5050

22 Full Time Sales People

multiple levels for dominance in the County League. Outside of their two-year contract, Webster and Clayton would also play a third time in 1926, intended to be on Thanksgiving, for a second County League Championship Game between the two schools.

In the three years of competition with Clayton in the Turkey Day Game, Webster would win these contests with scores of 13-7, 26-0 and 41-0. In May of 1925, *The Echo* newspaper reported that, "Kirkwood High, our old rivals, seem about to re-enter the League, although they have taken no definite action as yet. They asked Mr. Roberts to have Webster play Kirkwood in the Thanksgiving game. Although this was impossible as we have already agreed to play it with Clayton according to a two-year contract, this friendly move on the part of Kirkwood seems to show a desire to get back into organized athletics again. Prospects seem bright for a better and stronger County League next year with the breach mending thus quickly." Kirkwood did re-enter the County League in 1925, as did Normandy, but Kirkwood would not play again in the Turkey Day Game until 1928.

In the second game against Clayton in 1925, Webster Groves was peaking in terms of its league dominance. The 1925 team, considered the best team that Charley Roberts ever coached, had several players of notable achievement, six of whom were voted onto the County All-Star Team for their respective positions; Joe Lintzenich at halfback, who would later be a star and team captain for Saint Louis University, play for the Chicago Bears in 1931 and 1932 and tie a National Football League punting record at 94 yards, Clarence "Buddy" Sample at fullback, who was also an incredible track athlete that would break numerous high school track records, three of which were considered world

The 1927 W
Club Banquet

records, Harold Hack at right guard, Emmet Senn at left guard, Kirby Thornton as captain and right tackle and John "Gang" Greene at quarterback, who was chosen over three other players as the *Saint Louis Times* newspaper noted, "Three candidates for the quarterback position caused many an hour of study, and even the data on the season's performance of this trio would be ordinarily confusing. John Green[e] of Webster was chosen over Boldt of Clayton and Smith of University City not on a record of touchdowns or a total of yard gainage, but chiefly because of his valuable generalship. Green[e] was a master at out guessing the enemy and his strategy rivals anything displayed this season by any local varsity. Besides carrying the ball eighty-five yards through a broken field against Maplewood, Green[e] has maneuvered the oval on five occasions for a total of 375 yards, and upon only one occasion during these feats did he carry the ball over the line for the touchdown, but signaled for a mate to carry over the honor marker."

In the 1925 season, Webster Groves would amass a 5-2 record, losing to only two teams, Benld, Illinois and Male High School of Louisville, Kentucky, a nationally ranked high school team. These two teams, and a third, East Saint Louis High School, were the only teams able to score against the 1925 Webster squad, the notable distinction being that no Missouri school was able to score a single point against them. Also, this season would be the first year of the newly created Missouri State High School Activities Association (MSHSAA), of which the County

League would join with its member schools; Webster, Clayton, Kirkwood, Maplewood, University City, Normandy, Ritenour and Wellston.

After three years of Turkey Day Games against Webster, Clayton was beginning to regret the cold and otherwise muddy conditions of the games at Webster, in which they kept losing. Clayton, therefore, declined to play the game against Webster for a fourth straight year in 1927. Webster also, in the spring of 1927, withdrew from the County League after its second year of membership within the Missouri State High School Activities Association. The stated reason for its withdrawal was that, according to the April 7, 1927 edition of *The Echo* newspaper, "At present the County Constitution requires its members to use county rules in all contests wherever they may be played. Webster High has been playing outside teams such as Louisville, Ky. and Dayton, Ohio and has been entering outside track meets such as the Missouri State Meet and Stagg's Meet at University of Chicago. The local officials believe that we should be allowed to contest in equal terms with schools such as Kansas City and St. Louis in the state meet and be allowed to use the Chicago rules in the Chicago meet and not be handicapped by being forced to use St. Louis County rules." Webster would remain outside of the County League until it rejoined in 1931. Webster sought and found a replacement for the 1927 Turkey Day Game in a Saint Louis team named Beaumont High School, who they played and beat by the score of 6-0. Beaumont at that time was not considered a very strong football school, but this year they had an exceptional season for them, in that they held the four top football schools of the City of Saint Louis to scoreless ties. Webster beating Beaumont only 6-0 to a school that had ended the season 0-5-4, may now have begun to show the lessening power of Webster's football squads. This factor and another would set the stage for a renewed contest between Webster and Kirkwood in the 1928 Turkey Day Game.

Between the years of 1924 and 1927, it is rumoured that Kirkwood played other teams on Turkey Day during its suspended relations with Webster, but there is no evidence that shows them doing it. There is in existence a 1927 Kirkwood football schedule that has a "pending" game listed with University City on Thanksgiving, but yearbooks at University City High School, the earliest dated book being 1927, show no Turkey Day games were played with Kirkwood in the years 1926 or 1927. In 1928 Webster and Kirkwood did agree to resume play of the Turkey Day Game, with Kirkwood having at its helm a new and, who would later prove to be until his retirement, longest running head coach, Ernie Lyons. Ernest Lee Lyons was born in Waverly, Illinois on September 11, 1898 and graduated college from the University of Illinois. The renewed rivalry with Kirkwood would earn Webster two more victories by the end of the decade, but the addition of Ernie Lyons would set Kirkwood's football program in a new direction

Bud Sample, Webster track legend

Roger Slater, 1924
Webster football captain

THE GOLD AND BLACK

In the early 1920s, there was a gradual shift from Webster's colours of orange and black to those of gold and black. In all of the years from 1920 until 1924, there was always a mention of orange in at least one article of the yearbook, but starting in 1917 Webster started being referred to as the "Gold and Black" by some newspaper reporters. By 1925, in both the 1925 *Echo* yearbook and the 1925 *Turkey Day Program*, Webster referred to itself as the "Gold and Black."

By 1926, the *Echo* yearbook was back to referring to Webster as the "Orange and Black" and it seems that it was at this time that Webster made the decision to stick to its original colours. There has never been found a reason for the gradual switch to gold and black, nor has been found the decision to remain orange and black.

By Shawn Buchanan Greene
Webster Alumnus 1987
Written August 13, 2007

GIVE ME A...

What generations today do not understand was the difficulty of obtaining your school's letter for athletics prior to the 1980s. Certainly, in the early years, letters were only able to be earned and worn by athletes… and they had to be earned; it was not enough just to be on the team. At Webster High School in the 1932-33 school year, the requirements in football were "that the gridder must play in at least eighteen quarters" for the season. Each sport had its own requirements, but essential to each sport's criteria was that some standard of regular play occurred. In the 1917-18 school year at Webster, the W Club was formed, which after its foundation, inductees had to first earn a letter in a sport and then be voted into the organization by its members. Such conditions gave athletes a great desire to display their letters on sweaters and expensive lettermen's jackets. During the 1980s, these standards lowered, so that now letters are awarded to anyone who joins and remains on the team.

By Shawn Buchanan Greene
Webster Alumnus 1987
Written September 27, 2007

THE W CLUB

**Kirkwood Football
Head Coach Albert
"Hap" Bernard**

E. Fitch, J. Payne, H. Kiesker, R. Brown, Paul Maschoff, O. Kiesker, Walters, C. Burdick, Melville H. "Mutt" Martin, B. Payne, Sperry Gould, Vic Schwentker

**Webster Football (5-1-1)
Head Coach Charles A. Roberts
County League Champions**

Chauncey "Chunk" Baldwin, Steve Thornton, Clifford Dunn, Sherman Senne, Sam Woods, Bill Kleisle, Dwight Ingamells, "Meat" Copley, Ferd Stork, Ernie Nolkemper, Ed Shannon, "Hog" Johnson, Morris Mathis, Robert Patterson, Eugene Larson

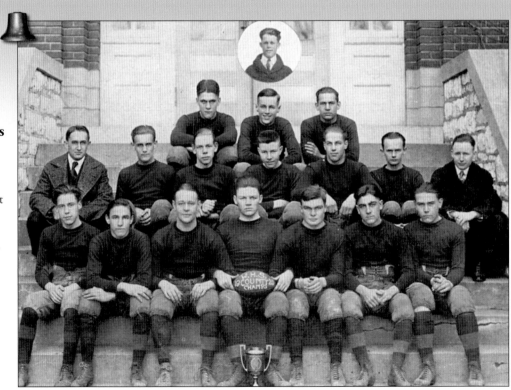

Kirkwood Football (4-3)
Head Coach Albert "Hap" Bernard

Row 1: Julian Payne, Bobby Dentzer, Morton Lange, Sam Nichols Row 2: Spencer Gould, Paul Maschoff, Burdick, Barton Payne, Hilbert Kiesker, Otto Kiesker, Ray Brown Row 3: Fletch Walker, Red Harrison, Melville H. "Mutt" Martin, Courtney Shands, Willard Cunningham, Edwin Fitch, Vic Schwentker, Unknown, Bob Williamson, Coach Hap Bernard Row 4: Asst. Coach Neville, Principal Frank Tillman, Ed Howell, Unknown, Kirtley Baskett, Joe Wise, Scott Dickson, Chub Brown, Asst. Coach Erffmeyer.

1921 Webster
Football

Webster Football (6-0-1)
Head Coach Charles A. Roberts
County League Champions

Sam Woods, Douglas Gibson, Dwight Ingamells, Dick Haswell, Ferd Stork, George Buchanan, Chester Greene, George Senne, Quentin Gaines, Thomas Wohlschlaeger.

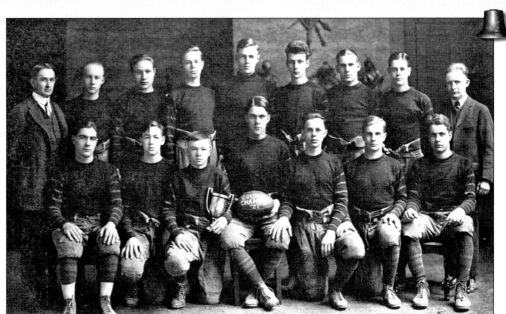

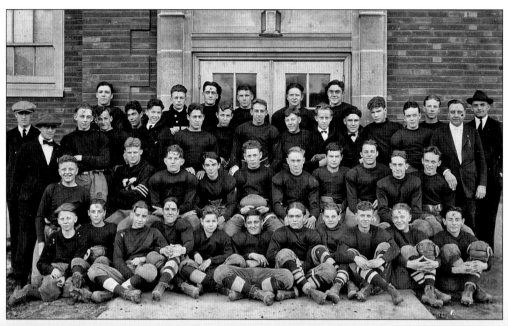

Kirkwood Football - Head Coach Albert "Hap" Bernard
Row 1: Unknown, Bob Dentzer, Eugene Niccols, Frank Elson, John Holscher, Elmer Tiesler, Chip Sturdy, Dick Robinson, Don Howell, Vernon Rowe, Morton Lange Row 2: Unknown, Julian Payne, Theodore Jacoby, Bill Taussig, Melville H. "Mutt" Martin, Irving Byerly, Bob French, Ed Howell, Charley Betty, Joe Wise Row 3: Merrill Wilson, Albert Bernard, Robert Winkler, Ralph Behrens, Edward Sanders, Louis Wingert, Chester Brown, Spencer Gould, Victor Schwetker, Lawrence Shallcross, Unknown, John Murphy, Harrision Howester, Bob Williamson, Scott Dickson, Frank Tillman, Harvey Neville Row 4: John Andrews, Wray Huckins, Jack Walsh, Paul Maschoff, John Royer, Courtney Shands

Webster Football (5-2-1)
Head Coach Charles A. Roberts
County League Champions
Leland Billings, Douglas Gibson, John Haldane, Bertram Mann, Ralph Metcalf, Hal Phillips, Gershon Ward, Thomas Wohlschlaeger, Sam Hodgdon, Burch, George Senne, Schnellbacker, Quentin Gaines, Carpenter Barnett, Chester Greene

Webster's Roger Slater

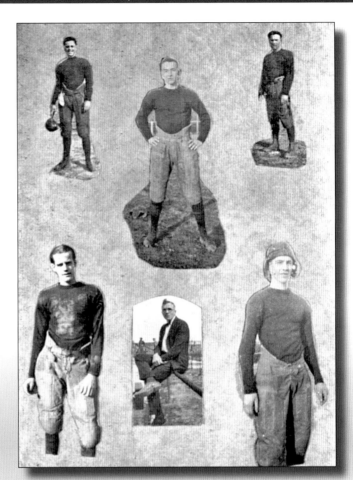

Webster Football

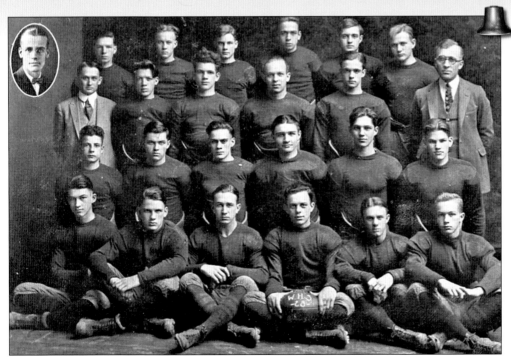

Webster Football (5-2)
Head Coach Charles A. Roberts
County League Co-Champions
George Senne, David Tompkins, Quentin Gaines, Carpenter Barnett, Henry Metcalf, Walter Vesper, B. Schnellbacher, Nathaniel Fritz, Randall Wardan, Roger Slater, Kirby Thornton, Walter Boswell, Joe Lintzenich, John Greene, E. Curson

49

1924

CLAYTON - 0 | WEBSTER - 13
Thursday, November 27, 2:00 p.m. at Kopplin Field

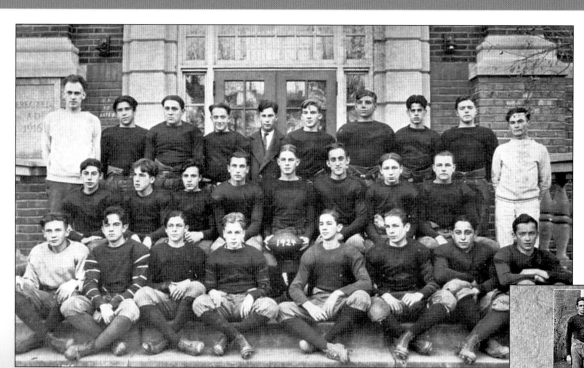

**Clayton Football
(2-4-1)
Head Coach
Sam Hall**

Ed Mutrux, Falzone, Jack McAtee, Adie Boldt, Haffner, Kenney, Lewis, Mike Creach, Carson Chase, Jablonsky, Harold Tzinberg, Wittmeyer, Mueller, Sweet,

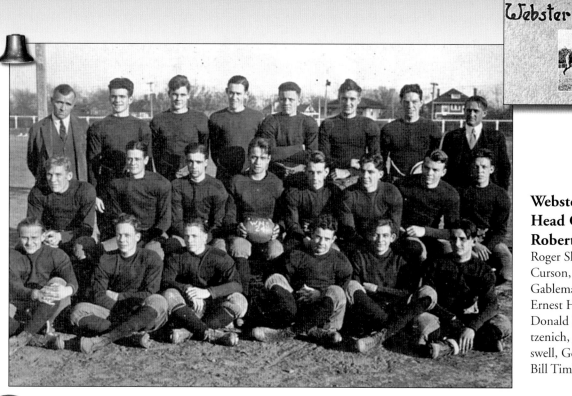

**Webster Football (6-1)
Head Coach Charles A. Roberts**

Roger Slater, Chester Greene, Curson, Kirby Thornton, Harold Gableman, Schell Furry, Bill Lacy, Ernest Hoffsten, Dave Strain, Donald Hart, Ted Barker, Joe Lintzenich, John Greene, Walter Boswell, George Wood, Harry Tyrell, Bill Timberlake, Harold Hack

Sam Hall and his backfield

Clayton FootbalL (7-1) - Head Coach Sam Hall
Adie Boldt, Jack McAtee, Haffner, Kenney, Lewis, Mike Creach, Carson Chase, Jablonsky, Harold Tzinberg, Wittmeyer, Mueller, Paul Kiebler, Floyd Creach, Ben Roman, Talbott, Fisher

Program
AND
OFFICIAL SCORE CARD

ANNUAL
FOOT BALL GAME
CHAMPIONSHIP NUMBER

WEBSTER .. vs .. CLAYTON
WEBSTER ATHLETIC FIELD

Thursday, November 26, 1925

PROGRAM COURTESY OF THE ADVERTISERS

Webster Football (5-2)
Head Coach
Charles A. Roberts
County League
Champions
Row 1: Coach Charley Roberts, Kirby Thornton, Harold Hack, Coach Henry Tudor
Row 2: Emmet Senn, Joe Lintzenich, John Greene, Leslie Wolf Row 3: Bud Sample, Jack Hall, George Wood, David Ward Not Pictured: Harry Tyrell, George Gisburne, Walter Boswell

1926

CLAYTON - 0 | WEBSTER - 41
Saturday, November 28, 2:00 p.m. at Kopplin Field

Clayton Footbal (4-3)
Head Coach Sam Hall
Wittmeyer, Lewis, Mueller, Paul Kiebler, Talbott, Fisher, McGrath, Hyman Miller, Kinum, Rabenau, Phillips, McNeely, Davis

Games played on Turkey Day at Kopplin Field were usually muddy affairs

Webster Football (4-3-1)
Head Coach Charles A. Roberts
County League Champions
Harold Hack, Hunt, Bert Miller, Bud Sample, Phil Yeckel, Harvey Miller, Ray Knickman, R. Nicholson, R. Jones, W. Perkins, B. Kenamore, M. Tyrell, Emmet Senn, E. Finkenaur, John Greene, L. Snyder, W. Ward, O. Pettingill, A. Goodloe, G. Gottsberger

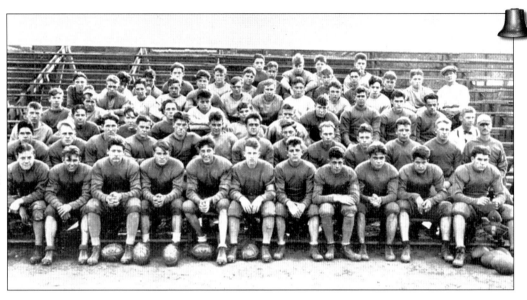

Beaumont Football (0-5-4)
Head Coach Lewis

Michael Barnhouse, Vladimir Anastasoff, Milton Ens, Carl Weidner, Holtman, John Lone, Theodore Close, Herbert Bohringer, Robert Menges, Elmer Nickel, James Bryon, Jimmy Duby, William Hoyer, Edward HeilmanPeter Brarae, Burr Barnard, Fred Busse

KIRKWOOD HIGH SCHOOL
Foot Ball Schedule 1927
September 23—Central High at Kirkwood
September 30—Belleville at Kirkwood
October 7—Maplewood at Kirkwood
October 15—Benumont High at Maplewood
October 22—Clayton at Kirkwood
October 28—Ritenour at Kirkwood
November 4—St. Charles at Kirkwood
November 12—Normandy at Normandy
November 18—Open
November 24—University City (pending)

Webster's first band in 1926 was not a marching band

Webster Football (3-4-2)
Head Coach Charles A. Roberts

Row 1: Gottsberger, Nicholson, E. Basch, Bruce Miller, P. Yeckel, Nesbit, H. Miller, Buchanan, Knickman, P. Sibley, Curtis, Salveter Row 2: Moore, Skinner, R. Schmidt, R. Wood, Alt, Snyder, C. Yeckel, Wedemeier, Bilchrist, Baster, Tyrrell, B. Miller Row 3: Morehouse, Moody, Bopp, J. Miller, Pierson, Peters, Senn, Johnson Row 4: Coach Robertsw, Stark, Leck, Brown, Barker, D. Sibley, Coach Gaines, Rodenroth, Christoffersen

Kirkwood Football - Head Coach Ernest L. Lyons

Kirkwood's
starting offense

Webster Football (3-3-2) - Head Coach Charles A. Roberts
Row 1: Coach Gaines, Salveter, Wood, Westrup, Baster, Freschi, L. Larson, Tyrrell, Yeckel, J. Larson, Schneidermeyer, Henderson, P. Sibley, Coe, Alt, Coach Roberts Row 2: J. P. Larson, Greene, Scott, Senn, Coester, Nahm, Ramsey, Pahmeyer, R. Schmidt, Fuchs, Hicks, F. Guth, Crippen Row 3: D. Coyne, Weidemeier, Bopp, Bailey, W. Jones, Broaddus, J. Patterson, Stork, Barrie, Flint

Kirkwood Football - Head Coach Ernest L. Lyons

Webster Football (6-2) - Head Coach Charles A. Roberts

Row 1: Coach Roberts, K. Gustafson, Stork, Leck, J. Larson, Freschi, P. Sibley, R. Schmidt, Nisbet, D. Sibley, P. Johnson, Coach Gaines Row 2: Broaddus, Cole, Coester, Scott, Gisburne, Flint, Rustemeyer, A. Bopp Row 3: I. Hicks, Bryant, C. Honig, R. Evans, Zell, King, Senn, R. Flynn, G. Brown Row 4: Westrup, Kraft, Barrie, G. Bopp, Curtis, Hillmeyer, E. Link, Young, Miller, C. Carr Row 5: Jackson, H. Payne, Fuchs, R. Hall, Hutchinson, Moeller, O. Conrad, J. George

JOE LINTZENICH

To have such a father as Joe Lintzenich is such a blessing. He was kind, gentle, strong, protective and a great gentleman. I never saw my father play football but those who did told it like this, "to think of and see Joe in his early years is to think of strength, strength of body and strength of will. If you wanted proof, you put a football in his hands and let him run. Those who saw him do it said he had no equal." That was written by his best friend all his life until his death, John M. (Jack) Joyce, the president and founder of the 7-Up Company.

My father loved my mother and all his family, therefore I realized early in my life that I was one of the lucky ones who had no "baggage" to carry into later life. That is quite a gift. I remember what kind of friend my dad was to many of his friends he had a lifetime; Larry Musel, Bill Kalhorn, Ed Rydrick. He loved his country. He enlisted at 35 years old to fight in the Navy in WW II. To think my father fought in Japan on the battleship North Carolina and my husband Jack Buck fought in the same war in Germany at 18 years old.

My father was proud of me when I went to Broadway – He even knew my lines and hoped against hope I would remember them; I was also proud of him. He was a man's man but he was handsome and dressed so well the women loved him too. He loved my mom – "Mama" he used to call her. He taught me how to drive, once! He said "How fast could you stop if a child ran out that driveway!" after I threw him against the front window – we got a driving instructor. He could sing and dance – the only thing he couldn't do was tolerate men treating women badly. He loved my husband and once introduced me as "Jack Buck's wife." He told me about Webster growing up. At Christmas he cut down the family tree and brought it home on a wagon with Maggie and Mouse (his two mules).

Thank you, Daddy, for everything.

By Carole Lintzenich Buck, Written June 13, 2007

CHARLES A. ROBERTS
WEBSTER FOOTBALL HEAD COACH 1907-1931

"Coach!" That name recalls the man who, for the past seventeen years has given his time and energy unstintingly for the betterment of Webster High School. Coach Roberts is a part of the institution. Without him there would be a feeling that something was missing.

Before school in the morning his room is a den where all the important matters of the day are discussed. One might compare him to a judge, settling all the petty arguments and passing sentence on various phases of school life. Then, at other times, he has his audience spellbound with the tales of his boyhood and instances of big games that happened long before our time. The usual topic, however, is the next game and what ought to be done in it that wasn't accomplished in the last game. The bell often rings in the middle of one of these discussions, but they are always resumed at some future date.

In the classroom he is ever patient and willing to explain the mysteries of the realm of mathematics which, to us, is often utter darkness. Between the closing hours of school and dusk is a short period in which he functions for the school, but along a different line. Most of the students know the results of these hours only in the terms of a championship team. Only a few, however, know of that long hard practice after a tedious day in school in which both "Coach" and players become exhausted. Then he prods the players with these words: "Go like a bullet," or "Hit him and turn him end over end!" It is in these hours that the personality and the character that are his influence the lives of the boys.

He instills in the players, through some unseen power, that courage to fight clean and hard to the finish; that fighting spirit which will not acknowledge the end of the game until the last whistle When he has taught a boy to give all he has that Webster might win, then he has helped build that boy's character.

"No one fears to trust him with the innermost of secrets. He comforts the weary mind, and advises the prospective athlete."

"As a teacher he is a Solon; as a coach he is a genius; and as a friend he is a Jonathan. Freshmen may come, and seniors may go, but he stays on forever."

Written for the 1925 Echo Yearbook

1927 W Club Banquet

"Don't ask me the names of any Kirkwood players I was up against, because we wouldn't have anything to do with them. The only thing I really remember was that Coach Roberts was one of the finest gentlemen who ever walked the face of the earth. He taught math on the side, but he talked football most of the time."

Steve Thornton, Webster-Kirkwood Times, *1984*

ERNEST LEE LYONS
FATHER, ATHLETE, COACH, FRIEND

Within a single week, Ernest Lyons lost three people dear to him: his father, mother, and baby brother all perished in the devastating flue epidemic of 1918. This tragic experience shaped his life in a profound way and hardened his resolve to make something of himself.

Born in 1898 in the prairie town of Waverly, Illinois, my grandfather spent his early life working in the farm fields with his mother, and of course, going to school. Of his brothers and sisters, my grandfather enjoyed learning. After his parents' deaths, Wilson Smith, the editor of the Waverly newspaper saw something special in the rawboned, straightforward young athlete. Smith took him under his wing and helped him get into the University of Illinois, an academic accomplishment for my grandfather, and something not everyone could do back in those days. He diligently paid his way by night as a security guard at the University Armory; a great job for a student wanting time to study.

Unfortunately, with the full curriculum of Engineering courses, as well as day jobs, he had no time left over for his major love: athletics. However, he decided to switch to Physical Education and was soon happily involved in sports as well as learning!

Graduating in 1923, my grandfather took a job as teacher and football coach in Sabetha, Kansas. This was not the only new and pleasant development in his life: His new bride, Myrtle Eva Carter of Tolano, accompanied him on his journey. In 1928 he came to Kirkwood's school system as their new head football coach and Physical Education teacher. While they lived on Woodbine and Geyer, a magical young child came into their lives. Her name was Audie. He then took his young family to New York where he earned a Masters degree at Columbia University.

Obviously a sports enthusiast above all else, he went to many games around St. Louis. He became friends with many of the Cardinal "Gas House Gang" who came to play ping-pong at his home. Often he was invited to the press box to watch baseball games. During Kirkwood High football games my mother tells me, "After a game, no one could ever tell whether we had won or lost by the expression on his face or his personal demeanor. Under pressure of a game, he never let it get him down." My grandfather truly had grace under pressure.

Appointed the athletic director of Kirkwood Schools, he was also the Kirkwood High School golf team coach. The most exciting time of the year was the Turkey Day Game, an occasion that was anticipated with no less significance than Christmas. Beating Webster Groves in the annual game was almost as sacred as Thanksgiving and the Pilgrims. The Lyons family never had turkey with the trimmings but went out to dinner after the game.

My mother, now of junior high age, would help him sort athletic equipment in the warehouse. They had a special bond: taking his daughter many places. Watching him refereeing a plethora of football games at stadiums throughout the area was just one of the fun things they did as father and daughter. She also walked with him when he played golf (she was a good golfer herself). In fact, playing golf was his responsibility for many years and he was named to the St. Louis Association Hall of Fame in 1956.

My grandfather's funeral in May of 1957 had to be postponed a week so many folks had time to arrive from both coasts. Not a year goes by in which my mom does not meet someone who does not remember her father. A smile will cross their face and they will mention how much they liked him and what a great man he was.

Kirkwood Football Head Coach 1928-1948
Written by Dane Marti, grandson, and Audie
Lyons Marti, daughter (Kirkwood Alumna 1950).
Written May 6, 2007

THE COUNTY LEAGUE AND THE MISSOURI STATE HIGH SCHOOL ACTIVITIES ASSOCIATION

The Saint Louis County League, commonly and simply known as the County League, was likely created in 1906. It is first documented in football by Kirkwood and Webster Groves when they played for the County League Football Championship, which Kirkwood won 17-12 at The Stadium, now Francis Field, at Washington University. The County League provided many championships in athletics, which it normally awarded a number of points and a cup to the championship team. There was also a year-end cup awarded to the school that had amassed the most points in the County League for athletics.

The County League in its beginning was considered a lesser competitive league than its neighbour, The Saint Louis City League. In the State of Missouri, there were many leagues, but there was no centralized body to declare a "Missouri State Champion." It was not until the late 1910s and 1920s that the County League gained prominence. In the winter of 1925-26, a meeting occurred at the Hotel Statler in Saint Louis amongst influential men throughout the State of Missouri. Of those in attendance was the principal of Clayton High School, Carl Burris, and members of the University of Missouri coaching staff. The meeting resulted in the formation of the Missouri State High School Activities Association, commonly known by its acronym MSHSAA and pronounced "meesha." The original purpose of the association was to foster and create standards for Missouri high school athletics.

Because of the involvement of Carl Burris, who was the first secretary of the association and in large part to the strength of the County League at this time, the Saint Louis County League was the only county league to gain admittance to the Missouri State High School Activities Association as a single unit. In the first year of the Missouri State High School Activities Association, the County League standings were:

	Won	Lost	Tied	Pct.
Webster Groves	5	0	0	1.000
Clayton	5	1	0	.833
Kirkwood	3	1	0	.750
Maplewood	3	2	0	.600
University City	2	3	0	.400
Normandy	1	2	1	.333
Ritenour	1	6	0	.143
Wellston	0	3	1	.000

The Missouri State High School Activities Association did not start a championship series in football until 1968. The league, much like its championship series is not mandatory and teams each year must submit an application to participate in any of its championship playoffs, which in football is known as the Show-Me Bowl.

By Shawn Buchanan Greene
Webster Alumnus 1987
Written April 13, 2007

"*Once more the thump of cleated toe against pigskin, once more a hallyhoo and sound of scuffling from the fenced field, once more cheery clamor and throaty song echo from the steaming locker-room; — how can anyone fail to thrill to such an atmosphere? How can anyone be immune to the gridiron itch?*"

The Echo, Thursday, October 6, 1927

ECHOES FROM THE PAST

Webster High School's first yearbook was printed for the Class of 1911 and was named *The Senior*. There was no yearbook in the years 1912, 1913 and 1914, likely due to the lack of funds to create it, but a yearbook was made in the year 1915. There was some debate as to what to name the 1915 yearbook, but it was finally decided to follow precedent and to name it also *The Senior*. In the fall of 1915, the sophomore class was challenged to print a newspaper by their second period writing instructor, Miss Stapleton. The newspaper, named *The Echo*, was printed in six issues starting December 20, "each issue just about five cents ahead of bankruptcy." In 1916-17, the newspaper had eight issues and its first two years of existence were largely credited to future Olympian and Webster alumnus, George Pierce Messengale. At the end of the year in 1916 and 1917, the newspapers were bound as an ad hoc yearbook, and called *The High School Echo*. In the 1917-18 school year, the newspaper was reduced to four issues, the fourth being the first *Echo* yearbook, which has been printed annually, without interruption, ever since that time.

Kirkwood High School's yearbook came much later than Webster's in 1938, the year that they also adopted their mascot name the "Pioneers." Most early Webster yearbooks did not give meaningful mention of the Turkey Day Game until 1922 and the series with Kirkwood would be interrupted from the years of 1924-1926. Clayton High School and Beaumont High School served as Webster's Turkey Day adversaries during those years, while it seems that Kirkwood tried, but was unsuccessful in finding their own adversary. Below are the reprinted sections from Webster's *Echo* yearbook and Clayton's *CLA-MO* yearbook regarding the Turkey Day Game. It should be noted that while Beaumont High School did have a yearbook, the season account was not very detailed and there was no mention of Webster or the Turkey Day Game.

ECHO 1916 – THANKSGIVING 1915

And then came the biggest game of the year, because Kirkwood is our deadliest rival in sports. Webster was thought to have a team far superior to that of Kirkwood, but the Red and White's team fought grandly, and indeed, during the first half kept the ball in Webster's territory, and succeeded in scoring one touchdown. But towards the end of the game, Webster by sheer force overcame them and marched across their goal line three times in quick succession. It was at this time that Irland distinguished himself by tearing around right end for a ten yard run that led to a touchdown; and a few minutes later, intercepting a forward pass, he carried the ball to Kirkwood's 10 yd. line and from there, Halman made the second touchdown of the day. Avis kicked goal. The final score was – Webster 19; Kirkwood 6.

ECHO 1922 – TURKEY DAY GAME 1921

The most exciting game of the year was the annual battle with Kirkwood, in which Webster won out by a 7-6 score. The game started out in great style for Kirkwood. In about five minutes, they had a touchdown, but missed goal. This resulted in their losing the game as later events proved. After this pleasant surprise, Webster dug in, and the teams battled over the field for the next two periods. The last quarter opened the score still 6-0. The crowd had just about given Kirkwood the game, and Kirkwood was so sure of another touchdown when they advanced to our twenty-yard line again, that it seemed a shame to hold there. There was still about two minutes to play, but the team hadn't quit fighting yet. The whole team seemed to be ravin', rarin', fightin' fools, and then Webster got the ball. Senne called a trick play that was older than himself, and "Cop" caught the ball on the pass, set out for home, and kept going. Three of the Kirkwood men almost caught him, but he slipped them somehow, and only one more was left. The Kirkwood back was head across to "Cop" at full speed and it seemed that he couldn't miss him. Just as he was about to tackle him, "Big Inkie" came cruising up and dived under. The rest was easy; Copley scored and Stork kicked goal. "Big Ink" was carried off unconscious and was in bed for a day or two, but as he said, "We won, so what's the difference?"

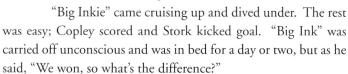

George Massengate

ECHO 1923 – TURKEY DAY GAME 1922

The weeks preceding Thanksgiving were filled with anxiety. Critics virtually gave our ancient rival, Kirkwood, the victory. But on the fatal day, our team came out before the three thousand odd spectators with a fighting spirit that Princeton could not have withstood.

Webster's superiority showed from the first, but a blocked pass gave Kirkwood a touchdown, and a lead which she kept during the half. A blocked kick in the third quarter gave Webster her chance for the touchdown and goal kick that meant the most glorious victory ever won by the school. The game which was won by a score of seventy-six to nothing, was not such a great victory as this, where there was a difference of but one point.

ECHO 1924 – TURKEY DAY GAME 1923

Even our mortal enemies, Kirkwood, had to suffer another

one of those numerous defeats at Webster's hands. After a postponement of the eventful game, Webster trounced them to the tune of 7-0. Oh, how they wailed and tore their hair! They should have known that it takes nothing short of a regulation Army tank to stop boys that play like Carp, Red, Jiggs, Nat and Shorty.

> "On a fine Autumn day with a crisp wind blowing, certainly students turn out in crowds to support the team and the school which it represents. From another standpoint it can be seen that many boys, because of football alone, go to school who otherwise would have long since quit."
>
> *The Echo,* Thursday, November 11, 1926

ECHO 1925 – TURKEY DAY GAME 1924

On Turkey Day Webster opposed Clayton, our ancient rival. This game was much harder than everyone expected. Clayton held Webster scoreless in the first quarter. Later, in the second quarter, Webster scored by means of a long pass and line bucking. Beginning the next half, Webster scored on a blocked punt. The attempt at extra point failed. A few minutes after the kickoff a Clayton back broke through the line, picked up a loose ball and raced for a touchdown. Soon the game ended with a 13-7 score, the result of the last game of the 1924 season.

CLA-MO 1925 – TURKEY DAY GAME 1924

Finally and gloriously came the great battle with Webster. Teeming with over-confidence, the Webster team was expected to pile up at least forty points, but the fighting spirit of the Orange team netted a mere 14 to 7 result in favor of the Roberts' eleven. The game was a fight from start to finish, with Clayton holding its own and even carrying the fight to the enemy. Green[e] of Webster fumbled and Lewis, our left end, scooped up the ball and ran 70 yards for Clayton's first score. After this play Webster became demoralized and the game ended with Clayton rapidly advancing up the field.

ECHO 1926 – TURKEY DAY GAME 1925

The Thanksgiving Day feature game of the season, to have been played with Clayton, was postponed two days on account of heavy rain. However a large and spirited crowd witnessed the frolic, which proved to be one of Webster's easiest victories. The final score was 26-0. Again Lintzenich's superior punting was of exceptional brilliancy. However, Sample's line plunging and Greene's generalship were also worthy of much praise.

CLA-MO 1926 – TURKEY DAY GAME 1925

The day of days dawned cold and gray, with a hint of rain in the air. We showed up at Webster in uniform at the appointed hour, with the rain coming down in torrents. We were primed for the big battle, but Webster wished to call off the contest because of the inclement weather. Officials agreed to play the game the following Saturday at Webster. The day was cold and clear,

but the field was still muddy and sloppy from Thanksgiving rains. Webster ruled a big favorite because of their tremendous weight advantage. The County Seat eleven lost all chance for a victory after Harold Tzinberg, veteran 192-pound [87 kilogram] tackle, was removed from the fray with a broken leg. Clayton fought throughout and threatened repeatedly with its dangerous aerial attack, which it had been noted for, but Webster's line plunging ability gave them a 26 to 0 victory and the County championship.

ECHO 1927 – TURKEY DAY GAME 1926

The Thanksgiving Day game, which was the deciding one for the championship of the County League, topped the scales with a count of 46-0. It was truly a mud fight with Sample as the star.

CLA-MO 1927 – TURKEY DAY GAME 1926

The Webster game was postponed as is the annual custom and then was played in a sea of mud as per usual. After the first quarter there was little hope for the much outweighed Orange and Blue. The score w as not indicative of the hard fight which Clayton carried on throughout the game, however. When the players were finally dug out of the mud and noses counted, the score was found to be 41-0.

ECHO 1928 – TURKEY DAY GAME 1927

Thanksgiving, however, brought a roseate ending to a relatively unprofitable season. Beaumont, who had held four leading city teams to scoreless ties, Webster repulsed by carrying the ball across the line on the sixth play of the game, this, perhaps, was the brightest event of the season.

ECHO 1929 – TURKEY DAY GAME 1928

Before a record crowd of several thousand fans on Thanksgiving Day Webster's fighting team fittingly brought down the curtain of the football season by defeating Kirkwood by a score of six to nothing. Bob Ramsey scored the touchdown that won the game, and Westrup and Freschi gave splendid support by punting.

ECHO 1930 – TURKEY DAY GAME 1929

After a rest of ten days or so, Webster journeyed to Kirkwood on Turkey Day. After the snow had been cleared and purple lines drawn on the field, a large crowd swarmed the bleachers to freeze their feet while Webster downed the Red and White. Bill Freschi should receive considerable credit for his remarkable returns of Kirkwood's punts. However, the team as a whole was responsible for the victory, as they gave Bill the much needed interference, and then they held the line to keep the Red and White from scoring.

In the early part of 1930 the economy in America was fine, but it quickly made a drastic downturn from which it would take an entire decade and a half and a second world war for it to recover. The Great Depression in America affected the entire world and likewise became a world depression. Radio became the dominant mass media during this decade and a new animated character, Mickey Mouse, made his debut in cinemas. By 1939, another theatrical milestone would be reached when *The Wizard of Oz* would become the first widely distributed movie to use colour.

In the 1930s the Turkey Day Game reached a level of maturity and stability that had otherwise not existed in the game. The scores were less lopsided than in previous years and, finally, Kirkwood was able to win some games, four in total for this decade.

1930 was another magical year for Kirkwood, as the team won that year's Turkey Day Game for the first time in 17 years. There is very little written documentation regarding Kirkwood teams until 1940, so it is difficult to comment on the character of the team. From a box of newspaper clippings that had been kept by Charley Roberts, a few details of the game were printed as a part of the 1949 *Turkey Day Program*. In the program it mentions "Kirkwood's outstanding man on the offensive was Norcum Patrick. Brink knifed through center for Kirkwood's touchdown. Martin of Kirkwood blocked a punt by Freschi, the ball rolled back 30 yards and out of the end zone for a safety. George Nisbet scored the touchdown for Webster after Harkey had blocked a punt." There is in existence a 1930 Kirkwood offensive-line team photograph, with the players' names written on it and a large hand scrawled note, "We Beat Webster." Also, there was an alumni match that was played the following day between Kirkwood and Webster. For many years, the score of this game was mistakenly listed as a game played in 1924, as many of the players listed were from that era. The star of the game, John "Gang" Greene, scored the winning point, with the game ending in victory for the Webster Alumni, 7-6.

There was a bit of a controversy during the 1931 season in that Kirkwood halfback Malcolm Patrick had grown a mustache. Patrick had played on the 1930 team and it was accused by many that Patrick had to be older than the school stated, because of his mustache. The fact is that he was only 17 or 18 his senior year and his ability to grow a mustache and his level of play were all issues related to his maturity rather than his chronological age. The 1931 team's 0-0 tie at the end of the Turkey Day Game was a large disappointment to the players, in that they fully expected to win the game. The game was played on 15 centimetres of snow as Kirkwood Principal Murl R. Moore wrote; "We expected a great team and a great one we had. Kirkwood was undefeated but tied twice. One of the games was with Webster in the traditional

T. D. game which was played on a field covered with at least six inches of snow. That game was scoreless and seemed more like a defeat as we were certain it would have been a run away victory on a decent field."

In 1929, Webster Groves hired a new Superintendent of Schools, Willard E. Goslin, who would later be a nationally recognized proponent of "Educational Progressivism." Goslin's tenure was the focal point of public outcry when he, in the 1931-32 school year, "promoted" long time Webster High School Principal James T. Hixon to the position of Director of Research, due to "philosophical" differences held between the two gentlemen. The community outcry was so loud that Goslin was forced to reinstate Hixon as the High School Principal for the 1932-33 school year. After the removal and reinstatement of Hixon, Goslin turned his attention to Hixon's close friend and outspoken supporter during his removal, Charley Roberts. After the first game of the 1932 season, Roberts stepped down as head coach of the football team as part of a recondite "deal," which elevated him to a formally created position as athletic director. Until this time, while controlling athletics at Webster High School, Roberts' role as athletic director was only unofficial.

The coaching duties for the remainder of the 1932 football season were passed to Roberts' six-year assistant coach, Froebel Gaines. Hixon, Roberts and Gaines were all friends and when the football duties were passed to Gaines, he was told that his post would be temporary, as there was already another coach, John McArtor, which the school district planned to hire after he finished college. Frank Froebel Gaines graduated from Sidell Township High School. After high school, he attended Millikin University for a period of time and then transferred to and graduated from the University of Illinois. It is said by Webster 1967 alumnus and historian Charles Schneider that Froebel liked the exoticness of his middle name and chose to go by it, rather than his forename. In fact, Schneider was only able to find his forename through military records, as Froebel Gaines had only ever listed his name and signed his school contracts as F. Froebel Gaines.

In 1932, Froebel Gaines became Webster's second head coach since the founding of the Turkey Day Game and he was the first coach at Webster to devise a system that organized teams around a "varsity," "reserve" and "B" team format. Until this time, Webster had only its varsity team and a secondary squad known as the "scrub team." Under Gaines' new organizational system, the varsity team would be comprised of the best players of the school which were mostly senior and some junior class students. The reserve squad was comprised of the remaining junior class students and the B team was a composite team of sophomore and freshman students that could begin getting some experience and playing time on the field that they might not have otherwise been able to get under the old organizational model.

In 1933, the first mention of the Webster Groves mascot "Statesmen" was made in the *Echo* yearbook. Prior to this publication, those that attended Webster Groves High School were always referred to as "Websterites" or, in the case of athletic teams, would commonly take the name of the coach and add "-men" to it, who would in the case of football become the "Gainesmen." So was the case in all of the years in the twenties, when the Webster football, basketball and track team players referred to themselves as the "Robertsmen." The origination of Statesmen is obvious, in that it refers to the school's namesake, Daniel Webster, who was a prominent statesman in New England.

In the three years, from when Froebel Gaines took command of the Webster Groves football team, he amassed a 16-8-1 varsity record and a 1-2 Turkey Day Game record, winning the Turkey Day Game only his last year as head coach. Originally hired to coach baseball and teach geography and given his "temporary" status for three years as head coach of the football team, Coach Gaines relinquished his post to his two-year assistant coach, John McArtor, who was now considered ready to take control of the Webster squad. John Trusten McArtor was born May 6, 1908, in Saint Louis, Missouri and attended Northeast Missouri State Teachers College, before coming to the Webster Groves School District. Froebel Gaines, although not a prominent figure in Webster Groves varsity football history, would later make a name for himself coaching B team football and as the varsity baseball head coach. Since its dedication on October 24, 1976, one of the baseball fields at Memorial Park in Webster Groves has borne his name.

With McArtor's ascendancy to the head coach position of the football team, Goslin forced the stepping down of Roberts as athletic director, once again causing a hailstorm of community opposition, as *The Webster Reporter* notes, "Charles A. Roberts, an institution within an institution, has stepped down and out from the athletic department, has severed his connections with the sports after a brilliant career comparable with that of any individual in the country. We do not know just why Mr. Roberts has been removed as athletic director, a post made for him after the installation of a new superintendent, when he was asked to give up active coaching of the football team, but we do know there are many, many men and women of this city who regret any action that had to do with his withdrawal." After his removal as athletic director, Roberts was left only as the head coach of the track team, also being forced to surrender his job as basketball head coach.

At the time that Froebel Gaines took control of Webster's football team, the Webster Groves Chapter of a high school branch of the YMCA, known as the Hi-Y, whose purpose it was "to create, maintain, and extend throughout the school and community, high standards of Christian character," began to develop "pep" events to build school spirit around the Turkey Day Game. The first events began in 1932 and 1933 in the form of the group visiting businesses in the Webster area to get a larger audience to the Turkey Day Games, in response to waning attendance figures. By 1934, the Hi-Y sponsored a pep parade before the Turkey Day Game, with the group reporting in the *Echo* yearbook that there was an "overflow" crowd in attendance at the game. The day after the game, the Hi-Y held a victory dance "and many of the Kirkwood students showed their friendly spirit by attending the entertainment."

The next year, in 1935, the Webster Hi-Y sponsored for the first time a Pep Bonfire and again their Pep Parade. As the 1936 *Echo* yearbook reports; "On Wednesday, November 28, members of the Hi-Y scoured the town for inflammable material and after several hours of back-breaking toil had accumulated a huge pile of material. The pep meeting then got under way. A crowd of several hundred boys and girls gathered around the fire. Coaches spoke, cheer-leaders yelled, students sang, firecrackers exploded, parades started, and then as a fitting climax – the fire department arrived." By 1937, the Webster Groves Chapter of the Hi-Y was, although unconfirmed, thought to be the largest Hi-Y Chapter in the United States and by the end of the 1930s, Kirkwood had formed its own Hi-Y chapter. Also in 1937, Webster organized for the first time a marching band, due to the inspiration of art teacher Pete Myers and with the help of the high school band director, Hans Lemcke. Although the Turkey Day Game was played in Kirkwood that year, the 1937 Webster marching band was the first marching band to perform during halftime at a Turkey Day game that year.

It is important to document that a possible factor in Webster's dominance in the game for its first twenty-three years was that Kirkwood was a consolidated school district until some time in the late 1940s. The official name of the school district is Kirkwood School District, R-7; the "R-7" designating it as the "Rural 7" school district. Because there was no other school district west of Kirkwood until you reached the City of Eureka, students came to Kirkwood High School from areas such as Jefferson Barracks, Manchester and Ellisville. Essentially, any student living in a district without a high school could apply to the County Superintendent of Schools for assignment and attend almost any place that they chose. The Webster Groves High School by many accounts had a larger student body than Kirkwood in the early years and they were often described by many sources as simply being bigger physically than their Kirkwood counterparts for many of those years.

In 1938 in Kirkwood, the first yearbook was published under the name of the *Pioneer*. The name *Pioneer* resulted from a contest by the Kirkwood school newspaper, *The Kirkwood Call*, to name a school mascot, winning over the names "Red Birds" and "Red Hawks." It is because the *Pioneer* yearbook came so late to the school that earlier details of Kirkwood High School's history are so difficult to find and verify, unlike Webster High School whose earliest yearbook was printed in 1911. According to 1937 Kirkwood alumnus, Sherwood Hughes, prior to the *Pioneer* yearbook the last issue of *The Kirkwood Call* newspaper served as the yearbook, printing photos of all of the academic year's sports teams and reporting summaries of the seasons.

The fall of 1938 was also a fractious time between the two schools. According to 1941 Kirkwood alumnus, Bud Leonard, there were many verbal exchanges between Kirkwood and Webster students in the weeks prior to the Turkey Day Game, culminating in a large gathering of students at the fifth putting green at Westborough Country Club, which was the putting green located closest to the intersection of Sappington Road and Lockwood Boulevard, near enough the border between the two communities, that had to be quelled by the Kirkwood, Webster and Glendale police. Once news reached the administrations of the two schools, an edict was made, probably due to the influence of James Hixon, that the Turkey Day Game would be cancelled permanently if anything like it ever occurred again. In order to save the game, Leonard, who was a varsity football player and president of the Kirkwood Hi-Y, conceived of a joint school dance to ease tensions between the schools' student bodies with hopes of saving the game.

A FIFTY YEAR LOVE AFFAIR

Although I had no coaching assignments when I came here in 1930, my interest in football was still red hot. Kirkwood's squad that fall was loaded with lettermen and everyone expected an outstanding season. I watched the preseason practices regularly and, having played college football, was occasionally asked by Ernie Lyons, head coach here for many years, to work with the kickers and passers – something I dearly loved doing. I wish I could report that the 1930 team was all that it was expected to be, but such was not the case. After a miserable start, some changes were made as a result of a practice game with U. City. We took what was considered our second team over to scrimmage U. City's second squad and our boys clobbered the young Indians but good. Gene Kelly, a name familiar to many, was in charge of the Kirkwood boys and, as a result of that battle, convinced Coach Lyons that some new faces should be given a try. Two important changes made put Jack (Little Mutt) Martin at fullback and Malcolm Patrick at halfback. These two changes and others worked wonders. Kirkwood won the remainder of its games and, on Thanksgiving Day, beat Webster for the first time in many, many years.

We could hardly wait for the '31 season to roll around. We expected a great team and a great one we had. Kirkwood was undefeated but tied twice. One of the games was with Webster in the traditional T. D. game which was played on a field covered with at least six inches of snow. That game was scoreless and seemed more like a defeat as we were certain it would have been a run away victory on a decent field. Many of the boys making up the starting lineup of that 1931 team are still living. The ends were John Hamaker and Dave Ruhl. Tackles were Jack Rose and Harold Murtfeldt and the guards were Vernon Reisenleiter and Bob Young. The center was Dick Prough and the backfield was made up of Jim Pierce, quarterback, Jack Patterson and Malcolm Patrick as halfbacks and Jack Martin at fullback. (It is my belief that all of these boys are alive except Reisenleiter and Rose). Our Line was a great one and they played both ways back in those days. Our offense was equally great. Patterson and Patrick were unstoppable around the ends and Martin ran over and through everything between the tackles and up the middle. And when a pass needed to keep the defense honest Pierce was there with an accurate arm. That 1931 team was truly a great one. The only other undefeated team in Kirkwood's history came 25 years later.

Something I particularly remember about the 1931 season were the complaints about Malcolm Patrick. He had grown a shadow on his upper lip (I don't believe any of the other boys could have grown a moustache had they tried) so he was constantly accused of being over age. And, although he looked older, he was only 17 or 18. One member of that team, Jack Martin, and I became very close friends and we were hunting buddies for over 25 years.

By Murl R. Moore
Kirkwood School Principal
1947-1963
Excerpt from the Kirkwood Historical
Society Review
December 1980

F. FROEBEL GAINES
WEBSTER FOOTBALL HEAD
COACH 1932 - 1934

My father Frank Froebel Gaines, Commander U.S.N.R. (Ret.) 1899-1975, was born in Sidell, Illinois, the third of seven siblings and he was a veteran of WWI & WWII. He attended Millikan University and then the University of Illinois, receiving his teachings certificate in 1923 in the same year he married my mom, Ruth Clara Williams. He became a father with the birth of my sister, Sherry Ruth and obtained his first teaching/coaching position in Paducah, Kentucky. Subsequently, my parents moved to Flat River, now Park Hills, Missouri, in 1924 and to Webster Groves in the fall of 1926. I, Don Melvin, was born in January of 1927. My dad assumed the coaching of baseball at Webster Groves High School the following spring, together with the teaching of geography in the classroom. Varsity football was added to his duties in 1932 with the understanding that it was only temporary, as another coach would be arriving in 1934 or 1935 (John McArtor).

"B" team football (primarily sophomores) was added to his duties from 1937 through 1942. "Froe" as most people called my dad was pleased and proud of his "B" teams, (undefeated 1937-1940 and 1942). My dad was an innovator and his teams were the first to use the new "T" formation at Webster Groves, but baseball was his passion. His teams from 1927 through 1966 were 412-154, which is quite a record. Two of those players went on to the major leagues, Bud Byerly and Charley James.

My dad pushed for an annual state high school baseball tournament and wrote his thesis on same for his master's degree in physical education. He was an excellent and much sought after football and basketball official for over twenty years, working both sides of the river for high schools, small colleges, Big 8 and the St. Louis Knights (that's six different rule books.) Additionally, he served on newspaper boards (*Star-Times*, *Globe-Democrat* and *St. Louis Post-Dispatch*) Selecting the outstanding athletes and teams in the area.

Harry Caray, a personal friend and an infielder in the 1930s said of my dad in his book, *Holy Cow* (on page 35) "an astute baseball mind he knew the game very well, he knew how to deal with different personalities, something you really need to know these days to work in the major leagues." In the summers of 1947 and 1948, my dad worked as a scout for the Philadelphia Phillies.

In his leisure time, my dad loved to hunt game birds, fish for trout, play cards (poker and bridge) and he served his community as a "Kiwanian" (He was Lieutenant Governor of Division VIII in 1963.) My dad was a loving father with a good sense of humor, somewhat strict, loved to debate (he'd take either side or even change sides), could be tight with a dollar ("needs" vs. "wants"), but everyone enjoyed his company.

By Don Melvin Gaines
Webster Alumnus 1945
Written July 10, 2007

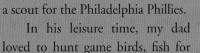

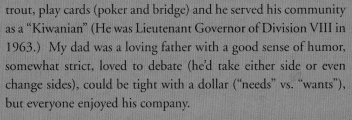

"AN ASTUTE BASEBALL MIND **HE KNEW THE GAME VERY WELL**, **HE KNEW HOW TO DEAL** WITH DIFFERENT PERSONALITIES, **SOMETHING YOU REALLY NEED TO KNOW THESE DAYS** TO WORK IN THE MAJOR LEAGUES"

Harry Caray, *HOLY COW*

1930

KIRKWOOD - 8 | WEBSTER - 0
Thursday, November 27, 2:00 p.m. at Kopplin Field

Kirkwood Football – Head Coach Ernest L. Lyons

> "FOR THE FIRST TIME SINCE 1913, KIRKWOOD BEAT WEBSTER!"

Webster Football (4-2-2) Head Coach Charles A. Roberts

Row 1: Flint, Honig, Greene, Carr, Hall, Stork, Becker, Brockman, Larson, Nisbet, Freschi, Coester, Pollock, Henderson, Scott, Harkey, Barrie, Hicks, Westrup, Evans. Row 2: Coach Gaines, Burgess, Kraft, Bryant, Horne, Cook, Breen, Hillmeyer, Milentz, Cox, Moler, Moeller, De Salme, Zell, Harvey, Kelly, Coach Roberts. Row 3: Lewis, Ward, Anderson, McLagan, Bourgeois, Hicks, Close, Kelly, Bopp, Corner, Broaddus, Smith, Wilson, Lysell, Miller, Callan, Curtis.

Kirkwood Football (6-0-2) – Head Coach Ernest L. Lyons

Kirkwood's Malcolm Patrick

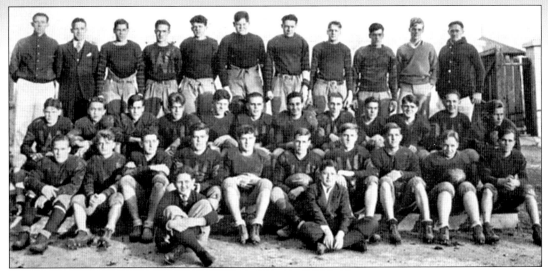

Webster Football (2-4-2) Head Coach Charles A. Roberts

Row 1: Hoffman, Hoffmann. Row 2: Wright, Morey, Hillmeyer, Zell, Greene, Carr, Moeller, Link, Bopp, Smith. Row 3: Larson, Smith, McLagen, DeSalme, Cook, Burgess, Breen, Prehn, Arlene, Corner, Westrup, Rossiter. Row 4: Coach Gaines, Ward, Harvey, Anderson, Hicks, Miller, Wright, Moeller, Miller, Robbins, Coach Roberts.

1932

KIRKWOOD - 6 | WEBSTER - 0
Thursday, November 24, 2:00 p.m. at Kopplin Field

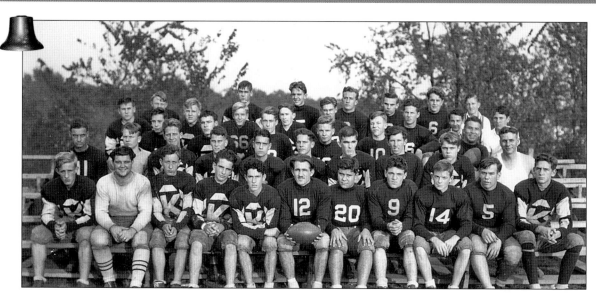

**Kirkwood Football
Head Coach
Ernest L. Lyons**

Kirkwood's Inky
Reisenleiter

Webster Football (4-3-1) – Head Coach F. Froebel Gaines

JJackson, Baumstark, Perkins, DeSalme, Anderson, McLagan, Cook, Smith, Breen, Becker, Westrup, Robins, Burgess, Prehn, MacKeen, Miller, Larson, Blake. Row 2: Coach Gaines, Blake, Hicks, Coggeshall, Timberlake, Langworthy, Breen, D'Agosting, Wright, Moeller, W. Miller, Howe, Tyler, Hudler, Tucker, Rossiter, Ward, Coach Smith. Row 3: Sandidge, Goodenough, Scott, Cummins, Smith, Dorsay, McArdle, Pierson, Mahler, Sparger, Heitert, Linstead, Heitert, Foote, Miller.

Kirkwood Football - Head Coach Ernest L. Lyons
Tenney, Tepper, Wilhelm, Betty, Krienkamp, Gadsby, Berkeley, Peeples, Loveridge, Johnson, Patterson.

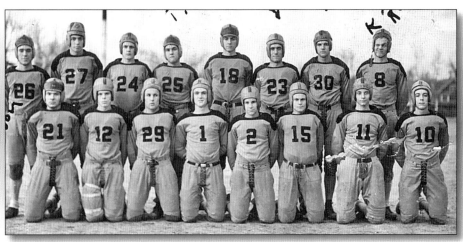

1933 Webster starters

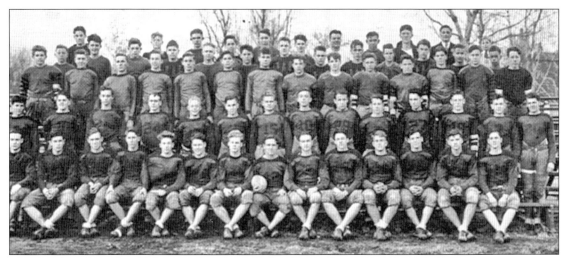

Webster Football (5-4)
Head Coach
F. Froebel Gaines
Peterson, Moeller, Tyler, Veaper, D'Agostino, Blake, Robins, Anderson, Foote, Coggeshall, Hicks

Kirkwood Football (4-4) – Head Coach Ernest L. Lyons
McMorron, Krienkamp, Cox, Van Patton, Kleybusch, Wallach, Leavitt, Cheney, Leveridge, Ben Peeples, Bill Heffelfinger.

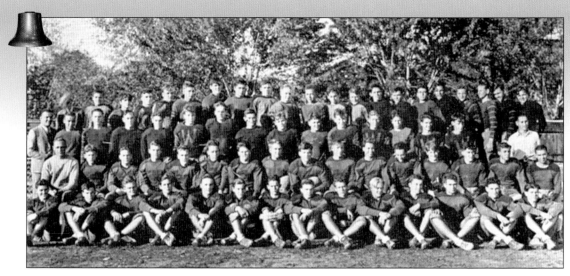

Webster Football (7-1-1) – Head Coach F. Froebel Gaines

Row 1: Kohlmann, Breen, Guthrie, Murphy, G. Heitert, Buck, Willingham, Wright, Kelley, J. Heitert, Bowring, Alger, Grace, Wider Row 2: Keel, Larson, Mier, Yaeger, Lindstedt, Peters, How, Tyler, Blake, Schricher, Frailey, Hudler, Robins, Keane, Moller, Coach Gaines Row 3: Coach McArtor, McKeon, Schumann, Paxton, Nabors, Ely, Beimdiek, Chapman, Wood, Horr, Jackson, Ruengert, Thiel, Jones, Peterson, Schiffman Row 4: Winters, Cole, Bcker, Spann, Reck, Wolf, Chadwick, Anderson, Sneed, Heaton, Coffman, Summa, Wilbur, Gross, Higgins, Krueger, Huber, Hacker, Schultz, Blanner, Gray.

KIRKWOOD - 0 | WEBSTER - 7   1935

Thursday, November 22, 2:00 p.m. at KHS Athletic Field

1935 KIRKWOOD SCHEDULE

Belleville	................0-19 loss
Clayton	....................0-6 loss
Normandy	...........12-24 loss
Hannibal	..................6-7 loss
Crystal City	.............7-6 win
St. Charles	..............19-0 win
Chaminade	...........21-0 win
Wellston	...................6-0 win
Webster	....................0-7 loss

Kirkwood Football (4-5) - Head Coach Ernest L. Lyons

LE	Meder
LT	Barnett
LG	De Salme
C	Donald Ducheck
RG	Cox
RT	Wallack
RE	Tenney
QB	Brady
LHB	Shands
RHB	Leavitt
FB	Kauffmann

1935   Souvenir Program   1935

25th Annual Football Game

Kirkwood High School

-- vs. --

Webster Groves H. S.

.. at the ..

Kirkwood High School Stadium

Thanksgiving Day

2:00 P. M.

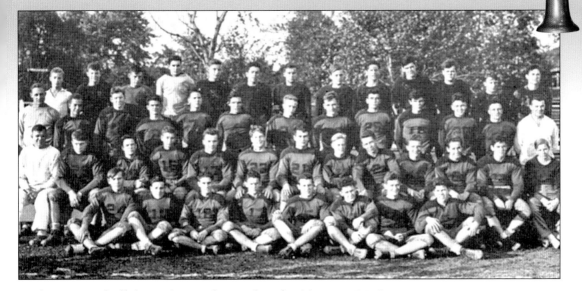

Webster Football (5-3-1) Head Coach John Trusten McArtor

Row 1: Schreiber, Cole, Nabors, Willingham, Kelley, Trefts, Chapman, Pendarvis. Row 2: Coach Smith, Ely, Mier, Wolff, Heitert, Robins, Alger, Heitert, Frailey, Hacker, Summa, Gross, Winters. Row 3: Coach Keel, Coffman, Jackson, Jones, Shewman, Huber, Heaton, Reck, Krueger, Schnebelen, Hoff, Spann, Coach McArtor. Row 4: Coffman, Hundley, Peterson, Anderson, Buck, Higgins, McKeon, Reaves, Schulz, Chadwick, Wood, Wilbur, Lee.

Kirkwood Football (7-2) – Head Coach Ernest L. Lyons

Row 1: Reisenleiter, Thatcher, Loveridge, Johnson, Farrow, Morgan, managers Grotha & Brackbill Row 2: Signor, Davis, Dillingham, Leavitt, Hughes, Martin, Meder, McCartney, Gene DeSalme Row 3: Dr. Gaines, Bux, Berkley, Matthey, Duchek, Venarde, Morrisseau, Crosby, Fleck, Coach Lyons Row 4: Coach Wiggins, MacMillan, Barnett, Gray, Thompson, Hill, Cox, manager Thompson, waterboy Daegele.

Webster Football (2-5-1) – Head Coach John Trusten McArtor

Row 1: Waldschmidt, Furhman, Peterson, Reck, Hacker, O'Herin, Krueger, Ely, Gross, Huber, Pendarvis, Higgins, Schnebelen, Succarth, Coffman. Row 2: Winters, Coach Smith, Horr, Grinnell, Swahlen, Henkle, Devine, Reaves, Roeder, Graybill, Anderson, Woods, Cummins, Curtis, Coach McArtor, Coach Keel. Row 3: Meyers, Meyers, Copeland, Applebaum, Ashcroft, Coester, McKee, Pacey, Murphy, Carvell, Burch, Wood Row 4: Tillay, Wood, Winters, Smith, Burton, Buck, Bohn, Hinson, Morris, Brown, Goerner.

Kirkwood Football – Head Coach Ernest L. Lyons

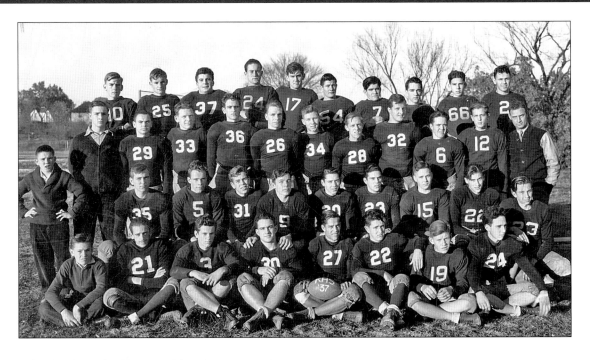

Webster's and the Turkey Day Game's first marching band.

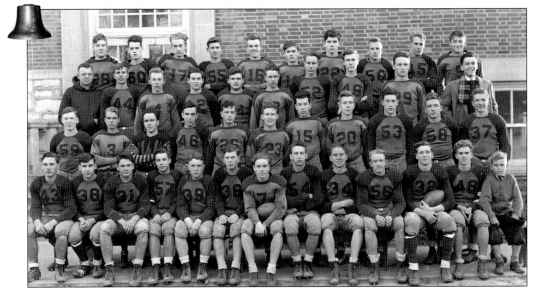

Webster Football (3-3-2) Head Coach John Trusten McArtor

Row 1: Mckee, Pacey, Ashcroft, Applebaum, E. Adams, Henkle, Goerner, Brinnell, Roeder, Coester, H. Goerner, Carvell Row 2: Adams, Detert, Tillay, Cummins, Lothman, Fillo, Hinson, Peterson, Woods, Reck, Hacker Row 3: Coach Smith, Winters, Oliver, Martsolf, Vogt, Hart, Devine, Lenzen, Wood, Higgins Row 4: Smith, Morris, Brockman, Gerell, Elzemeyer, Maus, Wilson, O'Herin, Querveaux, Greenwood.

1938

KIRKWOOD - 6 | WEBSTER - 13
Thursday, November 24, 2:00 p.m. at Kopplin Field

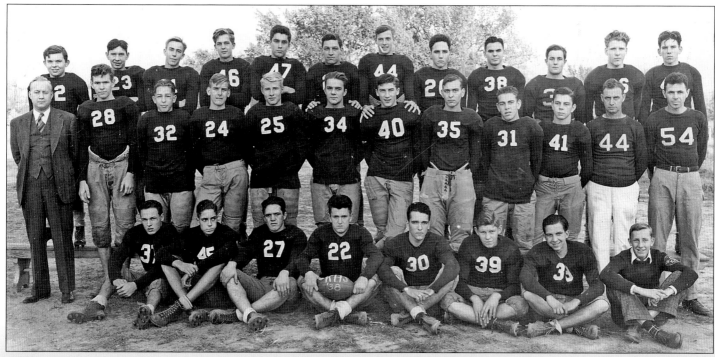

Kirkwood Football – Head Coach Ernest L. Lyons

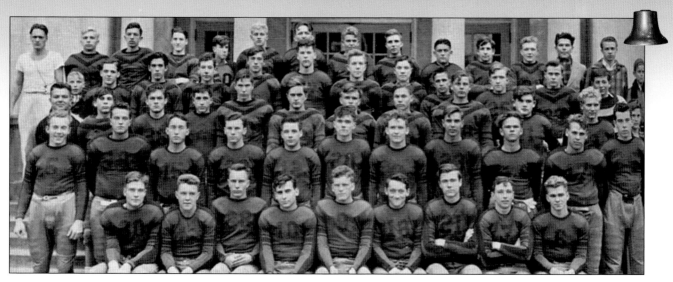

Webster Football (6-2-1) – Head Coach John Trusten McArtor

Row 1: Smith, Adams, Devine, Pacey, Murphy, Greenwood, Lenzen, Peterson, Carvel. Row 2: Oliver, Lothman, Pearson, Armstrong, Applebaum, Brien, Fillo, Winters, Fuhrman, Quevreaux, Hinson. Row 3: Coach McArtor, Maus, Maus, Sears, Wreath, Waggoner, Brackman, Seifert, Gerell, Vogt, Sudfield, Quevreaux.

Row 3: Bartz, Ecoff, Crews, O'Neil, Woodard, McMath, Peterson, Hilleary, Conner, Landon, Gustafason, Dupre. Row 4: Coach Cooper, Foote, Smith, Akers, Akers, Heidorn, Fieldson, Tendick, Goerner, Bartz, Kirk, Wright, Calvert, Hart, McWay.

KIRKWOOD - 6 | WEBSTER - 0

Thursday, November 23, 2:00 p.m. at KHS Athletic Field

Kirkwood Football – Head Coach Ernest L. Lyons

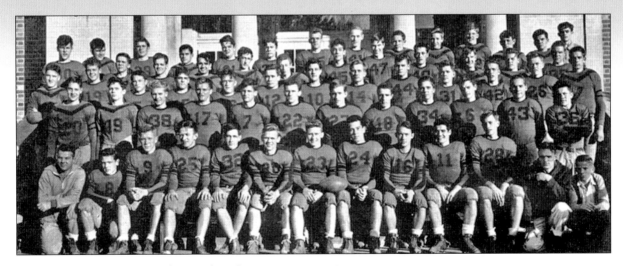

Webster Football (2-4-2) – Head Coach John Trusten McArtor

Row 1: Coach McArtor, Dassler, Peterson, Fieldson, Sears, Auinbauh, Fillo, Hinson, Pearson, Chapman, Woodard, Coach Cooper. Row 2: Stacy, Doisy, Sudfeld, Brackman, Gruer, Armstrong, Landon, Tschannen, Bryson, Berthold, Woods, Dixon. Row 3: Akers, Lothman, O'Herin, Dorsett, Bartz, Forsyth, Overman, Ballard, Gustafson, Paschen. Row 4: McMath, Maus, Ecoff, Luth, Hanford, McKeague, Crews, Wreath, Schwarz, Akers, Buxton, Carvell. Row 5: Miller, Goerner, Pottoff, Bohn, Mullen, Elzemeyer, Linss, Watkins, Culling, Barbre, Martin, Burnett, Maus.

75

THE BEAT GOES ON

Prior to 1939, very little information can be found about the Kirkwood High School Band program. However, in 1939 a significant change took place when Burton Isaac was appointed District Music Coordinator and the Director of the Kirkwood High School Orchestra and Band. Under Mr. Isaac's leadership the size, quality and stature of both the band and orchestra grew significantly. The Marching Pioneers were formed and became an integral part of the half-time performances at all football games, particularly Turkey Day. In 1938 and 1959 the first sets of band uniforms were purchased for the band and were financed completely by the Kirkwood Lions Club. In 1975 Isaac oversaw the formation of a parent support group, The Association for Instrumental Music (AIM). He retired in 1976 following a very successful 37-year career in Kirkwood and passed away in 2001.

In 1976, John Kuzmich was hired as the District Music Co-ordinator and Assistant Band Director. Stan Topfer was hired as the Director of the Kirkwood High School Bands. Bob Baumann was hired in 1978 as the Middle School (Nipher and North) Band Director and would later become an assistant at the high school. Marching Band became an extension of the band program as an after school activity. It continued to grow and involve itself in the many activities at Kirkwood High School. Football games, Turkey Day and the Green Tree Parade were the focus of their activities. The indoor concert bands grew into two bands – Symphonic and Concert Bands and the Jazz Band under the direction of John Kuzmich grew in size and popularity. In

1977 AIM purchased new uniforms for the band, which were intended to update the look of the Marching Pioneers and serve as temporary uniforms until funds could be raised to purchase new uniforms. Elaine Boyd joined the staff in 1981 as a part-time choir director and Assistant Band Director. Elaine served as the interim Music Coordinator during the 1984-85 school year and inaugurated the new elementary instrumental music delivery model, which is still in place today.

In 1985, I was appointed District Music Coordinator and Director of Bands. Bob Baumann and Elaine Boyd continued as assistant directors. Jason Rekitte was hired as Band Director at Nipher Middle School in 1992 and Steve Upton replaced Elaine Boyd in 1992. Through the leadership of new Superintendent Thomas Keating, the financial support of the school board and fund raising efforts of AIM, new marching and concert uniforms (the ones you see today) were purchased. Marching Band returned as part of the regular curriculum and the size of the band program grew from 90 to 150 over the next 16 years. The Marching Pioneers performed in Veiled Prophet and Veterans Day Parades and the Pommies became an integral part of the half time performances. Turkey Day half-time extravaganzas included Parachutists (3 times), a Salute to the 150th anniversary of Kirkwood, a pigeon release and a good old fashion melodrama entitled "Heroes." The often award winning Turkey Day Band Hall became an important part of the Turkey Day week activities. The quality of the indoor concerts bands (Concert and

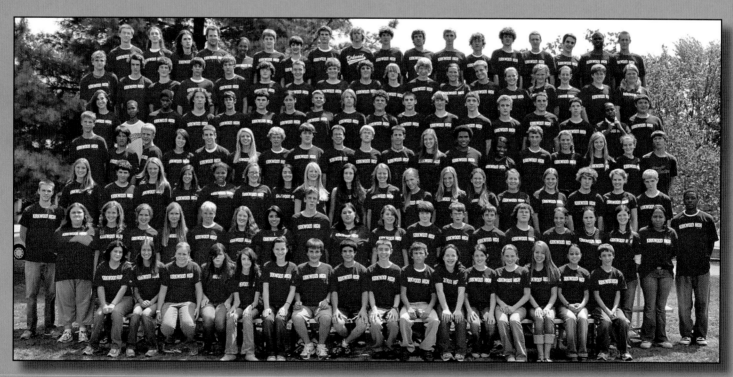

Kirkwood band in the 1940s

Symphonic) grew significantly during these years, as did the Jazz Band under the direction of Bob Baumann. The Symphonic received Division I ratings in the MSHSAA state music festival for 12 consecutive years and the Symphonic and Concert Bands received gold and silver ratings and other special commendations at festivals in Atlanta, Chicago and Nashville. The Musical Pit Orchestra, Solo and Ensemble Festival activities and the Wind Section for the Orchestra were extra-curricular activities available to members of the band. As a result of this growth, the district voters approved construction of the Thomas N. Keating Performance Center and an opening night gala was held on April 29, 1995. This center included an 821-seat theatre, new band and choir rooms, practice and storage rooms and renovation of the existing band room to be used by the growing orchestra program. Following my retirement in 2001, Joe Akers was appointed District Music Coordinator and Band Director and continued the activities, traditions and accomplishments of the band program.

The tradition lives on.... In 2003, Jason Rekittke was appointed Music Coordinator and Kirkwood High School Band Director in 2003 and Jeff Melsha was hired as Band Director at Nipher Middle School. Bob Baumann retired in 2005 and Rebecca Friesen was hired as Band Director at North Kirkwood Middle School. Both Rebecca and Jeff serve as Kirkwood High School Assistant Band Directors. Jeff also directs the Kirkwood High School Jazz Band and choreographs the Pioneer Pride Half-Time Shows. Rebecca also directs the Woodwind Chamber Ensemble. Luis Actis, Nipher Middle School math teacher, joined the band staff in 2005 as the Percussion Instructor. Bob Baumann and I continue to teach part-time in the elementary instrumental program and offer our services at other times to the band program.

As you will see on the field today, the great tradition of the Kirkwood High School Bands continues. The Marching Pioneers – now the Pioneer Pride Marching Band – continues to be an integral part of the Turkey Day game and Turkey Day Week activities. The newly formed Wind Ensemble, The Symphonic and Concert Bands, the Woodwind Chamber Ensemble and the Jazz Band continue to receive Division I ratings in MSHSAA state music festivals and have received gold and silver awards at music festivals in Chicago and Atlanta.

A dedicated music staff and talented students keep the Kirkwood High School Band tradition alive. Go Pioneers!

By Thomas Poshak
Music Coordinator, Director
Kirkwood High School Band 1995 – 2001
Written September 9, 2007

K formation in 1966

JOHN TRUSTEN MCARTOR
WEBSTER FOOTBALL HEAD COACH 1935 - 1940

Out of all the remarkable personalities that were identified with "100 Selma," none were more respected and fondly remembered than Coach "Mac" McArtor. John Trusten McArtor was a gifted educator, a winning coach, a mentor and counselor, a genuine friend, a sharp wit, a practical joker, a handyman and carpenter, a committed father, and one of the early pioneers (no pun) that created the outstanding reputation of Webster Groves High School. Trusten was destined to lead, teach, and coach. And he earned the respect to make him not only effective, but now a legend.

Mac grew up on a farm in Northeast Missouri and felt just as comfortable talking about corn and cows with his Webster friends at Walter Weir Gas Station as he was praising his football and baseball kids. He graduated from Kirksville State Teachers College in 1931. Mac was quite the guy on campus. He was honored with Outstanding Scholar and Outstanding Athlete, but always a friend to all. He was the captain of the football team as a tenacious guard.

James T. Craig said on October 6, 1988:

"… I admired him (Trusten) from the beginning. He was an ideal athlete. I envied his ability. I went to football games at Kirksville and saw how hard Trusten tackled. He was fast and strong. On offense he'd block out opposing players, giving Gus Beavens, our all-state fullback, a big hole to plunge through. Undoubtedly, he influenced me. I thought that I'd like to do what Trusten did. I wanted to see if I could play as well as him. I tried out for the football team…"

Equally impressive was Mac's baseball and basketball record. He was a catcher at Kirksville, and during the summers, he played on just about every baseball team in northern Missouri and semi-pro baseball in Nebraska. The basketball team nicknamed him "Pest." He could smother the opponents with a defense that drove them nuts!!

Mac's close friends always knew his most admirable college achievement was the courtship of Nina Starbuck. There were no closer teammates than Trusten and Nina.

Webster Groves required two years teaching experience. So after graduation in 1931, Trusten began his teaching and coaching career, first at Centralia High School where he started the football program, and then Shelbina High School. In the fall of 1933, he came to "100 Selma." Mac and Nina married on March 4, 1934. Nina also taught at Webster Groves High School for seven years. She was equally respected as a "permanent substitute" at WGHS.

(In those days, Webster did not allow the hiring of couples.)

In 1940, Trusten and Nina built their home at "530 Lilac Avenue," a home that Mac designed and helped construct. In November of 1940, first son, Eugene, was born … just in time for the Turkey Day Game. This home raised four children who made their own names at WGHS. Nina, now Grandma and Great-grandma Mac, still lives in the "house Mac built," now 67 years later.

Just as Mac's Webster teams gained prominence, WWII started. Mac left WGHS to work for Curtiss Wright, one of the major aircraft manufacturers during the war, as the director of employee recreational programs. During this time, he would also earn a Masters Degree in education from the University of Missouri to add to his credentials. Following the war, Mac coached and taught in St. Louis at Southwest High School.

The McArtor dinner table and backyard were full of stories and inspiration. Mac would refer to his mentors like Don Faurot at Kirksville while teaching life's lessons to his three sons and daughter (as well as the backyard full of neighbor kids who were always there, no matter what season). Mac knew backyards were for raising kids, not grass. And the many mud holes, destroyed tomato plants, and broken storm windows from errant balls attest to his patience.

Mac's kids were all good athletes (thanks to the encouragement of Nina and Mac). They vividly recall going to high school football practices with "Pops." As young boys, the brothers remember games, practices, and locker rooms watching the big boys under the guiding hand of their Pop which defined their lives. Younger sister, Ninalee, was the "lady in jeans" in the family and clearly Mac's little princess.

Mac and Nina both worked several secondary jobs to make ends meet in a growing family. But family was always first. Today, his sons and daughter fondly recall their father's acceptance of dogs, ponies, and convertible automobiles. They inherited Mac's talent for fixing everything. (Mac knew virtually everything could be fixed with 2x4's, spike nails, and adhesive tape.)

Lessons taught on the athletic field at an early age would serve the family well in 1956. Mac was seriously injured in an accident. The McArtor family had been coached in self-reliance, sacrifice, the can-do spirit, mutual support, and a strong Christian faith. Nina was now mom and dad, primary breadwinner, and caregiver. She rallied her family with courage and confidence to deal with the unfortunate circumstances. While teaching full-time, Nina put herself through graduate school to earn a Master Degree from Washington University, St. Louis, in order to provide for the family.

It was during this challenging time that Mac's friends and students reflected their heartfelt affection and respect for the fallen Coach. Living in Webster Groves was an additional blessing with close neighbors and enduring friends.

Nina's love and sacrifice would see the four children through high school and college. Dozens of orange "Ws" from several sports would decorate the wall, as well as three black letter jackets. Three "Roberts Awards" for Sportsmanship and Leadership would also be displayed. Nina saw four kids in college, as Coach Mac made a valiant recovery and comeback.

With the kid's core values taught early by Nina and Mac, faith and perseverance pulled the family through this uncertain time. Nina remained the strength of the family and Mac became, once again, the beloved coach and mentor to all that knew him.

Where does inner strength get developed? On a cold Missouri dawn behind a mule and muddy plow? On fourth-and-goal with the game on the line? During the last lap of a mile race? During the last inning of a dusty double-header on an August afternoon? Wherever the source, both Mac and Nina had that inner toughness yet gentle demeanor. They led by example, as evidenced by the four children.

Nina's and Mac's impact on their teams, classrooms, friends and neighbors was made evident upon Coach Mac's death in 1977. The loving testimony of so many people was comforting to Nina and family. It filled an album.

Mac's players loved playing for him and appreciated the life lessons he taught in addition to the sport of football or baseball. Coach Mac highly respected sports and was a student of the games. Coach did not tolerate those who did not show the same respect or give their best effort. This respected competitive leader, once settled in his chair with newspaper and pipe, would offer a soft lap or an encouraging word to all.

Trusten's many accomplishments as an athlete and a coach have been recognized within the Missouri sports community. In 1988, Mac was named to Kirksville's (now Truman State University) Hall of Fame. And when the University named an "All Century Team," Trusten McArtor was selected to represent a remarkable era of athletes and accomplishments.

Legends are remembered by stories, and everyone can recall something special about Trusten, Mac, Coach, Pop, J. T., and (yes) The "Pest." At 96 years old and still loving and always teaching, Nina is clearly in her own All-Century category.

Perhaps the most memorable day of Clan McArtor was Thanksgiving. For Orange and Black Statesmen, the day is full of pageantry and competition, chilly afternoons, marching bands, and combat against Kirkwood. Some things are timeless. Turkey Day games and the pride in Webster Groves High School are two.

John Trusten "Mac" McArtor helped shape them both.

Nina Starbuck McArtor, Commercial Subjects Teacher, Webster High School 1935; Eugene S. McArtor, Webster Alumnus 1958; T. Allan McArtor, Webster Alumnus 1960; John W. McArtor, Webster Alumnus 1961; Ninalee McArtor Gallaher, Webster Alumna 1966

Police Halt Webster-Kirkwood Class Fight

Police of Glendale, Kirkwood and Webster Groves spent a busy night when, besides the usual Hallowe'en pranks, they were called upon to disperse a crowd of about 200 students and alumni of the Webster Groves and Kirkwood High Schools, who had met for an arranged "gang fight," a prelude, according to students, to the football game between the schools on Thanksgiving Day.

After two attempts, fights were stopped by police in Kirkwood. Following a few individual skirmishes at the Kirkwood and Pittman Schools, the "battlegrounds" decided upon three days ago, the Webster warriors returned to their own bailiwick only to receive word the Kirkwood crowd was advancing to meet them, down Lockwood boulevard, on foot, in their own cars and by hitched rides.

Webster enthusiasts, according to potential participants, went to meet them. The two crowds came together on West Lockwood just west of Sappington road in Glendale, but were dispersed by police of the three towns before any actual encounters.

Rivalry between the schools is keen, and, students said, after the usual insults were cast back and forth, the mass fight was arranged for Hallowe'en. Police said several of the students carried clubs. A number of girls were in the crowd.

An Article from the Kirkwood Monitor
Printed Friday, November 4, 1938

80

71 YEARS AGO, TODAY

Kirkwood High School football was much different back in the early years of the 19th century, but one thing has never changed: The Kirkwood-Webster Turkey Day Football Game is always the hi-light of the school year.

Ernie Lyons was our coach in 1936 and was much admired and respected by all his players. The Kirkwood football field is named in his honor. In 1936, Ernie Lyons had only one assistant. Compare that to the seven or eight assistants today's teams have.

In 1936, the Kirkwood High School student enrollment numbered about only 600 students. The football squad consisted of only 29 players. The first season practice didn't take place until the day after Labor Day, when the school year started.

We received uniforms that had been well used in previous years. The team pants were made of heavy canvas material - (a far cry from today's light weight uniforms). We were issued leather helmets (no face masks in those days.) Each player had to furnish his own heavy leather shoes with hard rubber cleats. We had no exercise or conditioning machines, as today's teams have.

In those early years, players played both offense and defense. If a player was substituted in any quarter, he couldn't return until the next quarter. Because the teams were such small squads, we couldn't have dedicated offensive and defensive teams.

The night before the Turkey Day Game, we had a big wood fire on the school grounds. The Cheerleaders led the crowd in songs and school cheers. On Thanksgiving morning, students decorated their parent's cars with red and white crepe paper and, with the team players in various cars, they drove through Webster honking horns and shouting "Beat Webster!" Game Time was always 2 o'clock.

In 1936, only about eight students drove to school. (Compare that to the many student cars at the high school today.)

The 1936 Turkey Day Game was played at Webster's Field, which was located in back of their high school. The field had very little grass and the game was played in rain and snow and most of the field was ankle deep in mud.

Our fast and lightweight team could not run well in the deep mud and lost the game to a better team 12 to 0. The Kirkwood team of that year had an overall record of 7 wins and 2 losses. Schools were not integrated at that time, so we never played with or against black players.

I'm 87 years old now and still remember my years at Kirkwood High School and the Kirkwood-Webster Game as being among the happiest time of my life.

By Sherwood Hughes
Kirkwood Alumnus 1937
Written February 2, 2007

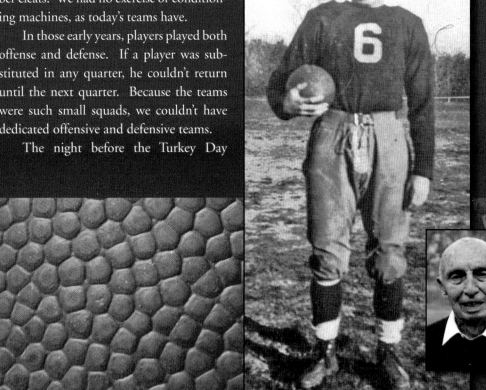

SHERWOOD HUGHES in 1936 and 2007 and still a Kirkwood fan.

THE 1940S..........................

Unresolved affairs left from the Great War, combined with connected events from the Great Depression, caused another devastating world war to erupt. While swing music became ever more popular, so did the sounds of "big band" music. By the end of the decade, another form of music called "rhythm & blues" would also be introduced. The decade of the 1940s is best described in its first half as the most destructive decade in world history, while its second half may be viewed as one of the more prosperous as the world rebuilt itself.

By the 1940s, the Turkey Day Game reached equilibrium and, in it, friendship. In 1939, both high school Hi-Y chapters did organize a joint school dance the Saturday following the Turkey Day Game, naming it the Friendship Dance. Bud Leonard states that the name "Friendship Dance" resulted from a "complete lack of imagination" and he fretted for some time afterwards about the name selection. Despite his concern, the name remains to this day. The climax of the dance was the crowning of two queens, with the dance intending to show that, as the 1940 *Echo* yearbook has written, "good-fellowship and sportsmanship are the basis of the Hi-Y movement."

Although the creation of the Friendship Dance is quite notable and significant in itself, another very important tradition started a year later as a part of the dance, which is the passing of the Little Brown Jug to the losing team. The jug was painted with a "K" and a "W" representative of each school, separated by a football. As stated, instead of the winning team receiving the jug, it is the losing team that receives it, with the caption on the jug reading "The Turkey Day Game Consolation Award."

On the back are inscribed the scores for each year's Turkey Day Game, starting in 1940. Since the introduction of the tradition, there have been three jugs passed between the schools.

The jug is a reflection of the unique sense of humour of its originator, Bud Leonard. Firstly, Leonard borrowed the tradition from the one held between the University of Minnesota and the University of Michigan, in which the winner of their contest won a jug. Bud, however, wanted his own twist to the tradition, which is why the loser of the Turkey Day Game receives the jug. A part of the joke in exchanging the Little Brown Jug is that the losing school would have to keep it in their trophy case, so that despite all of the school's other victories, they would still have to display it next to their trophies as a reminder that they had lost the Turkey Day Game.

The total record for the Turkey Day Game between 1940 and 1949 was four wins for each school and two ties, making this the most balanced decade between the schools. The teams tied in the years 1942 and 1944, which in regards to the Little Brown Jug meant that the school that had lost the previous year would have to continue to display it in their trophy case. In the spring of 1941, John McArtor took a job at Maplewood High School to coach and be athletic director, resulting in McArtor's one-season old assistant coach, Ray Moss, becoming Webster's new football head coach.

Raymond Woodson Moss was born September 2, 1913 in a small Missouri town named Hallsville. Football was not a recog-

The 1943 Turkey Day Game

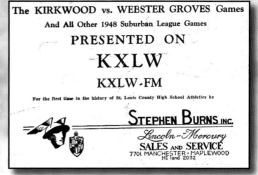

FRIENDSHIP AND A LITTLE BROWN JUG

nized sport at Hallsville High School when he attended, making it that much more impressive and characteristic of his natural athleticism that he was a star end with the University of Missouri for three years, was elected co-captain of the team in 1938 by his teammates and was chosen to be on the All-Big Six Team his senior year.

In 1943, Kirkwood was blessed with one of its finest athletes in an All-Star named Henry Christmann. Christmann may have been the most gifted athlete for Ernie Lyons to coach and was described in a newspaper account as being a "tall, long-striding, hard-smashing ball carrier." Despite a weak offensive line his senior year, Christmann led the team to a 5-3-1 record, scoring the majority of his team's points, with his team winning the Turkey Day Game.

Although *The Echo* newspapers of 1926 and 1927 indicate that there were "moving pictures" of football games, at present the earliest known recording in existence is from 1944, filmed by the parents of Kirkwood's King Martin, who was Kirkwood's first four-year letterman. In the years from 1941 to 1944, film making saw resurgence with the creation of propaganda films that were being developed as a part of the war effort. This made access to equipment and the creation of 16 millimetre films commoner during the war with educational institutions having the greatest access to the medium. Radio broadcasts had also been made of the game, the first known broadcast occurring in 1948 by KXLW-FM Radio.

In 1945, Webster fielded what was considered the best team in the county with a record of 7-0-1. Showing the importance of the Turkey Day Game, Webster declined playing the best City of Saint Louis team on Thanksgiving, which was a customary arrangement between the best city and county teams at that time,

so that they could instead play Kirkwood. Webster won the game 12-0, making their final season record 8-0-1.

In 1948, an old rock quarry, known by Webster old-timers as Forty Acres, gave way to Webster Groves' new football field, dedicated as War Memorial Field. The field would be used for the Turkey Day Game in the years from 1948 to 1956, because its size could better accommodate the large Turkey Day Game crowds. The 1948 season is also important in that it was the first year that players switched from wearing leather helmets to plastic, although face guards were still not in use. After the 1948 season, Kirkwood's longest running coach until that time, Ernie Lyons, decided to leave his post as head coach of the Kirkwood football team. Kirkwood High School hired for the next season Bill Lenich, a graduate of Joliet Township High School, in Joliet, Illinois. William T. Lenich, who only had an initial in lieu of a name, was a high school letterman for four years in football, basketball and track. He received his college education at the University of Illinois, where he lettered three years in football and was elected the team's most valuable player. Nicknamed "Wild Bill" in college, he was honoured by being chosen to participate in the annual Blue-Gray College Classic, his senior year. The next year, Lenich signed a contract to play center for the American League Milwaukee Chiefs professional football club, in Milwaukee, Wisconsin. After a short career in professional football, Lenich became a high school football coach, taking the reins of the Kirkwood football team in 1949. The contest between Ray Moss and Bill Lenich in 1949 would begin the Turkey Day Game's longest running rivals in the game's history.

1940 KIRKWOOD - 12 | WEBSTER - 6

Thursday, November 28, 2:00 p.m. at Kopplin Field

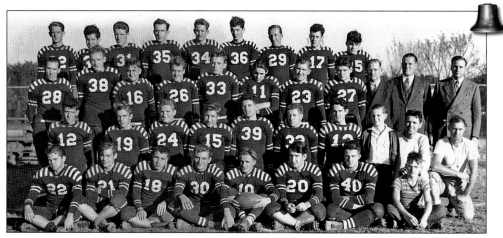

Kirkwood Football (4-2-1) - Head Coach Ernest L. Lyons
Koprivice, LeFort, Mabie B., Mabie E., Gray, Pinker, Redfern, Hoester, Tillman, Munroe, Kumpf, Pastel, Wills, Knowlton, Sparks, Rice, Philips, Hahn, Fairleigh.

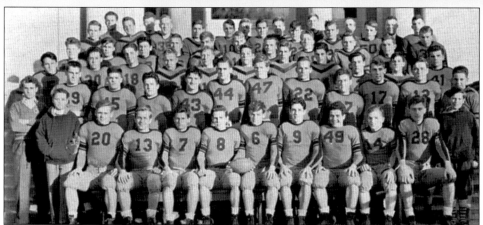

Football Queen
Catherine Kremer

Webster Football (4-4-1) - Head Coach John Trusten McArtor

Row 1: Sick, Auinbaught, Ballard, Gruer, Dassler, Berthold, Crews, Chapman, Ferguson, Woodard, Balser Row 2: Jones, Gartizer, Dorsett, Dixon, Richardson, Holt, Hamilton, Wood, Bartz, McCrory, Forsyth, Stadelhofer Row 3: O'Herin, Schwarz, Stacey, Berg, Leedham, Millburn, Jordan, Dickson, Bowe, Waldschmidt, Burnett Row 4: Buxton, Maus, Mullen, Mittler, Wesel, Gerstung, Buhrmaster, Johnson, Beesly, Sullivan, Cassidy Row 5: Bambei, Coach Moss, Lothman, Hundley, Linss, Ritzen, Applebaum, E. Busch, Blough, B. Busch, Miller, Hedges, Matt, Dr. Colgate, Schmid, Coach McArtor, Hilleary.

84

KIRKWOOD - 13 | WEBSTER - 19

Thursday, November 20, 2:00 p.m. at KHS Athletic Field

1941

Kirkwood Football - Head Coach Ernest L. Lyons

Koch, Frier, Collins, Johns, Detjen, Busch E., Stein, Miller, Browndyke, Jewett, Allen, Nooter, Shay, Busch B., Muth, Whitemore, Reuter, Buhmaster, Martin, Boyles, Feldman L., Grinnell, Holmes, Colton, Feldman H., Buschman, Schlawter, Baird, Cassidy, Schoknecht, Drew, Keller, Brandt, Heidinger.

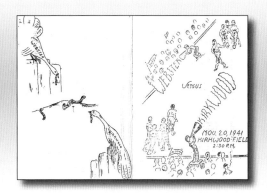

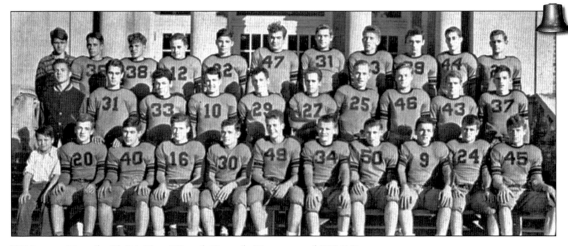

Football Queen
Virginia Gray

Webster Football (7-2) - Head Coach Raymond W. Moss

Row 1: Mullen, Busch, Miller, Boettger, Sullivan, Lothman, Buhrmanster, Cassidy, Busch, Schmid, Hundley Row 2: Coach Moss, Gartizer, Mullen, Applebaum, Hewitt, Miller, Linss, Schlei-ffarth, Gerstung, Hilleary Row 3: Schumert, Pitts, Stein, Johns, Mozley, Matt, Kemmerling, Johnson, colton, Koenig, Doyle

85

Football Queens
Kirkwood's Maxine Cooper
and
Webster's Martha Berry

Kirkwood Football (1-5-2) - Head Coach Ernest L. Lyons

Row 1: Managers Stanhope, Tolliver, Heineman Row 2: Vincent, Novotny, Chasson, Gardner, Weber, Rother, Redman Row 3: Wolbrun, Wittaker, Fuzner, Carmody, Kingsley, Wiesman, Wagner Row 4: Hartmann, Pastel, Hahn, Means, Coleman, Wills, Schul-enberg, Johnson Row 5: Wiese, Kolb, J. Christman, Staten, H. Christman, Calquhoun, Wagner Row 6: coach Lyons, Broderick, Knowlton, Scott, Mueller, Krabbe, Coach Wiggins, Mr. Hendricks

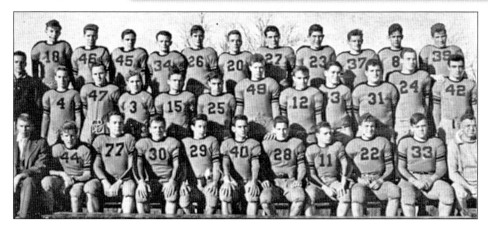

Webster Football - Head Coach Raymond W. Moss

Row 1: Hoefl, Beedle, Schweider, Lay, Ditty, Smith, Fleschner, Mudd, Buercklin, Dahlheimer, Olds, Whyte Row 2: Noth, Hanson, Weinischke, Zumwalt, Lindholm, Toft, Dring, Wolff, Zeiss Row 3: Hicks, Summa, O'Kelley, Kuhlman, Delong, Knickman, Elster, Whyte, Carothers, Salveter, Cliff Row 4: Coach Moss, Hellmich, Fitzgerald, Dickey, Mueller, Greene, Schwarz, Odor, Von Hoffman, St. Pierre, Stauber

Football Queen
Joetta Greer

Kirkwood Football (5-3-1) - Head Coach Ernest L. Lyons

Row 1: Berger, Howard, Wilson, Carpenter, Mr. Hendricks, Suits, Matthews, Wiese, Blase Row 2: Coach Lyons, Chasson, Means, Agnew, Klossner, Edwards, Richter, Rother, Ehrman, Jordan, Coach Conklin Row 3: Carmody, Redfern, Sturtevant, Thompson, Young, Martin, Chartrand, Jones, Kingsley Row 4: Colbrunn, Christmann, Wills, Clinite, Hartman, Redman, Knierim, Harper, Krabbe.

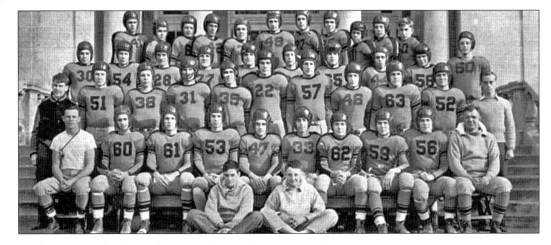

Football Queen
Ruth Richardson

Webster Football (6-2) - Head Coach Raymond W. Moss

Row 1: Colton, Hinkle Row 2: Coach Moss, Grinnell, Honig, Boyles, Johns, Jewett, Schlatter, J. Allen, Stein, Coach Smith Row 3: Carlson, Busch, R. Peterson, Jones, Borman, Browndyke, Nooter, Martin, Croghan, Calvert, Koch Row 4: Hotze, Shay, McGrew, Miles, Muth, Gilman, Keller, Reifstick, Duerr, Barker Row 5: Frier, W. Allen, Rallston, Stephens, B. Peterson, Deutsch, Schmid, Heidinger, Sick, Schlatter, Moore.

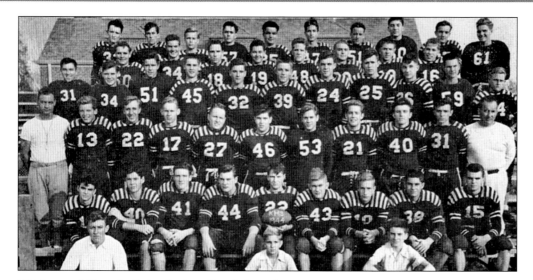

Football Queen
Susan Thias

Kirkwood Football (1-6-1) - Head Coach Ernest L. Lyons

Row 1: Managers Peacock, Peters, Franz Row 2: Fletcher, Stevens, Knickmeyer, Martin, Hunter, Fray, Thompson, Wilson, Lester Row 3: Coach Lyons, Coleman, Bridge, Neff, Spies, Zollner, Crancer, Housman, Carter, Langenbeck, Coach Conklin Row 4: Kohler, Petigo, Moeller, Robinson, Howard, Niewoehner, Fitzpat-rick, Ehrnman, McGlone, Earley, Jordon Row 5: Means, Thompson, Pliler, Haxton, Spencer, Finler, Carpenter, Gatchell Row 6: Colbrunn, Chartrand, Agnew, Essen, Hall, Young, Burkhardt, Knierim, Harper, Krabbe.

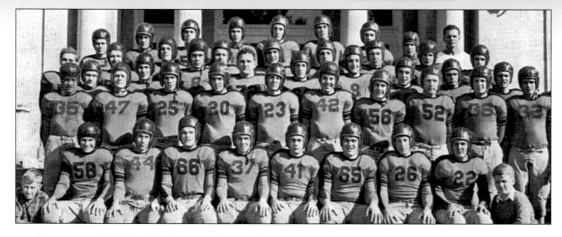

Football Queen
Mary Stuart Conzelman

Webster Football (5-4-1) - Head Coach Raymond W. Moss

Row 1: Powell, Duerr, Shay, Ford, Heidinger, Frier, Keller, Gilman, Higginbotham, F. Peterson Row 2: Rozier, Boss, Hiatt, W. Allen, Sprick, Schlatter, A. Carlson, Phillips, Wills, Owen Row 3: R. Peterson, L. Allen, Eschenroeder, Miles, Stephens, Busse, N. Carson, Collins, Sturges Row 4: B. Peterson, Ripley, Davis, Rollston, C. Jordan, Muth, Underwood, J. Jordan, Cordes Row 5: Buck, McGrew, Schmid, Donnellan, Barker, Waddock, Deutsch, Tschannen, Coach Moss

Football Queen
Joan Falvey

Kirkwood Football (3-3-2) - Head Coach: Ernest L. Lyons

Row 1: Managers Peacock, Peters, Franz Row 2: Fletcher, Stevens, Knickmeyer, Martin, Hunter, Fray, Thompson, Wilson, Lester Row 3: Coach Lyons, Coleman, Bridge, Neff, Spies, Zollner, Crancer, Housman, Carter, Langenbeck, Coach Conklin Row 4: Kohler, Petigo, Moeller, Robinson, Howard, Niewoehner, Fitzpatrick, Ehrnman, McGlone, Earley, Jordon Row 5: Means, Thompson, Pliler, Haxton, Spencer, Finler, Carpenter, Gatchell Row 6: Colbrunn, Chartrand, Agnew, Essen, Hall, Young, Burkhardt, Knierim, Harper, Krabbe

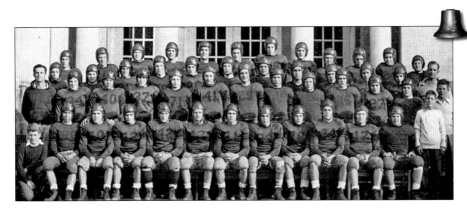

Football Queen
Dorothy Worley

Webster Football (8-0-1) - Head Coach Raymond W. Moss - Suburban League Champion

Row 1: F. Peterson, Schaefer, W. Peterson, Owen, Stephens, Rippley, A. Carson, N. Carson, Cordes, Schmid, Phillips, Brown, Truex Row 2: Coach Moss, Stein, G. Schlatter, Allen, Rollston, Deutsch, Busse, Runon, Parker, Graf, DeBoer, Kastner, C. Schlatter Row 3: Kuhn, Quigley, Sprick, Hundley, Hinkley, Martin, Murray, J. McKelvey, Tschannen, Holling, Finley, Coach King Row 4: French, Jordan, Paschen, Crossman, B. McKelvey, Meier, Cooper, Comotto, Hemenway, Peat, Noonan, Stahlhut

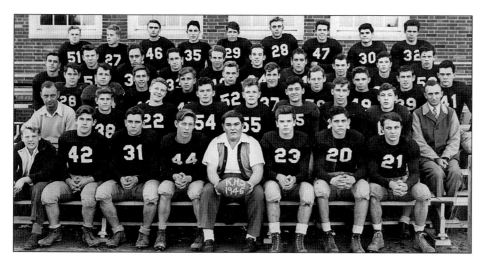

Football Queen
Patricia Baskett

Kirkwood Football (5-3-1) - Head Coach Ernest L. Lyons

Row 1: Burkhardt, Loeser, Marcolina, Gan, Flori, Gleiber, Jackson, Hunter Row 2: Coach Lyons, Spallinger, Wegner, Leigh, Munroe, Dart, Franklin, Heising, Mr. Bormier Row 3: Hall, Fleener, Sturdy, Wuest, Chomeau, Thompson, Richter, Woods, Meyers, Pollock Row 4: Hebberger, Chiles, Dwyer, Schulte, Boogher, Bass, Rettig, Ruppoert, Price, Moore Row 5: Almstedt, Garder, Fendler, Smith, Pratt, Zimmerman, Seaver, Berger, Maas.

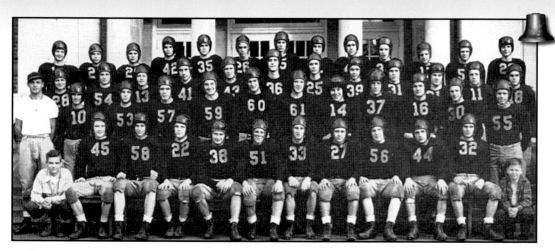

Football Queen
Ann Williams

Webster Football (5-5) - Head Coach Raymond W. Moss

Row 1: Hudspeth, Hundley, Cooper, Martin, Hutsell, Sprick, Comotto, DeBoer, Stein, Finley, French, Hanson Row 2: Coach Moss, Baureis, Kuhn, Tschannen, Hinkley, Meier, Paschen, Schlatter, Zink, Busk, Shattuck, Sick Row 3: Menke, Quigley, Stahlhut, Schoen, Jordan, W. McKelvey, Hobbs, Fedder, Hedley, Grace, Person, Koester Row 4: J. Becker, Nolte, Ritzen, Noonan, Graf, Peat, Davis, Eyler, J. McKelvey, Conrad, Stadelhofer, Clausen, D. Becker.

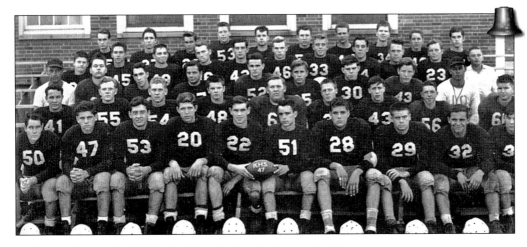

Football Queen
Kitsy Jordan

Kirkwood Football (6-2) - Head Coach Ernest L. Lyons

Row 1: Hall, Jackson, Dart, Pratt, Meyers, Hebberger, Rettig, Hallof, Maas, Ruppert Row 2: Hunter, Monroe, Gardner, Flieber, Autenrieth, Rutledge, Jones, Egley, Kincade Row 3: Coach Lyons, Koehler, Betts, Wood, Moore, Wuest, Moore, Hull, Coach Nagel Row 4: Fogerty, Sturdy, Wood, Eggers, Smith, Chomeau, Zimmerman, Bass, Disney, Hauk, Droege Row 5: Fawcett, May, Berry, Buchanan, Fleener, Butcher, Boogher, Felgenhauer, Ferber, Loeser.

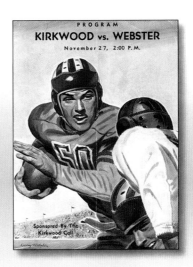

Football Queen
Charlotte Lawson

Webster Football (7-2) - Head Coach Raymond W. Moss

Row 1: Manager Menke, Noonan, Ritzen, Koester, Hinkley, Person, Paschen, Becker, Manager Schlatter Row 2: Hedley, Conrad, Nolte, Quigley, Stahlhut, McKelvey, Graf, Oliver, Wood Row 3: Coach Bryant, Forsythe, Spotts, Shield, Frith, Simpson, Fitzgerald, Schultz, Zavertnik, Greene, Coach Moss Row 4: Fedder, Kaufman, Reardon, Conway, Rutishauser, Jenkins, Davis, Rodgers, Peat, Lamoreaux.

Football Queen
Billie Bartelsmeyer

Kirkwood Football (7-2) - Head Coach Ernest L. Lyons

Row 1: Managers Meyer, Stafford Row 2: Rodgers, Hauk, Fogerty, Berry, Daegele, Davis, Rott, Brown, Jackson Row 3: Coach Lyons, Beck, Zimmerman, Chomeau, Ferber, Autenrieth, Bryant, Lindemeyer, Stinson, Whipple Row 4: Jones, Betts, Hase, Robertson, Evans, Diekroeger, Perry, Drescher, Ruppert, Coach Schoknecht Row 5: Summa, Egley, Bierk, McClaren, Disney, Boogher, Ferber, Unverferth, Spencer, Russell Row 6: Maas, Bowe, McFarland, Schmick, Harrison, Sites, Felgenhauer, Kunkel, Curlin, Herman, Stebold.

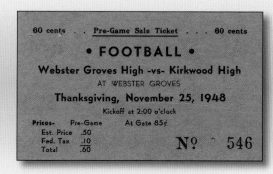

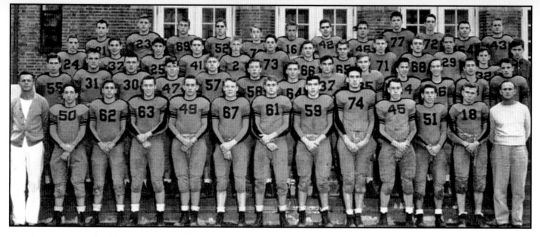

Football Queen
Joan Sousley

Webster Football (4-6) - Head Coach Raymond W. Moss

Row 1: Coach Moss, Mathis, Schultz, Fitzgerald, Harrison, Conway, Lippincott, Reardon, Rodgers, Breckenridge, Rauschkolb, Forsythe, Coach Bryant Row 2: Costello, Muth, Hutchison, Richmond, Straub, Schlatter, Huffmann, Spotts, Ward, Wilson, Whitney, Krewinghaus, Duckworth Row 3: Wilson, Woodson, Haase, Johnson, Gundelfinger, Lee, Keefer, Peavy, Pittman, Miller, Durkee, Bland, Schlatter Row 4: Metcalfe, Hodges, Rose, Warren, Diekroeger, Powell, Warren, Miller, Cook, Gale, Rosebrough, Gremp

Football Queen
Jill Meyer

Kirkwood Football (1-8) - Head Coach William T. Lenich

Row 1: Managers Whitlow, Thompson Row 2: Pottgen, Curlin, Rott, Wesseling, Brown, Richter, Davis, Daegle, Evans, Summa Row 3: Lindemeyer, Betts, Malsbary, Munroe Robertson, Diekroeger, Beck, Ferber Row 4: Hagemann, Perry, Koprivica, Gariel, Neuhaus, McGlashon, Wolff, Hicks, Greene Row 5: Bryant, Staub, Meredith, Crancer, Bopp, Mabie, Clawson, Jones, Hase, Davies Row 6: Coach Lenich, Coach Duchek, Coach Schoknecht.

Football Queen
Sandra Smith

Webster Football (7-2-1) - Head Coach Raymond W. Moss

Row 1: Gale, Miller, Johnson, Huffman, Durkee, Schlatter, Miller, Semmelmeyer, Straub, Warren, Lee, Wilson Row 2: Costello, Haase, Rosebrough, Krewinghaus, Gundelfinger, Weinischke, Pittman, Woodson, Peavey, Diekroeger, Metcalfe Row 3: Hartman, Coolidge, Dupsky, Brannacker, Goodspeed, Dunkel, Crooks, Butler, Simmons, Carlson, Cook Row 4: Forsythe, Jones Zwygart, Brickey, Dahl, Rose, Robinson, Duckworth Row 5: White, Carter, Hutchison, Keefer, Cruickshank, Ehlers, Brown, Corey.

ONE-TOO-MANY WINLESS MEMORIES
OF TURKEY DAY GAMES

You can't have lived in Kirkwood for any length of time and not become involved with the Kirkwood-Webster rivalry. They are two communities with affluent people who are leaders in the metropolitan area and who became competitive because of their proximity.

When I was in World War II, I would never call home on Thanksgiving until late in the evening because I always wanted to know who won the Kirkwood-Webster football game.

When we were young, winning the football game was always the indication of a successful season and it always proved in our minds that if we won we were much better than the people in Webster Groves.

When you grow up and mature and are constantly associated with people from Webster Groves either in business or socially, and find out how nice those people were and are, the rivalry takes on a different character. But beating Webster Groves at football was the big thing when we were young.

My family has had a disastrous history in this particular area. My father, J. C. Hoester, Jr., played football for Kirkwood and we have a picture of the Kirkwood team and written on the football itself are the words "County Champs." But dad lost to Webster Groves.

Dad played, I believe in 1917, and went into World War I. In 1916, my mother's brother, Sardius Van Dam, played for Kirkwood. That year Webster Groves had a player by the name of Al Lincoln and Webster Groves beat Kirkwood either 76 to 0 or 77 to 0. The family always said that the Kirkwood boys all went off to win the war to end all wars, while the Webster boys stayed home and played football.

My dad's younger brother, Harrison Hoester, played on the team in the early 1920s. He played two years and they called him "Hippo." He was six feet, four inches [193 centimetres] tall and weighed over 200 pounds [90 kilograms] and in those days he was one of the very biggest men on the field. He lost to Webster Groves both years.

When I played for Kirkwood in the Turkey Day game in 1941, we tried a trick play. Bert Fenenga was the coach of the Cleveland High School football team and he was the person who conceived the play.

The play was based on the fact that if a ball is fumbled by a player and it goes out of bounds before it can be recovered by either team, the ball is put back into play on the spot where it went out of bounds, and it goes to the team who last had possession of the ball. The idea was to intentionally fumble the ball in such a way as to gain yards.

The Cleveland High School coach conceived the idea of batting the ball out of bounds. I was the quarterback and I threw the ball up in the air and the fullback, Leonard Kumph, would bat the ball forward and toward the sideline hoping the ball would go out of bounds for a gain. The ball would then be brought to 15 yards from the sideline. And we would work our way down the field. You, of course, couldn't score a touchdown that way but it was a real interesting play. You have never heard how loud the boo birds from Webster Groves could be if you weren't at that Turkey Day game in 1941.

We, Kirkwood, lost the game 19-13, but I had some consola-

SCHOOL HONKS

Sometime around the end of the 1940s, Kirkwood and Webster students who were now driving cars frequenter than in previous years began to use their car horns to express their school spirit. The key for the honks has never been found in any written material, but they have been passed from one generation to the next in both communities and they continue to this day. In several interviews conducted amongst members of the 1940 teams, the honks have been pinpointed to have started some time between 1947 and 1950. For what may be the first time, here is the key for the honks and their accompanying words.

Honks: a bell denotes a honk and a dash denotes a pause.

Kirkwood honk:

🔔 - 🔔 - 🔔🔔🔔 - 🔔🔔 - 🔔🔔🔔

Our – team – has no fear – follow – the Pioneers

Webster honk:

🔔 - 🔔🔔🔔 - 🔔🔔🔔 - 🔔 - 🔔

We – are the States – men from Web – ster – High

tion 25 years later. The Webster Groves High School Class of 1941 was having its 25th anniversary party for the June graduating class. Webster Groves had a film library of past Kirkwood-Webster games and the people in charge of the party got the 1941 Turkey Day game, not realizing that the June class of 1941 would have played "their Turkey Day game" in November of 1940.

My consolation came in reminding my friends from Webster Groves how dumb they were not to figure out that they wanted the 1940 film instead of the 1941 film.

The story doesn't end there. My cousin Pete Van Dam, who was a track star for Kirkwood and who ran the hundred yard dash fro Kirkwood, played halfback for Kirkwood in the late 1940s and early 1950s. He broke always for a 40 or 50 yard run but was caught on the six or seven yard line and Kirkwood couldn't score. The game wound up a nothing-nothing tie. The guy who caught him played as the catcher on the Webster Groves baseball team and catchers are notoriously slow – but Hank Kuhlman was a great player.

The rivalry went to every sporting event that Kirkwood and Webster Groves played. I had some consolation in the fact that I was on the wrestling team for four years and individually never lost a match to Webster Groves.

I got some intellectual consolation many years later when a social studies teacher from Webster Groves and I got into a newspaper war on which community, Kirkwood or Webster, was the "Queen Of The Suburbs." How could Webster be the original "Queen" when Kirkwood was incorporated as a city many years before Webster Groves?

Even with the consolations I spoke of, it's not like winning the Turkey Day game. I sure wish we had won. To me the tradition of the Turkey Day game is far more important and creates far more character than cancelling the Turkey Day game to play in the state championship game.

The Kirkwood-Webster rivalry is the oldest high school rivalry in the state and probably the oldest rivalry west of the Mississippi. Ninety-nine percent of the people in Kirkwood and Webster can't tell you who won the state football championship last year, but a very large percent can tell you who won the Turkey Day game.

Written by Robert G. J. Hoester
Kirkwood Alumnus 1942
Written for the Webster-Kirkwood Times, Nov. 25 – Dec. 1, 1994

SCORES & SUMMARIES 1901-1949

EDITOR'S NOTE: Some of this information was taken from an article titled "Scores and Stars 1910-1949" from the 1949 *Turkey Day Program*. What has been added is the missing information from that article, such as what is known prior to 1910 and descriptions of the games between 1924-1927. Also, the information from the 1949 game has been added, which had not yet been played. There is a notation in the "Scores and Stars 1910-1949" article that states that the information contained within it was from the files of the Webster Groves High School's *Echo* newspaper and yearbooks and from clippings kept by Coach Charley Roberts. The article also notes that publications were irregular between 1910 and 1922, so that details from games for that period are limited. What that and this article therefore contain, is as much detail that can be found in any one place regarding the early years of play between Webster and Kirkwood, and even some other Turkey Day Game rivals.

1901-KIRKWOOD 0; WEBSTER 22.
October 18, 1901 *Watchman Advocate*
In a foot ball game played last Saturday between the Webster Groves and Kirkwood high school team, the score was Webster Groves, 22; Kirkwood, 0.

1902-KIRKWOOD 0; WEBSTER 16.
Webster scored a touchdown in the first half and the extra point was scored. Coggeshall scored two touchdowns in the second half, but both extra points were missed.

1902-KIRKWOOD 5; KIRKWOOD ATHLETIC ASSOC. 0.
There was no scoring in the first half. On the kickoff in the second half the ball was tipped by one of the Athletics who failed to capture it before it crossed the goal line. A Kirkwood player fell on the ball scoring a touchdown. The "umpire" originally did not count the score, but later admitted his fault and awarded the points.

1903-KIRKWOOD 14; WEBSTER 25.

1904-UNKNOWN.

1905-UNKNOWN.

1906-KIRKWOOD 0; WEBSTER 6.

1907-KIRKWOOD 5; WEBSTER 0.

1907-KIRKWOOD 6; WEBSTER 0.

1907-KIRKWOOD 5; WEBSTER 0.

1908-KIRKWOOD 17; WEBSTER 12.

First half Fred Heath of Webster scored a touchdown and Smith kicked the extra point. Shortly after, Urban Mudd of Kirkwood scored a touchdown, but Paul Simmons missed the extra point. In the second half Webster's Captain Thielecke scored a touchdown and Smith again kicked goal. Kirkwood came back and scored its second touchdown with Simmons making the extra point. The game was won by a Robb Lowe touchdown and the extra point was kicked again by Simmons.

1908-KIRKWOOD 5; WEBSTER 0.

1909-KIRKWOOD 0; WEBSTER 23.

1910-KIRKWOOD 10; WEBSTER 13.

"Cy" Merrill kicked a field goal from the 30-yard line. Sam Mc-Cartny made one of the touchdowns for Webster, and Chamberlain made one for Kirkwood.

1911-KIRKWOOD 12; WEBSTER 14.

Capt. Heath of the winners and Chamberlain of the losers were the individual stars. Merrell dropped a goal from the field for the Webster eleven.

1912-KIRKWOOD 12; WEBSTER 13.

One touchdown for Webster was made when the ball hit the goal post and bounded back into Kirkwood's end zone.

1913-KIRKWOOD 9; WEBSTER 5.

Fred Robertson kicked a 40-yard field goal for Webster. A safety accounted for two more points.

1914-CANCELLED.

Kirkwood's team this year may have been undefeated and untied. There was a disagreement between the schools this year that caused them to cancel the game.

1915-KIRKWOOD 6; WEBSTER 19.

Burrill Irland of Webster tore around left end for a ten-yard run that resulted in one of the two touchdowns he made. Capt. Halman made the third touchdown, and Northrup Avis kicked goal. Capt. Alter made the touchdown for Kirkwood. The game was played at Francis Field, Washington University.

1916-KIRKWOOD 0; WEBSTER 6.

Allen Lincoln made the touchdown. Bill Howze played a wonderful game for Webster. Quarterback Johnson and right halfback Higgins starred for Kirkwood.

1917-KIRKWOOD 0; WEBSTER 76.

Lincoln contributed six touchdowns and ten kicks after goal. His 46 points are said to have been the world's record at that time. Irland scored two touchdowns, and Proctor Wright, Percy Phillips, and Avis scored one each. Capt. Carl Stadelhofer blocked a punt which was recovered by Irland for one of his touchdowns. Overstoltz and Signor made telling gains for Kirkwood in one period of the game.

1918-CANCELLED.

The latter half of the football season was cancelled, along with school, due to an influenza scare.

1919-KIRKWOOD 0; WEBSTER 7.

In the last minute of the first half of the Webster-Kirkwood game, Percy Phillips broke through the Kirkwood line.

1920-KIRKWOOD 0; WEBSTER 7.

Steve Thornton scored the touchdown on a pass from Clifford Dunn. Thornton also kicked goal. Sherman Senne was captain for Webster, Payne for Kirkwood.

1921-KIRKWOOD 6; WEBSTER 7.

"Cop" Copley made the touchdown for Webster on an 85-yard run, and "Ferd" Stork kicked goal. White carried the ball over for Kirkwood.

1922-KIRKWOOD 6; WEBSTER 7.

Payne made the touchdown for Kirkwood. Chester Greene scored for Webster, and Quentin Gaines kicked goal.

1923-KIRKWOOD 0; WEBSTER 7.

Richard Shellabarger made the touchdown and the place kick. Capt. George Senne and Carpenter Barnett also starred for Webster. Kirkwood's outstanding players were Maschoff, Parks, Sturdy, Murphy, and Capt. Schwenker.

1924-WEBSTER 14; CLAYTON 7.

The first quarter was scoreless, but in the second quarter Webster scored by means of a long pass and line bucking. In the beginning of the second half Webster scored a touchdown on a blocked punt but missed the extra point. A few minutes after the kickoff, John Greene of Webster fumbled and Lewis, Clayton left end, scooped up the ball and ran 70 yards for a touchdown.

1925- WEBSTER 26; CLAYTON 0.

Joe Lintzenich's superior punting was of exceptional brilliancy. However, Bud Sample's line plunging and Gang Greene's generalship were also worthy of much praise.

1926- WEBSTER 41; CLAYTON 0.

In the first few minutes of play Webster scored the first touchdown on a 50-yard run by John Greene. Bud Sample scored the extra point by a run to the end-zone. Webster also scored a safety on a blocked kick. In the second quarter Sample scored two touchdowns, but both extra points were missed. By the end of the first half, Snyder scored a touchdown and Goodloe the extra point.

1927- WEBSTER 6; BEAUMONT 0.

Webster scored a touchdown on the sixth play of the game when Nesbit returned a punt, but he missed the extra point kick.

1928-KIRKWOOD 0; WEBSTER 6.

Bob Ramsey scored the touchdown. Capt. "Red" Tyrell of Webster was a hero on the defense. George Harsh, an outstanding star for Kirkwood, was "a demon on attack."

1929-KIRKWOOD 0; WEBSTER 14.

Bill Freschi scored all of Webster's points by ripping off runs of 60 and 70 yards, despite the two centimetres of snow covering the gridiron in Kirkwood. His kicking and running back of punts were features of the contest. Liberty punted for Kirkwood.

1930-KIRKWOOD 8; WEBSTER 6.

Kirkwood's outstanding man on the offensive was Norcum Patrick. Brink knifed through center for Kirkwood's touchdown. Martin of Kirkwood blocked a punt by Freschi, the ball rolled back 30 yards and out of the end zone for a safety. George Nisbet scored the touchdown for Webster after Harkey had blocked a punt. In a post-season game the Webster alumni defeated the Kirkwood alumni, 7-6. "Hub" Miller scored the touchdown for Webster. John Greene kicked the extra point. Klein scored for Kirkwood.

1931-KIRKWOOD 0; WEBSTER 0.

Most spectacular play of the game was a punt by Roy Greene.

1932-KIRKWOOD 6; WEBSTER 0.

Rabenau of Kirkwood intercepted a pass on Webster's 45-yard line and galloped over the goal without being touched. Charlie Burgess of Webster accumulated 58 out of 98 yards from scrimmage.

1933-KIRKWOOD 7; WEBSTER 0.

Kirkwood scored in the first quarter on a 20-yard pass from Ben Peeples to Jack Berkeley.

1934-KIRKWOOD 6; WEBSTER 12.

Webster's first touchdown was made by Jim Heitert, who ran 34 yards to score; the second, by Jack Howe, who sprinted 79 yards. Bill Heffelinger scored for Kirkwood after his team had advanced the ball 90 yards on a series of passes and runs. Russell Hudler did good punting for Webster. This game was played on a very muddy field.

1935-KIRKWOOD 0; WEBSTER 7.

Bruce Alger scored the touchdown for Webster, Julius Summa kicked the extra point, and Tom Nabors blocked two Kirkwood punts. There were flurries of snow.

1936-KIRKWOOD 0; WEBSTER 14.

Touchdowns were made by Harry Pendarvis and Jack Reck. John Higgins kicked the extra points. The game was characterized by a punting duel between Oliver Gross of Webster and Gene De-Salme of Kirkwood. Sherwood Hughes, 53-kilogram Kirkwood fullback, tackled Gross after a 30-yard run and prevented him from making a touchdown. Duchek was center for Kirkwood.

1937-KIRKWOOD 0; WEBSTER 28.

Jack Reck scored two touchdowns, and John Higgins and Sam Oliver, a junior substitute in the last quarter, scored one each. Higgins kicked an extra point, and Oscar Roeder booted a field goal from about the 20-yard line. The tackling of Henry Woods and Wilbur Hacker, and the passing of Dan Pacey were outstanding. Kirkwood had recently adopted the name Pioneers at the time of this game.

1938-KIRKWOOD 6; WEBSTER 13.

Kirkwood outplayed Webster in the first half. The Pioneers pushed over their touchdown on an eight-yard pass from Jack Faser to Vernon Gray in the end zone. Webster touchdowns were made by Dick Devine in the third quarter and Dan Pacey in the

fourth. Bill Lothman plunged through center for the extra point. The game was played on a muddy field.

1939-KIRKWOOD 6; WEBSTER 0.

Jack Faser led the Pioneers to victory.

1940-KIRKWOOD 12; WEBSTER 6.

Webster received the Little Brown Jug, which was instituted this year. The game was not decided until the final seconds when Harold Jenkins heaved a 38-yard pass to Kay Felker in the Webster end zone. McKee made the other touchdown for Kirkwood. John Sullivan scored for Webster.

1941-KIRKWOOD 13; WEBSTER 19.

Bob Buhrmaster, Paul Applebaum, and John Sullivan made touchdowns for Webster. Jack Pepin made on of the touchdowns for Kirkwood.

1942-KIRKWOOD 12; WEBSTER 12.

Bill Busch made both of the touchdowns for Webster. "Hank" Schoknecht played on the Webster team.

1943-KIRKWOOD 20; WEBSTER 14.

Both touchdowns for Webster were made by Dick Honig, the first on a pass from Jack Frier, the second on a pass from Bob Schlatter. Frier kicked the extra points. Kirkwood's touchdowns were made by Redman, Carmody, and Christmann. Hartman kicked one of the extra points, and Christmann ran around end for the other.

1944-KIRKWOOD 0; WEBSTER 0.

King Martin was captain of Kirkwood team. Logan Young was mentioned for passing and kicking, Charlie Coleman for running. Webster players mentioned were Jack Frier, Don Keller, and Charlie Stevens.

1945-KIRKWOOD 0; WEBSTER 12.

Norman Carlson and Dale Cordes made touchdowns for Webster. In the Pioneers' passing attack, passes to Burkhardt and Patterson took the ball deep into Webster territory.

1946-KIRKWOOD 6; WEBSTER 7.

Kirkwood's touchdown was made by Charles Meyer on a pass from Bob Schulte. Bob Stahlhut scored the touchdown for Webster, and Jim Sprick kicked the extra point.

1947-KIRKWOOD 14; WEBSTER 0.

Charles Meyer, Kirkwood's end and star of the game, made both touchdowns. The second was made on a long pass from Art Hebberger.

1948-KIRKWOOD 14; WEBSTER 7.

Jones and Maas made touchdowns for Kirkwood. Maas kicked the extra points. Rauschkolb of Webster scored a touchdown on a 70-yard run. Brickey kicked the extra point for Webster.

1949-KIRKWOOD 0; WEBSTER 6.

Webster scored one touchdown late in the third quarter, but missed the extra point.

THE LITTLE BROWN JUG

On November 30, 1940 a new tradition started as a part of the historic Turkey Day Game rivalry. Bud Leonard, whose idea it was to start the Friendship Dance, was inspired by the rivalry between the University of Michigan and the University of Minnesota and the tradition that they shared in awarding a brown jug to the winner of that football contest. Bud Leonard, possessing a unique sense of humour, decided that a jug should be awarded in the Turkey Day Game also, but as a twist on the Michigan-Minnesota rivalry, instead of it going to the winner of the contest, it would go to the loser.

The presentation of the jug was done at the Friendship Dance, given by the winning team's captain to the losing team's captain. The jug was intended to be kept in the trophy case of the loser for a year until the team who had possession of it was able to win the Turkey Day Game and thus force it upon the other team.

The original jug was commandeered from the parents of a Webster student, as reported by former Webster Groves High School principal and now Alumni Association Director, Pat Voss, "I was giving a tour at the high school a few years ago for a group of alums that had graduated in 1941. The cutest man asked if he could have his 'little brown jug' back and proceeded to tell me that he had taken it from his parents' basement so that it could be used at the Friendship Dance. That was the first that I had ever heard of it." The first jug was smaller than the jugs that would follow it, only measuring about 32 centimetres in height. There have been three jugs exchanged over the years with the years and scores recorded on the back of the jug. The first two jugs were kept at the Y.M.C.A. because it hosted the Friendship Dance until 1980. In 1987, the jugs were retrieved by Webster High School,

with jug number two currently being exchanged between the schools. The first jug has been missing since its retrieval in 1987. The first year and score on jugs one and two is 1940, although it is not known when the dates and scores ended for jug number one. The dates and scores on the back of the second jug end in 1959, which might be a later date than jug number one. The last jug to be used is clearly labeled "Jug No. 3" the first score that it bears is 1960 with the last date ending in 1975. Interestingly, Jug No. 3 was stolen in 1974 and there are no scores recorded on the jug for the years 1973 to 1975. Jug number three was stolen by a Webster alumnus in 1974 who found the jug unattended at the end of the 1974 game on a table in the swimming pool area that existed adjacent to Moss Field, where the restrooms for Moss Field were located. The culprit submerged the jug in the swimming pool and returned at night, climbing the fence of the pool and absconding with the jug. After a few parties in 1974, where the jug was used as the centerpiece, the jug was then kept in a bag in the culprit's parent's attic until P.J.'s Tavern opened in 1993. Fearing that he might be "strung up" for having kept the jug for so long, the culprit brought it to P.J.'s, where it has sat behind the bar ever since giving alumni a good giggle. From the time that the jug was stolen in 1974 until 1993, there was no jug exchanged between the teams.

The reason for the venue change for the Friendship Dance from the Y.M.C.A. to the high schools was because lagging attendance was costing too much for the Y.M.C.A. to want to host the dance. In the late 1980s, it was reported in the newspaper that the director of the Webster Groves Y.M.C.A., Bob Wanek, had possession of the old icons for reasons that he could not explain, with one jug's purpose being to prop open a door. Webster officials reclaimed the jugs and kept them in "The Vault" at Webster High School, until they mysteriously disappeared. One of the jugs reappeared one morning in October, 1993 in Kirkwood High School's front office, which is when the Little Brown Jug came back into use.

By Shawn Buchanan Greene
Webster Alumnus 1987
Written May 7, 2007

IT WAS BETTER TO BE A DANCER THAN A BRAWLER

The idea of a book on the Webster-Kirkwood Turkey Day Game sent me on a sentimental journey to a time almost three quarters of a century ago.

I'd gone to Webster in Jr. High (7th, 8th and 9th) and after moving to Kirkwood in the summer of 1938 continued on at Webster through my sophomore year. The Webster authorities learned of my transgression and rather unceremoniously threw me out of that school.

Having played B Team football at Webster, I tried out for the Kirkwood Varsity at the beginning of my junior year. The legendary Ernie Lyons and his assistant, Coach Kelly, both excellent judges of talent, immediately assigned me to the fifth team (it only had four players on it) where I excelled as a blocking and tackling dummy. Nevertheless as luck would have it, I started the first game and played every quarter of every game through 1939-40 culminating in my election as Captain before the Turkey Day Game of 1940. Incidentally, Kirkwood won both years.

The reason for my recounting the above was to explain the following. In 1938, groups of jocks from both schools massed for a fight on the grounds of Westborough Country Club. Fortunately the police were informed, arrived in force, and held the battle to a few small skirmishes. However the principal of each school issued an edict that a repeat would cause cancellation of the game and the series.

Because of my association with players of Webster and Kirkwood, you can understand this confrontation had to be thwarted. In addition, my girlfriend (later my wife of 62 years) was going to Webster. I decided that it was better to be a dancer than a brawler. This spawned a brilliant idea which, because of a total lack of imagination, we call "The Friendship Dance." The planning and implementation of the dance was performed by the Hi-Y Clubs of both schools.

In 1940, to have an award and borrowing from the Michigan-Minnesota Big Ten Game, we procured a little brown jug but awarded it to the loser in order to be different. The loser was then to display this jug in his trophy case.

Since we were on a roll, the two schools elected the first football queens who were to be crowned by the opposing Hi-Y presidents at the dance. Unfortunately, my future wife was runner up and I had to crown her best friend.

To my utter amazement after 68 years the sentimental journey seems to be going strong.

By William T. "Bud" Leonard
Kirkwood High School Alumnus 1941
Written April 9, 2007

MURPHY'S LAW

"The Brown Jug isn't awarded to the losers anymore," said the reporter covering this year's Turkey Day Game between the Webster Groves Statesmen and the Kirkwood Pioneers. "The lady said the jug has been missing for years."

What a shame, I thought. First Burl Ives dies, then the Brown Jug becomes part of an elaborate heist – I don't know what to make of it.

Taking a final drag off my cigarette, I drop the butt into a small opening of brown-colored, ceramic container. The strange looking jug – with a large "W" and "K" painted on opposite ends – has been sitting alongside my office desk for years. I don't know what to make of it.

I am thankful, however, that some poor sap other than myself was assigned to write the Turkey Game story this year. Eleven years I have been employed by this newspaper. Eleven years I have managed to duck the Turkey Game assignment.

I haven't been so lucky with other stories which come around on a yearly basis. Halloween stories are bad assignments – another haunted house story, another piece on how witches are really nice people.

But under the category of "stories I wouldn't assign my worst enemy, Turkey Day ranks right at the top.

Don't get me wrong. The annual Thanksgiving Day game is a great tradition. Having said that, however, reporters will gladly leap from second story windows to avoid having to write about it. After 14 years of coverage, getting "a new angle" on the Turkey Game takes more imagination than the average writer can muster. It's a lot easier to write about button collections.

Kevin Murphy as a 1973 C.B.C. Cadet

This year's football match-up story pitting the Pioneers against the Statesmen was handed off to reporter Janet Edwards, who, quick to realize she had a turkey on her hands, fumbled the assignment into the arms of an unsuspecting Marty Harris.

"But I don't know anything about football," said Harris.

"So what," I said. "I don't know anything about Halloween or witches, but anyone can fake 30 inches of copy."

My comments did nothing to lift her spirits.

"Just get some quotes form football players," I continued. "If you can't find football players, talk to cheerleaders. If cheerleaders are too busy, just stop anyone on the street. Nine out of 10 people will tell you they played in a Turkey Day Game whether they did or not."

Later, Marty would comment that "tight end" seemed a rather provocative title for football players. I was glad to see the story was being handled by a seasoned sports professional.

Crumpling a candy wrapper in my fist, I nonchalantly poked it through the hole of my brown, jug-shaped waste basket.

"What happened to the Brown Jug?" I asked Marty.

"There were a couple of small ones which haven't been seen in over a decade," she said. "Another, larger jug, hasn't been seen for a couple of years."

Now there's a good story. If I could get o the bottom of this missing Brown Jug business, I would be more than happy to write it I up for next year's Turkey Day game story.

Crushing out another cigarette on the edge of the container, I drop the butt into the jug.

Reader's Note: After Webster Groves High School reclaimed the first and second Little Brown Jugs from the YMCA in 1987, the Webster-Kirkwood Times borrowed Jug #2 for a photo session for a 1989 Turkey Day Game article. Forgetting to return it to the school, the jug sat next to Kevin Murphy's desk and used as an ash tray and trash can until the subject of the "lost jug" was brought to his attention. This is the jug now being exchanged between the schools.

By Kevin Murphy
Staff Columnist
Written for the Webster-Kirkwood Times, Nov. 20 – 26, 1992

RAY MOSS
WEBSTER FOOTBALL HEAD COACH 1941-1964

Our dad's favorite foods included broken pieces of bread in a glass of milk for a snack and corn meal hoecakes made on a griddle – common foods for a young man growing up poor on a farm in Hallsville, Missouri during the depression. Because of those circumstances our dad never expected to go to college. However, he accompanied a friend to Moberly, Missouri one day to visit the track coach at the junior college. This coach quickly observed that this strong, lean companion might also be a good prospect for his track team. From track, our dad moved into football. Thus began our dad's football career.

After two years at the junior college, our dad transferred to the University of Missouri where he majored in math and physical education. He had the privilege of playing as an end under Don Faurot and serving as co-captain of the football team along side All-American Paul Christman. Upon graduation, he was hired as the football coach in Monnett, Missouri where he was the most eligible bachelor in town – but not for long! On June 1, 1940 our dad married Jean Stoerger, an elementary education major, whom he had met at Mizzou. Shortly afterwards, he accepted the teaching and coaching position at Webster Groves High School.

The quiet demeanor of our dad carried over into his coaching. He was not a wordy man and so the words he spoke were always important. Before each game he emphasized two things: 1) enjoy the game, have fun and 2) playing the plan is more important than winning or losing. His standard of behavior was high and bad attitudes were not tolerated. He had a winning career and won the respect of, not only his own players, but other coaches as well.

During the early years of school integration, in the late fifties and early sixties, our dad often found himself seething over the prejudice that sometimes made it difficult for him to find a motel or restaurant that would treat all his boys equally when he had to take the team on the road, usually to Columbia. His belief was that everyone of any color was God's child.

On the home front, our dad worked hard to maintain a family of four children on a teacher's salary by refereeing basketball games during the school year and managing the Route 66 Drive-in Theater, and later, the snack stand at the Webster municipal pool, in the summers. And always, during the growing season, he was making the twice-a-day trips to "Memorial Field" at "Forty Acres," as Moss Field was then called, to "move the hoses" which watered his football field. During the fall weeks when football practice and the drive-in theater overlapped, he often survived on three to four hours of sleep and that continued until the children were school-age and Jean started teaching in the Clayton.

Our dad died of cancer at 68 on April 7, 1982. His quiet, winning ways were instrumental in establishing a standard that has helped make Webster Groves High School and the Turkey Day Game solid institutions.

By Gentry Moss Moellenhoff, Webster Alumna 1963
William Woodson "Woody" Moss, Webster Alumnus 1965
Candice R. Moss, Webster Alumna 1967
Kim Moss Kirsch, Webster Alumna 1971
Written April 2, 2007

Coach Lenard
"Bear" Bryant
and Ray Moss

WEBSTER GROVES WAR MEMORIAL FIELD AND MOSS FIELD

In a spirit of confidence in the future of Webster schools, the Webster Groves School District took a visionary leap and purchased forty acres of land outside the city limits of Webster Groves from Hydraulfe Press Brick Company in 1924. Originally, the area was bounded by Elm Avenue, East Glendale Road, Percival Drive, now known as Colebrook Drive, and by a creek running parallel to Chestnut Avenue.

After Webster voters approved the annexation of these acres in 1936, the school board, under the leadership of E. G. Curtis, who was the father of Congressman Tom Curtis, and Webster Groves city officials started talks on its joint future use and financing options. Plans coalesced around the need for a future school and athletic facilities for both school and city use.

The school district passed an $800,000 bond issue in December of 1944 that would fund a new cafeteria and gymnasium at the Webster Groves High School at 100 Selma Avenue and also a football and track stadium that would rival Washington University's Francis Field at the area that was now known as "Forty Acres." With the addition of city plans for an Olympic sized pool, Forty Acres would soon be considered the state-of-the-art athletic complex of the area.

Prior to construction of the facilities in the late forties, the acreage had consisted largely of an abandoned clay pit that had produced fire brick by Scullin Steel Works in the City of Saint Louis. No longer active as a mine since the 1920s, Webster area children often played pick-up games of Indian Ball, where Gaines Field is today, would swim in a flooded sink-hole near the batting cages adjacent to it, fly kites or watch Statesmen baseball games coached by the legendary Froebel Gaines on a rough field where Hixson Middle School now stands. The actual land that would be used for the football stadium and track lay fallow except for a couple of years that the city created a clay rimmed pond that when frozen became the city's first skating rink.

In order to build Roberts Gym at the high school, which was completed in 1947, the old Kopplin football field had to be sacrificed. The Webster football teams played their regular home games during these years of construction at Maplewood's football stadium, playing the Turkey Day Game at the Kirkwood High School Athletic Field for the years of 1945, 1946 and 1947. In 1948, the football field at Forty Acres was ready for use and its first Turkey Day Game played on November 25. The stadium was formally dedicated War Memorial Stadium, commonly shortened to Memorial Stadium, in May, 1949, in memory of the great conflict of World War II. The restroom facilities for the soon to be built swimming pool were to be used jointly with Memorial Stadium patrons, so in its first year, football game patrons were required to walk out of the stadium and walk a block down the street to use the restrooms and water fountains at Goodall Elementary School at the corner of Chestnut Avenue and Percival Drive. The new stadium was so well attended in its first year that the new parking lot was insufficient to park all of the cars, which caused cars to line the streets on every block for quite a distance away from the stadium, just as is done today. Harold Schaffer, who was the new owner of a nearby grocery store, parked cars on his lot for 50 cents, just like they did at the old Sportsman's Park for a Cardinals or Browns game.

Because it was able to better accommodate the large numbers of Turkey Day Game patrons, Memorial Stadium was the host of the Turkey Day Game from the years 1948 to 1956, until Lyons Field in Kirkwood was completed. Harry Carabina, a Webster Groves 1932 alumnus who lived one block away from the field, demonstrated his hall of fame talents by doing some radio broadcasts of the Turkey Day Games. We know him today as longtime Saint Louis Cardinals and Chicago Cubs broadcasting legend Harry Carey.

In 1976, Memorial Stadium was rededicated as Moss Field, honoring the field's first and legendary coach Ray Moss, who succumbed to cancer in 1982. Since its creation, Moss Field has been the home field of numerous generations of Webster players and three championship teams.

By John Lenich
Kirkwood Alumnus 1973
Written April 2, 2007

WILLIAM T. LENICH
KIRKWOOD FOOTBALL HEAD COACH 1949-1972

Growing up in the Lenich household football was such a part of our lives. It was more than just a game; it was a way of life. As a son of a high school football coach I quickly learned very early in life the importance of the game and how much influence the coach had on the lives of each and every player who put on the pads.

My father, or as most people refer to him, Coach Lenich, had such a major influence on me, my brother, and my sister along with many, if not hundreds of young men who have traveled through the hallways, and though the athletic programs at Kirkwood High School. Through his dedication and passion for the game and with his leadership skills he has taught many a young man valuable lessons in life. The lessons he taught go way beyond how to run a quarterback option play from the "Wish Bone" formation, or what is the best play to run when it's third and four with less than two minutes to play in the game. Like so many successful coaches, my father's classroom was the football field. As I look back, and as I go through my life I have become to understand his message. I would like to share four, of what I think, are the main lessons he taught. These are:

TEAMWORK: The importance of Teamwork and how valuable it is to work together to achieve success.

INTEGRITY: How the most valuable resource we have is the recognition that we are persons of integrity.

DEDICATION: Dedication to our assignments and how dedication is the keystone for our performance.

ENTHUSIASM: To have an enthusiastic positive attitude towards life and how a positive attitude can carry you though 90% of all activities.

I can tell you of many things he has done on behalf of so many people, things quite honestly, that as his son have made me extremely proud.

Coach Lenich has had a very successful and rewarding career as a player and as a coach. Highlights of his accomplishments from his playing days and coaching career are listed below.

PLAYING CAREER:
- Joliet Illinois Township High School. (1933 – 1936)
  - Starred in football and track.
  - In the 1936 season selected All Conference and All State for the position of Center.
- University of Illinois. (1936 – 1939)
  - In the 1939 season selected All American for the position of Center.
- Milwaukee Chiefs. (1940)
  - Played one season of professional football with one of the original AFC teams.

COACHING CAREER:
- St. Elmo Illinois High School. (1941)
  - Head coach for Football, Basketball, and Baseball.
- DeAndreis High School, St. Louis Missouri (1946 – 1948)
  - Head coach Football and Basketball.
- Kirkwood High School (1949 – 1973).
  - Head Coach Football and Golf.
  - Numerous Conference Championships.
  - Undefeated season in 1955.
  - Coached over 1,500 players.
  - Had profound impact of so many of those 1,500 players.
  - Finished his football coaching career with a winning percentage of over .675%.

Despite all the wins and agonizing losses, good times and challenging times, Coach Lenich always insisted his players hold their heads high, be proud of your accomplishments and "BE THE BEST YOU CAN BE."

By John Lenich
Kirkwood Alumnus 1973
Written April 2, 2007

IN THE OLDEN DAYS

The Turkey Day Game has gone through many battles — on and off the field. In the '30s & '40s, many fights and painting of the other school's property took place. In the late '40s, both schools passed a "peace policy." It started with a bonfire and pep assemblies. In 1949, I was asked by Coach Ray Moss to appear before the Kirkwood "Peace" assembly, held in the Kirkwood High School Auditorium. I was introduced by the Kirkwood principal and, of course, received many boos. However, after my speech, I got a standing ovation.

Cid Keane, John Schuette and I did the announcing for most of Jack Jones' coaching career and for some of the early years for Ken Manwarring. I remember one Turkey Day Game, at the end of Coach Jones' career, when both bands played as I tried to announce the starting lineup!

One Turkey Day Game, a good friend of mine was the head official. At one point in the game, whistles all blew and several penalties were called. My friend marked off 5 yards against Kirkwood, then 5 yards against Webster. Then they went 15 yards against Kirkwood and 15 yards against Webster. After all the penalties were marked off, I told the crowd that I was totally confused because the ball ended up right where it started! My friend looked up at me, threw his hands in the air, and started laughing – as did most of the crowd.

I know that when I played in '48 and '49, the players became very tense prior to the Turkey Day Game. Coach Moss, who captained the University of Missouri team in 1939, required that our black helmet and black shoes be shined prior to the game. We would sit in the hallway of Roberts Gym and coach would walk up and down for inspection. If not shined, you went into the locker room and shined as he wanted. Coach Moss and Coach Bryant were both the kind of coach that you would want to have coaching your son.

In 1980, after I opened Keefer's Sporting Foot, in Old Orchard, I was told that I had a malignant brain tumor. Ray Moss had been retired for many years and he offered to run my store while I was out. He ran my store for six months and ironically, after I returned to work, he developed cancer and passed away several months later. As you can see, Mr. Moss was not just a "coach," but a role model and friend. Because of what Ray Moss meant to Webster, it only took about 5 minutes at a Webster Board of Education meeting, to persuade them to name the field after him.

I can't remember the year, but Dale Collier was a close friend of mine, as well as the coach of the Kirkwood football team. At halftime of the Turkey Day Game, I was asked to be on the radio. I made the remark that I had to be for Webster, but since Dale was the Kirkwood coach, I hoped that the game would be close. Those were the kinds of relationships between Webster and Kirkwood… in the olden days.

By Lee M. Keefer
Webster Alumnus 1950
Written September 5, 2007

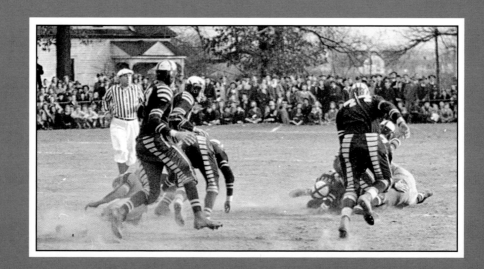

OUR STORY

We were so fortunate to grow up in the 1940s and live and go to school in Webster Groves. We had many great friends, teachers and coaches. We have many good memories that we will cherish forever. The highlight of the year was the Turkey Day Game and the friendship dance with Kirkwood. This was such a wonderful tradition and we all wanted to take part in it and carry it on. The day before the game we had a pep rally assembly. The cheerleaders would lead the cheers. The night before, some of the kids would go out to Kirkwood and yell out the car windows, "Beat Kirkwood!" A few other pranks took place but nothing bad, but maybe a few T. P. [toilette paper] jobs. [A T. P. job was a prank that involved throwing rolls of streaming toilette paper high into the branches of trees in the front yards of residences, making the yard unsightly and the paper difficult to remove.] The Friendship Dance was held the Saturday after the game. This was a fun evening and the crowning of both schools' football queens took place. My senior year I was crowned queen for Webster. This was a big honor and a complete surprise. We had a lot of friends at each other's school and didn't let the outcome of the game come between us.

My husband Jack Frier was a natural at any sport he took part in. As a freshman he didn't make the baseball team so he lettered in tennis. At Webster he played football, basketball and baseball. He did well in each sport until his senior year. Unfortunately, he got the whooping cough from his little brother the summer before his senior year. He played in the first four football games but would have to go out with a coughing spell. It also interfered with playing basketball. Jack has also been coached by five men who would later have fields named after them; Ray Moss, Tyke Yates and Froebel Gaines in Webster Groves and Don Faurot and John Simmons in Columbia, Missouri. Jack left high school in early January 1945 to join the Coast Guard. He went to the Coast Guard Academy and played on their baseball team. He was discharged in May of 1946.

I played on the field hockey team and the basketball, volleyball and baseball teams. I made all of the girl varsity teams. I loved playing sports and it was a big part of my high school days. When I was a freshman in high school I started dating Jack. He was a sophomore. When he was discharged from the service he went to the University of Missouri, where he lettered in football and baseball. When I graduated from Webster I got a job with the Electric Company. I dated Jack and spent many weekends in Columbia, Missouri. He graduated in 1950 and we were married on June 23. We will celebrate our 57th anniversary on June 23, 2007. Fifty-two of those years we have lived in the same house in beautiful Webster Groves.

By Dorothy Worley Frier
Webster Alumna 1946, Football Queen 1945
Written March 31, 2007

THE 1950S: ....

In the aftermath of World War II, America found itself in a geopolitical, ideological and economic "Cold War" with the Soviet Union. As the Korean War raged in Asia and the fear of nuclear weapons grew as a silent spectre, teenagers began to shake their hips to a new music style known as "rock 'n' roll." Rock 'n' roll had its beginning with a local Saint Louis musician named Chuck Berry, who armed with a guitar and his "duck walk," performed such songs as *Roll Over Beethoven* and *Johnny B. Goode*. Television, which had been released after the end of World War II, was now a common home device and many people were now moving from urban centers of living to the suburbs. By the end of the decade, racial segregation would end as schools across the country would be legally required to integrate.

The 1950s decade of football for the schools had the near equilibrium of the 1940s. In this decade, Webster would lead the series five wins to Kirkwood's four, with one tie. It is in this decade that one of the most important icons of the rivalry would be introduced.

The 1950s began with a game played on snow in subfreezing temperatures causing the players' jerseys to be frozen to their backs. Despite the cold, 6,000 fans still came to the game. Erv Dunkel was quarterback of the Webster squad and Guy Rose scored 19 of the 37 points for Webster. At the halftime of the game the score was 25-0 and it is said that the lone Pioneer left in the stands was Dave Jones, there to watch his brother Herb play, who would later be the mayor of the City of Kirkwood. The *Webster-Kirkwood Times* newspaper reported in its November 16-22, 1984 issue, "To this day there is considerable debate over whether Dave was watching out of loyalty to his brother, or because he was frozen to his seat."

When Murl Moore came to Kirkwood to teach in 1930, he started his employment with two other teachers, Edwin Tomlin and Paul Hunker. All three teachers lived in an apartment complex in University City, which was the home to many young, single professional men. One of the gentlemen living at the complex was Robert Stone, who at that time was employed by the Southern Railway Company. Moore and Stone became good friends and by 1951, Stone was the Vice President of the Frisco Railroad Company and Moore the principal of Kirkwood High School. One day in 1951, Stone gave Moore a call and asked if Kirkwood High School would like one of the brass bells from the steam locomotives that the railroad was replacing with diesel. Moore passed the offer to the Student Council, who voted unanimously to accept a free train bell. For a short period of time the bell had no purpose other than to be rung by mischievous students, seeking to prank Moore, who had the bell sitting out-

side of his office. Moore asked for the Student Council to find a purpose for the bell, which they did in making it the new trophy for the Turkey Day Game. The announcement regarding the bell was made in time for the 1951 game and was to be awarded for the first time in 1952.

Once again, just like in 1923, the schools were poised for something big to happen. At the 1952 Turkey Day Game the 68 kilogram bell, 181 kilograms when resting on its wheeled stand, was polished and ready for the winning team to claim it as their prize. Unfortunately, both teams fought hard to a 0-0 tie. Therefore, because Webster had lost the previous year's game by the score of 33-0, the Little Brown Jug would by default stay with Webster for one more year and, conversely; Kirkwood would be awarded the bell for the first time by default. The next year, in 1953 Webster Groves beat Kirkwood in the Turkey Day Game by the score of 33-13, to make them the first team to "win" The Frisco Bell, another notation being made that semantics is critical to the description of this game.

The year 1954 was noteworhty for Webster football, in that this was Webster's first and only undefeated and untied season. The team was led by the notable backfield greats Hank Kuhlman, Joe Heimlicher, Glenn St. Pierre and Charley James, who together were nicknamed The Four Horsemen, taken from University of Notre Dame backfield of the same name and likewise the biblical story "The four horsemen of the Apocalypse." According to Hank Kuhlman, the team prior to the start of the season had already made a commitment to themselves to be undefeated. Unusual to teams at that time, the backfield players averaged 88 kilograms, which was usually the size of a lineman. The backfield, therefore, was quite capable of moving the ball through the defensive lines of their opponents. Kuhlman also states that Coaches Moss and Bryant knew what they had with this team. "Moss," Kuhlman states, "was aware that our team could score large numbers of points against other teams and because of that, if we had a comfortable lead, he would limit my opportunities with the ball. He would say to me, 'Hank, you can have the ball for two plays and if you don't score, I'm going to give it to someone else.'" Kirkwood 1955 quarterback, Alan Coggan, states that his only memory of the Turkey Day Games in which he played was "getting the Hell beat out of me by Hank Kuhlman." Also unique to this team was that all four of Webster's backfield players were recruited to play for the same college team, the University of Missouri. There may be no other time in history when all four backfield players from one high school team were recruited intact to play for the same college team. In addition to having all four of Webster's backfield players, the University of Missouri was able to recruit

FOR WHOM THE FRISCO BELL TOLLS

all four of the All-State backs in the State of Missouri, two of which were Webster players. Besides the potent backfield, Hank Kuhlman and Charley James are clear that the success of the team was the result of all of its players and that they both regretted that the attention that the backfield received often overshadowed the contributions of the team's other players. The score of the 1954 Turkey Day Game was 46-7, which, according to Coggan, made Coach Lenich really angry because he felt that Moss had allowed his players to run-up the score of the game, as he states, "I never really felt like Coach Moss did run-up the points, but nonetheless, that's how Coach Lenich saw it," he says.

After the Supreme Court decision in the Brown versus Topeka Board of Education case on May 15, 1954, schools in Missouri and across the nation were ordered to end school segregation. According to Alan Coggan, "Black students were made really welcome at Kirkwood High School and we were really happy that they were there. Students would walk up and shake their hands and say 'welcome to our school.'" By all reports, the integration of black and white students in Kirkwood and Webster Groves was seamless and without controversy. With integration, Kirkwood gained its first two black football players; junior number 50 Robert "Boom-Boom" Cannon and sophomore number 41 Bill Moore. Bob Cannon was the fourth highest scorer on the 1955 Kirkwood team with 24 points. Although Alan Coggan states that "black students were made really welcome at Kirkwood High School," it is being noted that the 1955-56 school year was also the first year of Kirkwood's new high school at 801 West Essex Avenue, meaning that since its opening in 1955, the present Kirkwood High School has always been a racially integrated school. Webster Groves integrated their elementary schools in 1955, but waited until 1956 before integrating black students into the high school. Unique to Webster Groves was that it had within its city one of the few schools in the metropolitan area for black students, named Douglass High School. Students at Douglass were equally as proud and loyal to their school as Webster High students were to theirs. It was therefore thought by Webster administrators that they ought to give the high school students an additional year before forcing such a sudden change. The Douglass High School Class of 1956 was the last to graduate from the school, with the building meeting demolition by the next school year.

The 1955 Kirkwood team, not wanting to be outdone by the 1954 Webster squad, achieved also its own undefeated and untied season, which would be Kirkwood's second depending upon evidence from its 1914 season. Unlike Webster's squad, Kirkwood had no preconceived idea of achieving an undefeated season. It was not until three or four games into the season that the 1955 Kirkwood team took notice of what they might do. Uncustomary for this team was that Alan Coggan called all plays for the season on the field, which in seasons prior was done by Coach Lenich. Coggan had such football knowledge and command on the field that Coach Lenich acquiesced to the arrangement, reviewing plays with Coggan the day before a game and then letting Coggan take charge. The 1955 season ended with Kirkwood beating Webster 25-7 in the Turkey Day Game.

Cars driving in the 1950 Turkey Day Parade

Statesman John Crooks is chased by Pioneer Don Hagemann in 1950

Football Queen
Dorothy Reinke

Kirkwood Football (3-5-1) - Head Coach William T. Lenich

Row 1: Managers Sierbenz, Eckler. Row 2: Campbell, Moseley, Kilpatrick, Collins, Mabie, Meredith, Crancer, Bopp, Jones, Deichmann. Row 3: Klebolt, Gabriel, Burkhardt, Peters, Schneiderheinz, Trask, Schildmeyer, Malsbary, Varvel, Haney. Row 4: Webber, Butler, Doorack, Perkinson, Rapp, Koprivica, McClanahan, Charter, Wilkins, Schepp. Row 5: Coach Duchek, Coach Beltz, Baker, Heinz, Hagemann, Van Dam, Knotts, McClarney, Shafer, Wolf, Morrill, Coach Lenich.

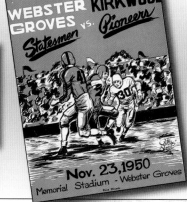

Statesmen Dunkel, Rose, Brickey and Crooks

Football Queen
Kathleen Bohren

Webster Football (9-1) - Head Coach Raymond W. Moss

Row 1: Manager Woods, Goodspeed, Massengale, Ross, Carlson, Miller, Butler, Ehlers, Rose, Crooks, Dunkel. Row 2: Coach Bryant, Cruickshank, Rau, Brannaker, Brickey, Sieger, Simmons, Meffert, Fisher, Perkins, Coach Moss. Row 3: Dupske, Lowe, Bollinger, Kirkland, Adler, Hodges, Boyce, Dunbar, Forsythe, Jones. Row 4: Allen, Gerhardt, Kick, Wright, Schewe, Hardy, Paden, Ryan, Weir.

KIRKWOOD · 33 | WEBSTER · 0
Thursday, November 22, 2:00 p.m. at Memorial Field

1951

Football Queen
Rosie Hull

Kirkwood Football (7-1) - Head Coach William T. Lenich

Row 1: Managers Trask, Boston. Row 2: Butler, Perkinson, Klebolt, Tancill, Shepp, Collins, Deichmann, Van Dam, McClanahan, Schneiderheinze, Peters. Row 3: Weber, Kirk, Doorack, Roth, Moseley, Campbell, Burkhardt, Hagemann, Mullen, Coach Lenich. Row 4: Coach Beltz, Braun, Ruppert, Johner, Henley, Rapp, Franke, Heinz, Shildmyer, Almstedt Row 4: Drath, Harris, Coggan, Herman, Koprivica, Bowman, Wilkins, Bowman, Charter, Langenbeck, Behrens, Coach Duchek.

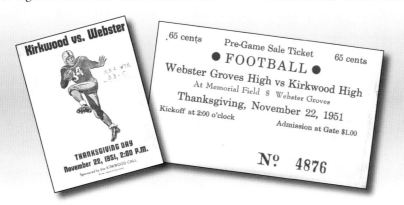

Football Queen
Susan Pender

Webster Football (3-6) - Head Coach Raymond W. Moss

Row 1: Moehlenpah, Scott, Kirkland, Bollinger, Wright, Schewe, Lowther, Adler, Ryan. Row 2: Kleitsch, Westrup, Hardy, Hodges, Gerhardt, Wilson, Manning, Shaiper. Row 3: Coach Bryant, Buercklin, Fitzgerald, Weinischke, Brown, Olds, Hammack, Kick, Erbe. Row 4: Ditty, Schwieder, Dahlheimer, Fleschner, Hansen, Mudd, Beedle, Coach Moss.

Football Queen
Gladys Heutel

Kirkwood Football (5-2-1) - Head Coach William T. Lenich

Row 1: Managers Farmer, Cole, Bowman. Row 2: Bowman, Shaw, Roth, Ruppert, Strauss, Rapp, Bowman, Almstedt, Ashlock, Rapp. Row 3: Coggan, Trask, Van Dam, Tancill, Hicks, Langenbeck, Heinz, Mullen, Alexander, Perkinson. Row 4: Coach Beltz, Coach Duchek, Kirk, Peterson, Cook, Braun, Harris, Henley, Moore, Herman, Coach Lenich. Row 5: Schmidt, Akin, Lott, Ebersole, Erbschloe, Kirk, Johnston, Bollin, Honey, Godi, Hill, Murphy, Cuendet, Bollinger, Hagemann.

Webster Football (7-2) - Head Coach Raymond W. Moss

Football Queen
Sally Diekroeger

Row 1: Manager Hoefl, Beedle, Schweider, Lay, Ditty, Smith, Fleschner, Mudd, Buercklin, Dahlheimer, Olds, Manager Whyte. Row 2: Noth, Hanson, Weinischke, Zumwalt, Lindholm, Toft, Dring, Wolff, Zeiss. Row 3: Hicks, Summa, O'Kelley, Kuhlman, Delong, Knickman, Elster, Whyte, Carothers, Salveter, Cliff. Row 4: Coach Moss, Hellmich, Fitzgerald, Dickey, Mueller, Greene, Schwarz, Odor, Von Hoffman, St. Pierre, Stauber.

Football Queen
Charlotte Ebersole

Kirkwood Football (3-5-1) - Head Coach William T. Lenich

Row 1: Managers: N. Bowman, Farmer, Krieger. Row 2: Coach Duchek, Hill, Ford, Harris, Honey, Tomasovic, Lott, Koch, Ebersole, Johnston, Dubail, Coach Lenich. Row 3: Murphy, J. Cuendet, Harting, Scholer, Mullendore, Ballin, Schmidt, Morgan, Coggan, Trask, B. Patton, Mackey. Row 4: Coach Beltz, Ashlock, B. Kirk, Scogin, R. Cuendet, J. Kirk, Dickinson, Sterbenz, McIntosh, Shrum, Schier, Winters. Row 5: Bollinger, Dall, DeBasio, Sands, Worfler, Harnish, Brown, Sengstock, Akin, H. Patton, S. Bowman, Allen, Rapp.

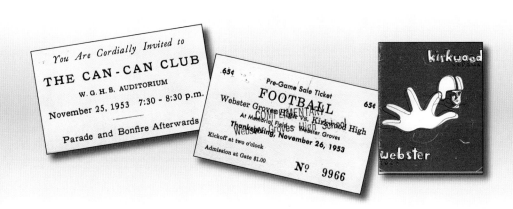

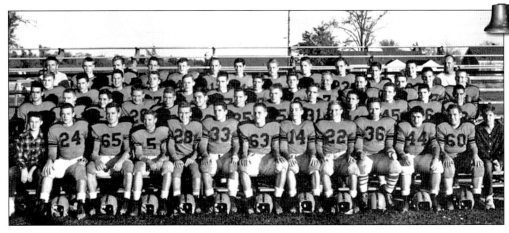

Football Queen
Julie Klasing

Webster Football (6-3-1) - Head Coach Raymond W. Moss

Row 1: Manager Pollock, Carothers, Hanson, DeLong, Mueller, Greene, O'Kelley, Stauber, A. Braun, Dring, Zeis, Kirby, Ramming. Row 2: Dames, Von Hoffman, Kropp, S. Brown, Schwarz, Patterson, Fowler, Schute, Madole, Knickman, Fitzgerald, Odor, Cliff. Row 3: Lippincott, Bruno, Marshall, Cooper, Peterson, Rogers, Bobbitt, Burton, Crigler, Wade, James, Sydow, Kuhlman. Row 4: Coach Moss, Hellmich, Bingham, Noonan, Detjen, Cox, Altenhofer, Link, Swartz, Ward, Nolan, Euhler, Coach Bryant.

Football Queen
Carolyn White

Kirkwood Football (5-4) - Head Coach William T. Lenich

Row 1: Coach Duchek, Hill, Ford, Harris, Honey, Tomasovic, Lott, Koch, Ebersole, Johnston, Dubail, Coach Lenich. Managers: N. Bowman, Farmer, Krieger. Row 2: Coach Beltz, Ashlock, B. Kirk, Scogin, R. Cuendet, J. Kirk, Dickinson, Sterbenz, McIntosh, Shrum, Schier, Winters. Row 3: Murphy, J. Cuendet, Harting, Scholer, Mullendore, Ballin, Schmidt, Morgan, Coggan, Trask, B. Patton, Mackey. Row 4: Bollinger, Dall, DeBasio, Sands, Worfler, Harnish, Brown, Sengstock, Akin, H. Patton, S. Bowman, Allen, Rapp.

Football Queen
Josephine Denty

Webster Football (9-0) - Head Coach Raymond W. Moss - Suburban League Champion

Row 1: James, Kuhlman, Noonan, Lippincott, Sydow, Cooper, Bobbitt, Detjen, Swartz, Link, Heimlicher, St. Pierre, Petterson. Row 2: Madole, Fox, Patterson, Ward, Euler, Cox, Thorpe, Busemeyer, Burton, Auten, Rogers, Bingham. Row 3: Manager O'Brien, Pemberton, Hopkins, Lansing, Everett, Schuette, Ford, Viehmann, Scott, Link, Ferry, Altenhofer, Mudd, Alt, Manager La Gear. Row 4: Coach Bryant, Coach Moss.

Football Queen
Phyllis Murray

Kirkwood Football (9-0) - Head Coach William T. Lenich - Suburban League Champion

Row 1: Manager Landrum, Elliot, Overbey, Fowler, Joy, Parent, Hallahan, Hunker, Gustafson, Brown, Morgan, Broadwell, Hoffsten, Byrne, Manager Aitch. Row 2: Thierbach, Minton, Boillot, Lehye, Almstedt, Marting, Putney, Cole, Coggan, Trask, Mackey, Cassidy, Reinhart, Moller, Haenni, Harris. Row 3: Coaches McClanahan, Clodfelter, Lenich. Row 2: Funk, Wood, Donahue, Bowman, Brock, Rohlf, B. Silver, J. Silver, Knoesel, Henley, Dobbs, Moore, Waterman, Cronin, Cannon, McClanahan, Prichett, Berger.

Football Queen
Fairlyn Margaret Forsyth

Webster Football (6-3) - Head Coach Raymond W. Moss

Row 1: Earnhardt, Whitecotton, Ferry, Auten, Pemberton, Alt, Hopkins, Everett, Mudd, Link, Serth, Link. Row 2: Knickman, Fox, Ford, Massengale, Freeman, Wolff, Viehmann, McFarland, Yoder, Thorpe, Smith, Robins Hanlon. Row 3: Morey, Patterson, Lang, Perabo, Stewart, James, Rimbach, Palmer, Lee, Caray, Werner. Row 4: Hindman, Cargill, Harlan, DuMont, Hawkins, Sample, Robertson, Reed, Snyder, Rutledge, Hicks. Row 5: Coach Moss, Coach Bryant.

1956

KIRKWOOD - 0 | WEBSTER - 7
Thursday, November 22, 2:00 p.m. at Memorial Field

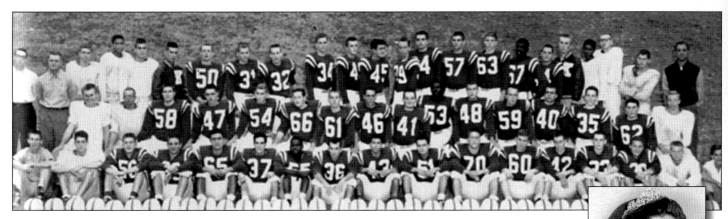

Kirkwood Football (4-5) - Head Coach William T. Lenich
Row 1: Manager Steele, Gissendanner, Fredrick, Neuhaus, Moller, McDougall, Cannon, Fowler, Cassidy, Ward, Dobbs, Henley, Weber, Bowman, Waitkins, Thomas, Manager Harris. Row 2: Brooks, Leyhe, Scholsky, Manczuk, Aitken, Donahue, Mullendore, Andrews, Scranton, Moore, Brell, Boillot, Dunn, Schneider, Wallace, Moholt. Row 3: Coach McClanahan, Coach Clodfelter, Handell, McCreary, DuBois, Webb, Scott, Gray, Corbet, Therlot, Waterman, Ernest, Schmidt, Mueller, Marting, Knoessel, Runnels, Harris, Cole, Lawrence, Funk, Trask, Coach Lenich.

Football Queen
Nancy Brown

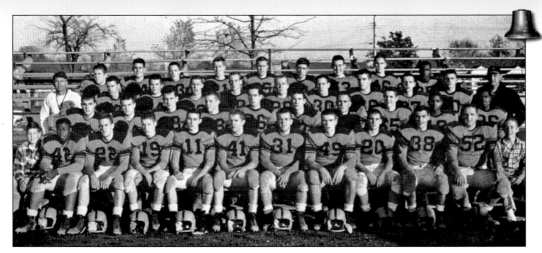

Football Queen
Judith Faris

Webster Football (4-4-1) - Head Coach Raymond W. Moss
Row 1: Auten, Robinson, Hanlon, DuMont, Patterson, Sample, Hicks, Snyder, Lang, Perabo, James, Dyer. Row 2: Caray, Robertson, Hindman, Cargill, Morey, Love, Reed, Terry, Barrett. Row 3: Coach Moss, Thalmann, McArtor, Himes, Dysart, Harlan, Brown, Alt, Charow, Nau, Coach Bryant. Row 4: Braun, Taylor, Nahm, Knowles, Koons, Gerhardt, Phegley, Williams, Crenshaw.

114

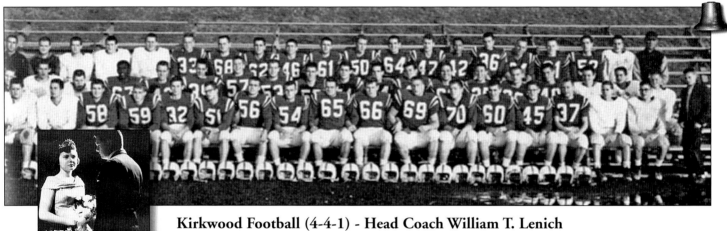

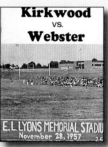

Kirkwood
vs.
Webster

E.L. LYONS MEMORIAL STADIU
November 28, 1957

Football Queen
Joan Gardiner

Kirkwood Football (4-4-1) - Head Coach William T. Lenich

Row 1: Rozier, Poole, Zokolsky, Aitken, Bowman, Trask, Dunn, Waterman, Ward, Henley, Dobbs, Mason, Lumas, Decker, Taft, Campbell, Peters, Huddleston. Row 2: Harris, Stobe, Larsen, Runnels, Schmidt, Andrews, Fredrick, Brell, Morley, Gissendanner, McDougall, Ernest, Neuhaus, Wolfe, Burcham, Minehart, Blevins, Whitehead, Winter. Row 3: Coach McClanahan, Coach Clodfelter, Knox, Howell, Schneider, Corbet, Scranton, McClintock, Nichols, Barton, Wainwright, Miller, Waitkins, McCrary, Blackwell, Rhode, Nentwig, Wilhelm, Heintz, Coach Lenich.

Football Queen
Lyn Dominguez

Webster Football (3-6-1) - Head Coach Raymond W. Moss

Row 1: Barret, Reid, Williams, Collier, Nahm, Thalman, Taylor, E. McArtor, Charow, Harlan, Dysart. Row 2: O'Brien, Carlin, Sheppard, Hubbel, Heller, Brown, A. McArtor, Munson, Earnhardt, Richardson, Sieber. Row 3: Coach Grahm, Coach Bryant, Coach Moss, Reeves, Stoddard, Brown, Card, Trenholm, Braun, Schwesig, Crenshaw.

Kirkwood Football (4-4-1) - Head Coach William T. Lenich

Row 1: Managers McNew, Luecke. Row 2: Douglas, Leyhe, Taft, Decker, Morley, Nichols, Trask, Barton, Schneider, Campbell, Wainwright, Nentwig, Wolf, Chiles, Meinhardt. Row 3: Dailey, Schultz, Saladin, Ross, Williams, Reed, Canda, Sarver, Bywater, Lindberg, Wilhelm, Robinson, Loomis, Mason. Row 4: Coach Batch, Waller, Morelock, Beard, Blackwell, Powell, Pool, Larson, Schmitt, Mueller, Blevins, Sokolsky, Hamilton. Row 5: Coach McClanahan, Ravens, Hobelman, Taylor, Mothersgill, Bond, Skinner, Wendt, Walsch, Williams, Heintz, Wohlgemuth, Tomlin, Coach Lenich.

Football Queen
Judy Briell

Football Queen
Marcia Catherine Otto

Webster Football (5-4-1) - Head Coach Raymond W. Moss

Row 1: Crenshaw, Sheppard, Hubbell, Carlin, B. Brown, Braun, W. Brown, Seiber, Munson, Schuette, Jones. Row 2: Barnett, Trenholm, Hipp, Schwesig, Perkins, A. McArtor, Hendricks, Crossman, Comfort, Robins, Jennewein. Row 3: Earnhardt, Collier, Davis, Hill, Clark, Phegley, Kieth, LeGear, Connelly, Reeves, Mr. Grahm. Row 4: Harland, Murdock, Heller, North, J. McArtar, Wisely, McGrath, Stuart, Richardson, Coach Moss, Coach Melvin.

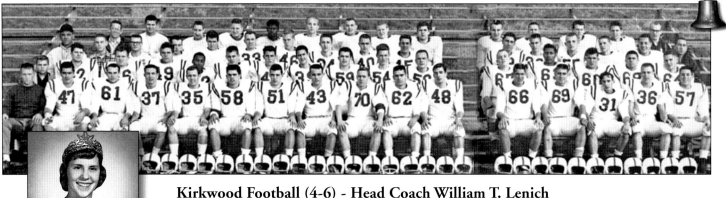

Football Queen
Suzy Zimmermann

Kirkwood Football (4-6) - Head Coach William T. Lenich

Row 1: Luecke, Loomis, Ravens, Sarver, Bywater, Williams, Queen Sandra Barnes Taylor, Leyhe, Wendt, Meinhart, Wilhelm, Ross, Morley, Reed, Taft, Wolf. Row 2: McNew, Douglas, Dailey, Wells, Weatherspoon, Waller, Landis, Frost, Schulz, Fellinger, Austin, Altmansberger, Brock, Canda, Nichols, Decker. Row 3: Coach Lenich, Dorlan, Daviess, Hoeh, Reid, Saladin, Bornemeier, Baker, Larimore, Wirtel, Zeigler, Summers, Lionberger, Edens, Graeler, Coach McClanahan. Row 4: Bond, Coach Baich, Kauflin, Summers, Cannon, McGill, Horn, Smith, Parsonage, Spenser, Reinhart, Hellstern, Knoesel, Dougherty.

Football Queen
Eleanore Thoene

Webster Football (6-3) - Head Coach Raymond W. Moss

Row 1: Perkins, Robbins, Kupferer, Harlin, Hinrichs, Hipp, LeGear, A. McArtor, Trenholm, Bill, Schwesig, Conley, Cook, Whitney. Row 2: Hill, Clark, J. McArtor, Beasley, Czarneski, Davis, McNeill, Townsend, Moir, Weston, Schroer, French. Row 3: Balker, White, Scott, Stewart, Wisely, Gordon, Mitsch, Pitts, Giger, Bedell, Malone. Row 4: Fahrenbruch, Braun, Riehl, Card, Zorumski, Reed

BRING BACK THE BELL!

In the fall of 1951, Kirkwood Principal Murl R. Moore was contacted by an old neighbour and friend, Robert Stone, who was the Vice President of the Frisco Railroad Company. The Frisco Railroad was in the process of replacing its steam locomotives with diesel and Stone asked Moore if Kirkwood High School would be interested in having one of the bells from a replaced locomotive. Moore passed the invitation to the Kirkwood High School Student Council, who accepted the gift.

Pete Bredehoeft, who was a member of the Student Council and a 1953 alumnus, was chosen to get the bell from the Frisco Railroad, not because of any special position that he held, but because he owned a flatbed trailer that he used to transport lawn equipment for summer jobs that he had mowing lawns. Bredehoeft arrived at the Frisco Railroad train yard alone, located in the City of Shrewsbury, to find that the bell weighed 68 kilograms. Unable to move the bell himself, the workers at the railroad yard generously offered to build a rolling stand, so that the bell could be easier moved.

According to Bredehoeft, seven to ten days later he was contacted by the Frisco Railroad yardmen to let him know that the bell and its rolling stand were ready, which together now weighed 181 kilograms. After bringing the bell back to the school, the Student Council needed to decide for what they would use it. While they discussed a use, the bell sat outside of Murl Moore's office. It became an obligatory prank of the students to ring the

bell and quickly flee before Principal Moore could catch them. This may have necessitated a decision for a use for the bell. The Student Council agreed in a vote to offer it to the winner of the Turkey Day Game and contacted the Webster Groves Student Council, who also approved the idea.

The Frisco Bell was introduced at the 1951 Turkey Day Game, which Kirkwood won 33-0, and was awarded for the first time to Kirkwood in 1952 after the game ended in a 0-0 tie. Because Webster Groves had possession of the Little Brown Jug from the previous year's loss, Kirkwood was awarded the bell by default. In 1953, Webster won the game and the bell by the score of 33-13, making Webster Groves the first team to "win" the Frisco Bell.

The first prank involving the bell was its theft from Webster in 1954 by a group of Kirkwood students; Mike Ebersole, Chuck Aiken, Harold Patton, George Lott, Alan Coggan and Harrison Trask. The students stole the bell by climbing through an unlocked window of Roberts Gym late at night and then wheeled it out of the front doors of the gym's entrance.

In 2007, the Frisco Bell will have been a part of the Turkey Day Game for 55 years. In all of that time, it has changed possession 25 times and five graduation classes have never had it in their school during their tenure; Kirkwood alumni 1966, 1972 and 1973 and Webster alumni 1984 and 1990. On behalf of them, let it be said to future generations... Bring back the bell!

By Shawn Buchanan Greene
Webster Alumnus 1987
Written May 17, 2007

Coaches Moss and Lenich shake hands before the 1952 game

THE 1954 UNDEFEATED SEASON

I grew up with my mother taking me to Turkey Day Games, mostly at Kirkwood since Webster Groves was without a field for several years until Moss Field was built. My house was only about 2 blocks away from the Field so I was able to watch more regular season games.

I was fortunate to play in 3 Turkey Day Games since making the varsity team as a sophomore. During the 3 years, we tied in '52 (0-0), won in '53 (33-13) and won in'54 (46-6). The 1954 football team has been the only undefeated team in WGHS history.

The '54 team was special because we had most of the '53 team back and our goal was to be undefeated in '54 as evidenced by the things we wrote when signing our year books (the Echo) that spring. We added two good players (Joe Heimlicher and Glen St. Pierre) that rounded out our backfield with Charlie James and me. Heimlicher, James and myself played Legion baseball in the summer of '54 and our team went to the National Tournament in Yakima, Washington (we won 3rd in the nation). We were late in returning home and missed some required football practices which would have made us ineligible for the first two games of the season. However, Coach Ray Moss was successful in getting the penalty for missed practices waived so we could participate right from the beginning of the season.

One thing that I am still amazed about – that I was able to catch up to and tackle the Missouri State 100 yard dash champion to preserve the 0-0 tie against Kirkwood in the 1952 Turkey Day Game. Another fond memory is defeating University City 33-7 in 1954 – when WG had not beaten them very often.

Our coach, Ray Moss, was a great influence on my going into football coaching because of his approach to the game and his sportsmanship of not letting the '54 team run up the score after the game was well in hand.

Our 4 backfield players received a lot of recognition (the 4 of us went to MU on scholarships and started on the freshman team and were undefeated) but the '54 team would not have done well without the likes of our Captain Olin Lippincott, Dan Sydow, Bill Detjen, Fletcher Bingham, John Swartz, David Cooper, Mike Noonan, Blaine Link and the rest of the team.

By Henry "Hank" Kuhlman
Webster Alumnus 1955
Written April 10, 2007

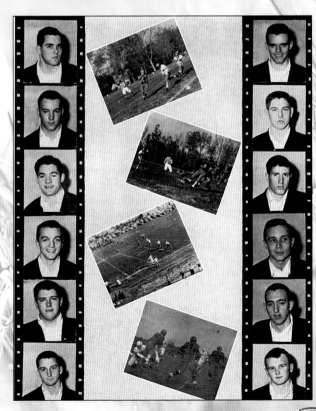

THE GREAT FRISCO BELL CAPER

The adventure by six Kirkwood High students occurred during the basketball season of 1954-55. I believe it was March, because the weather was warmer, but the exact month is up for debate. I am pretty sure that the perpetrators were four seniors; Mike Ebersole, Chuck Aiken, Harold Patton and George Lott. Two of us were juniors, me and Al Coggan. We had all gone to Webster to watch the Pioneers play the Statesmen. Webster won the game and Kirkwood fans were not enjoying a very good athletic year. We had already been clobbered in the Turkey Day Game by one of the best teams in the history of St. Louis football.

During the game we noticed the Frisco Bell, awarded to the school who had won the previous Turkey Day Game, on display either in the gym on the second level or in the lobby. I pretty much remember it being in the gym in clear view of everyone. There was no premeditation involved to steal it. I don't remember if we lifted it later that night, or the next night. But sometime during the game, or shortly thereafter, one of the seniors had the thought of stealing it, and we all thought it was a great idea.

Obviously the big problem was how to get in the WG gym without doing any damage, and avoid being spotted. We returned later, well after midnight, to "case the joint," and spotted a small window on the side of the building about twelve to fourteen feet [3.7 to 4.3 metres] above the ground. We figured that if we could somehow get someone up to the window, they could check to see if it was locked or not. A human ladder was quickly formed, with Al Coggan being the window checker. Al was the lightest, and once he got at the top he discovered the window was open, and rather easily entered with no damage or evidence of entry. Once

in, he simply went to the regular doors, pushed them open and in we went. Now the dilemma was how to get this 400 pound [181 gram] bell down to the playing floor, get it out and into the trunk of the car. The moving of the bell was not that difficult. Our football team may not have been very good that year, but we did have some really strong guys. The one thing that baffles me is how we got it in the trunk of someone's car. I don't remember having a pickup as they just weren't that popular in those days, but somehow we loaded it up, left without a trace. It was if by magic it had disappeared and we got the biggest kick out of visualizing the Webster Groves administrators trying to figure out what in Hell happened to the Bell.

Suddenly, we realized now that we had it what would we do with it? It stayed overnight in the trunk of the get away car, but we knew that was only a short term solution. I'm beginning to think by this time it was a Sunday, and whose ever car it was, was needed for transportation to school. A quick meeting was held by all and, I must have wanted to impress the guys, so I volunteered my garage, actually my parents' garage, as a hiding place. Somehow, without my parents' knowledge, we stashed it in the garage and did a great job of camouflaging it. I was always amazed my Mom never discovered it, since like most moms in those days, she was part Dick Tracy, CIA and blood hound.

So, it stayed hidden for a couple of days and then somebody sorta squealed. The next thing I remember was Kirkwood's principal Murl Moore getting on the trail. I think he called Al into his office and said he thought they knew what might have happened. However, they didn't know where it was, but Mr. Moore told Al "just get it back." Al came to me and basically said, "the jigs up, let's return it before this thing turns ugly!"

So we did. One of the guys found a pickup truck so we loaded it in the back and all six of us drove back to Webster Groves, right down Lockwood Avenue with the bell in full view. It was a nice touch of defiance, riding through Webster Groves with the Frisco Bell in full view. In retrospect, we probably avoided getting in trouble because no damage was done, and maybe the administrations of both schools were awed by our execution of the perfect prank.

By Harrison Trask
Kirkwood Alumnus 1956
Written June 26, 2007

MEMORIES OF 1955 KIRKWOOD FOOTBALL

No, we did not know we were that good until the season was over. This is why we went undefeated because we were never over confident. You really can't understand this team unless you look at the Webster Groves team of 1954. They were also undefeated and they beat us pretty bad in 1954. I was glad when it was over because I got tired of tackling Hank Kuhlman. I say trying because he ran over me several times. I did get back at him during the following basketball season. We beat them for the District so we could go to the State Tournament.

Except for Terry Mackey and Dick Rohlff, we were not big and strong. We were tough and smart and we never quit. We did not want to lose. There were very few mistakes made by anybody. I know the Turkey Day Game was supposed to be the big rivalry but beating University City and Ritenour were my fondest hope. Beating Webster was anticlimactic after going undefeated during the rest of the season.

During 1953 and 1954, I was probably the leading tackler from my safety position. In 1955 I rarely made a tackle because our great line and linebackers made most of the tackles.

Yes, we were integrated in 1955. Bobby Cannon started for us at right halfback as well as playing defensive safety. There was never a caustic remark toward him or toward anybody else at school. If all schools were like Kirkwood, there would have been less tension. There were no bullies or glory boys on our team or at the school, there were only individuals that had a lot of respect for each other. The athletes associated with everybody and did not have groups.

As far as Webster was concerned and all the other schools we played, there were too many friends at Webster and Maplewood to have real enemies. I even dated a Webster girl for a short while. Years later, I would run into Webster people in Dallas. I even saw and talked to Charley James from Webster's 1954 team around 1961 when he was playing AA ball.

I still get a thrill when I return to Kirkwood to see my brother Terry and his son Jeff who also played quarterback at Kirkwood in 1952 and 1977 respectively.

By Alan Coggan
Kirkwood Alumnus 1956
Written April 10, 2007

THE KIRKWOOD MESSENGER

The *Kirkwood Messenger* was published weekly from 1920 until 1959 by my dad, David Jones, Sr. My brother and I have continued the company as a printing business to this day. My brother, Herb Jones, KHS '51, who served two terms as mayor of Kirkwood, missed his senior Turkey Day Game with a serious knee injury. I, KHS '49, played in the '47 and '48 Turkey Day Games. The KHS Call was printed by the company starting in the 1930s. The Turkey Day programs were mimeographed until the end of World War II, in 1945.

Then Coca-Cola provided full color 8-page programs that were imprinted with team rosters by the *Messenger*. In the 1950s, Kirkwood and Webster started producing much more elaborate programs similar to today's programs. The *Messenger* printed them with the two schools alternately doing the design and layout. Herb and I recall, while still in school, folding and stapling 500 programs the night before the 1948 game. The school ran short as 12,000 fans showed up for the first Turkey Day Game at the new Webster field on Elm Avenue.

By David Lee Jones, Junior
Kirkwood Alumnus 1949
Written July 31, 2007

Messenger Printing Co., Inc.
Printing headquarters for over 100 publications
for schools and industry.

126 West Argonne Drive   Kirkwood, Mo. 63122
(314) 966-3413

THE GOLD AND PURPLE JAGUARS OF DOUGLASS HIGH SCHOOL

Summertime in Webster Groves is always hot, especially in August. It doesn't seem to be football weather, but when the Statesmen's legendary coach, Ray Moss, puts out the call for football tryouts, it's decision time. If you want to wear the Orange and Black, you trade in the comforts of home for the hard times at Kopplin Field.

Since the start of the 20th century that was a call answered by many young men, but not if you lived up on the hill beyond Shady Creek, now Kirkham Road, for these young men of "color" aspired to play for the Purple and Gold Jaguars and they played their home games on a rough field called "The Bottoms," near Deer Creek. The Jaguar program also had a glorious history of victories and championships after the Webster School Board approved extending Douglass School into a four year high school in the 1920s.

It was a "parallel universe," complete with a band, majorettes, cheerleaders, a fight song and a community parade from Douglass High School, along Holland Avenue and down to The Bottoms. There was no Turkey Day Game, but the Jaguars feared no one, playing teams as far as Evansville, Indiana and locally playing Sumner and Vashon high schools to find worthy opponents.

But it all came to an end for the cause of integration. After the United States Supreme Court decision in 1954, the dual black-white system in Webster had to end. Some students from Douglass High School, who were living in or near Kirkwood, such as Bob Cannon and Bill Moore, immediately entered Kirkwood High School. The summer of 1956 saw the last Douglass High School graduating class and, in a manner much the same

as Cortez burning his ships upon landing in America, the old Douglass High School was bulldozed, so that the school district might never turn back. The high school was no more, but there were still football players that didn't want to give up on a sport they loved. For weeks, the transferred members of the Douglass varsity football team that still wanted a senior year as players debated their options. They decided that their only option was to try out for the Statesmen team.

That August day, the former Douglass players rallied at the site of their old alma mater and walked down North Elm Avenue, crossed Shady Creek and went up North Gore turning onto Moody Avenue, back to Elm. In those days, Elm Avenue did not go through to Kirkham. They proceeded down Lockwood Avenue, turning onto Selma and at the old Lutheran Church, now the school board office, they took the path up to Kopplin Field where Coach Moss and Coach Bryant were holding tryouts. When they got up to Kopplin Field the Douglass six saw a long line of football players and for a long moment both groups stood and eyed each other. What thoughts these two groups had and what they said to their friends is lost to history, but we know that finally a white player, Jean Patterson, who knew the black kids from basketball pick-up games at the old Webster YMCA (there was a black YMCA and pool at Holland and Ravine, so there had been few chances of making friendships across the racial divide), approached them. Others followed Patterson's action and started talking to the Douglass six and in that moment, two races found a common denominator in the sport of football.

By Charles A. Schneider, Webster Alumnus 1967. Written Septtember 10, 2007.

Douglass Football 1954
Row 1: Kenneth Jackson, Arthur Ryland, Robert Johnson, Joseph Williams, Virgil Hudson, Raymond Anderson, Floyd Brinkley, Lewis S. Wilson, Benjamin Perkins Row 2: Charles Carr, Melvin Williams, Julius Dockett, Edward Robinson, Clyde Reid, William St. James, Robert Cannon, Douglass Barette, Neil Harris, Floyd Cobb Row 3: Coach William Bell, Joseph Washington, Robert Pace, Howard Pointer, Murl Scott, Nathaniel Waters, Raymond Babbitt, John Suggs, O. B. Cunningham, Arthur Jessup, Larry Washington, Robert Reid, Assistant Coach Leo Brinkley

KIRKWOOD HIGH SCHOOL ATHLETIC FIELD AND LYONS FIELD

One hundred years ago, football fields were just that - fields. There were no stands, goal posts, cheerleaders, programs, scoreboards, sprinkler systems and buses to take the teams to the games. The boys took the streetcar to the game, which was a local commuter, above-ground railroad transit system. In one instance it was reported in Kirkwood High School's newspaper, the *High School Journal*, that the football team traveled three hours by railcar to Ferguson, only to arrive and discover that Ferguson had scheduled a game with another team. The Kirkwood team was very disappointed and had no other recourse than to take the railcar back to Kirkwood, wasting six hours of their day traveling.

Because there were no stands, people stood around the field to watch the games. In the early years, the fields on which Kirkwood played were named for the people who owned them, such as "Jack Sturdy's field." The fields were easy for people to find, because towns were small and everyone knew where the fields were. Later, Kirkwood had a formal field located behind the high school on Webster Road, which changed names to Kirkwood Road for obvious reasons. The field behind the first Kirkwood High School was officially called the Kirkwood High School Athletic Field but was often referred to as "Edwards field." This was due to the close proximity of the Edwards home, now the Magic House, next door to Kirkwood's first high school. George Lane Edwards is of local fame, because he was the son and second generation of A. G. Edwards, of the accounting firm of the same name. In 1920, the Kirkwood School District purchased the George Lane Edwards property for the building of a new high school, and used the house as the Kirkwood School District office. By this time, athletic events had become really important to the school and the community.

During the years of 1948-1956, all of the Turkey Day Games were played at Webster's Memorial Field, because their field could better accommodate the large crowds of the Turkey Day Game with its stands, something that even still the KHS Athletic Field did not have. It has also been noted that the KHS Athletic Field was not an even playing surface, with it having a gradual rise from one end to the other. By 1955, Kirkwood had built a new high school at Geyer and Essex Avenues. Of course, there was to be a new athletic stadium built at this site, but it was not constructed and ready for use until 1957. For the first time, Kirkwood dedicated its field after a person, Ernie Lyons, who had served as Kirkwood's football coach for 20 years. From then, until this day, Ernest L. Lyons Field is the home of Kirkwood football.

By Susan Selbert Burkett
Webster Alumna 1958
Kirkwood Historical Society Collections Manager
Written August 2, 2007

KHS
Athletic
Field

Lyons Field 1957

THE 1960S

"The Swinging Sixties" began with a dashing, fictional English spy named, "Bond, James Bond" and ended with a three-day music festival in upstate Woodstock, New York. "Counterculture" quickly became the mantra of the decade as "hippies" began to stage Vietnam War protests across the nation. Despite the influx of British music resulting from The Beatles performing on the Ed Sullivan Show, a local Saint Louis married couple, Ike and Tina Turner also received national attention. Webster and Kirkwood students extended their rivalry to diners, such as Carl's Drive-In on Manchester Road and by halfway through the decade, Eastman Kodak would introduce a new home film format known as "Super 8," which would allow for the easy and affordable filming of 10 minute per reel home movies.

IN EFFECT, EACH SCHOOL VIEWED THE OTHER AS THE "ENEMY THAT YOU LOVED TO HATE."

In the Turkey Day Game, the 1960s continued with the same stability of the 1930s, 1940s and 1950s. Webster edged Kirkwood five victories to four, with one tied game in 1963. During this decade, like a continuing wave, the behaviour of the students regarding the rivalry began to intensify, but rather than the intensity being expressed with violence, it was done so with verbal barbs and pranks. In effect, each school viewed the other as the "enemy that you loved to hate."

Since the creation of the Friendship Dance in 1939, the two teams had played to win the game, but their feelings were usually brought and left on the playing field. Amongst the generation of those from the 1960s, the rivalry seemed to be expressed in year-round fashion and it is still done so by alumni of that era to this day. For example when a Kirkwood representative contacted his friend Greg Marecek, who is a 1967 Webster alumnus and founder of the Webster Groves Sports Hall of Fame, regarding how Kirkwood might go about starting their own organization, Marecek's first, and likely uncontrollable, response was to tell him, "Well, you first have to have some athletes that you can induct…" The children of Phil Greene found it odd that starting in junior high school their father, who is a 1965 Kirkwood alumnus, would take the place of their mother in driving the school car pool beginning in the month of November to their Webster school, that is, until all of the children were in the car and he turned off the radio and began to tauntingly sing the entire drive to school, "Kirkwood's got the bell, Kirkwood's got the bell… We're number one, and you guys sti-ink!" much to the vociferous protestations of the Webster children. This became a car pool ritual, until the children became old enough to drive themselves to school.

Until 1964, the Turkey Day Game was played as a league game between the two schools, but in 1964 it was changed to a non-league game for the first time in the game's history. The 1964 Turkey Day Game teams were full of colourful personalities that have strong ties to the communities. Webster Groves was an All-Conference team that year with the head coach's own son at center. The game was an epic battle between the Turkey Day Game's longest running rivals, Bill Lenich and Ray Moss. Webster won the battle, 19-13, with the pinnacle moment of the game being Bill Lenich's secretly devised trick play for this game, "The Triple Reverse Pass." The play, had it succeeded, would have tied the teams a second time in the game. To this day, no one is exactly sure whether left end Tom Holley had dropped the ball in the end zone or, as the story is also told, All-Conference halfback Walt Smallwood had dashed from the one side of the end zone to the other to swat the ball to the ground to stop the play. In the words of a smirking Tom Holley, "I don't remember the play, but I hope that I dropped the ball."

After the 1964 season, Ray Moss left his job as head coach of the football team after establishing a 151-88-17 career and 11-9-4 Turkey Day Game record at Webster, passing the reigns to his two-year assistant line coach, Jack Jones, but he remained Webster's athletic director until 1975. Jack Merle Jones was born November 22, 1938 and, having graduated from Beaumont High School, became Webster's second Turkey Day Game connection to that school. Jack Jones, prior to his teaching at Webster, was a three-year letterman flankerback at Northeast Missouri State Teachers College, when the team was ranked first in the State of Missouri.

In 1966, the Turkey Day Game resumed its league game status. Both Webster and Kirkwood had lost only one game that season to the same team, Normandy High School. Kirkwood used two quarterbacks that season, Bill Lenich, Junior, who handled many of the passing plays, and Dean Hoag, their stockier and shorter ground specialist. Prior to the Turkey Day Game, Lenich was injured and causing Hoag to play the entire game and cause a sensation for his aerial attack against Webster. Kirkwood won the game 19-7, handing Webster its second loss and winning the Suburban South Conference title. Most accounts of the game credit Hoag's extreme competitiveness as a major factor of his success in the game.

......A BITTERSWEET RIVALRY

At this time of the series, formal news networks and media became involved in the filming of the game. Radio station broadcasts and school produced 16 and 8 millimetre films of the games had started as early as 1944. In 1966, the national CBS (Columbia Broadcasting System) television network came to Webster Groves and produced an one-hour documentary, which was made scandalous by the community after its airing for its misrepresentations, called *16 In Webster Groves*. The documentary, while focused primarily on the students of Webster Groves High School, had filmed some of the broadcast at events such as the Friendship Dance. The next year, a local affiliate of CBS, KMOX-TV, again came to the game, this time to have highlights of the game broadcasted, along with four other long-standing Saint Louis area Turkey Day Games. Also, the attendance at the games began to exceed stadium capacity. Starting in 1962, attendance began to exceed 11,000 spectators, with the highest attendance occurring in 1965 with 11,905 persons. After this seam-breaking attendance, the schools decided to limit each school to 5,000 tickets, only available as a pre-game purchase. All attendees, including the bands and administrators, were required to have a ticket to attend future games.

1960

KIRKWOOD - 33 | WEBSTER - 12
Thursday, November 24, 2:00 p.m. at Memorial Field

Kirkwood Football (7-1-1) - Head Coach William T. Lenich
Row 1: Lionberger, Schulz, Bornemeier, Landes, Wells, Waller, Holdgraf, Douglas, Fellinger, Altmansberger, Parsonage, Weatherspoon, Smith, Wirtel, McNew. Row 2: Coach McClanahan, Saladin, Ziegler, Frost, Hoeh, Knoesel, Reid Dailey, McGill, Summers, Jarrett, Benecke, Larimore, Horn, Spencer. Row 3: Davies, Reinhart, Graham, Ryan, Edens, McHenry, Cracchiola, Wolf, Dickinson, Davis, Sanders, Snavely, Knott, Kohn. Row 4: Coach Batch, Loving, O'Neill, Kauflin, Obermeyer, Scott, Swift, Rice, Marcrander, Baker, Summers, Tibbles, Sutcliffe, Ravens, Coach Lenich.

Football Queen
Sharie Rulon

Football Queen
Katherine Ann Rerner

Webster Football (2-5) - Head Coach Raymond W. Moss
Row 1: Beasley, Card, Moir, French, Gordon, Pitts, Mitsch, Reihl, Beall, McArtor, Reeves. Row 2: Eberle, Tice, Zorumski, Rhodes, Culp, McKee, Reed, Machen, Card, Southworth, Rusan. Row 3: Stuessie, Higgins, Phegley, Wisely, Buckholz, Buchanen, Jones, Oliphant, McLean, Bischof, Davis. Row 4: Coach Moss, Coach Melvin, Witte.

126

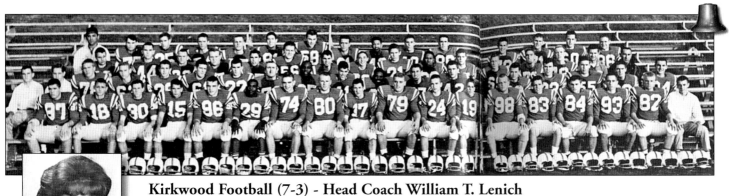

Kirkwood Football (7-3) - Head Coach William T. Lenich
Row 1: Snavely, McClanahan, Scott, Wolf, Wood, Graham, Marcrander, Coley, Pound, Steinkamp, Alsmstedt, Jarrett, Lionberger, Swift, Knott, Kohn, Benecke, K, Sadorf. Row 2: Rathert, Saenger, Sanders, Obermeyer, O'Neill, Luttbeg, Jerrett, Dickinson, Runnels, Martines, Reese, Busbee, Schaefer, Bowen, McHenry, Cracchiola, England, Eddins. Row 3: Kinker, Baldenweck, Boillot, Wohlgemuth, Beyer, Snow, Sterling, Schlueter, Keener, Whiteside, Kirk, Kemple, Ross, Taylor, Coach Batch, Coach McClanahan. Row 4: Coach Lenich, Talbott, McDougall, Herndon, Schwartz, Wolf, Waggoner, Waldmann, Jordan, Cleneay, Woodard, Wootten, Marshall, Royer, Wilks.

Football Queen
Libby Wright

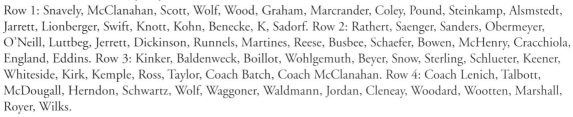

Football Queen
Linden Hanger

Webster Football (6-3) - Head Coach Raymond W. Moss
Row 1: Rhodes, Rusan, Brown, Reed, Zorumski, Tice, Stuessie, McLean, Higgins, Buchholz, Bischof. Row 2: Lowery, Schaeffer, Walker, Parsons, Eberle, Jones, Jost, Card, Machen, Ross, Reuter, Oliphant.

Row 3: Weisenfels, Brown, Hartman, Hall, Jennewein, Hale, Couch, Wilson, Best, Farmer, Rayburn, Schroeder, Mautz. Row 4: Hopper, Dillon, Lay, Robins, Alt, Gibbs, Taylor, Wilter, Weisenfels.

1962

KIRKWOOD - 10 | WEBSTER - 20
Thursday, November 22, 2:00 p.m. at Memorial Field

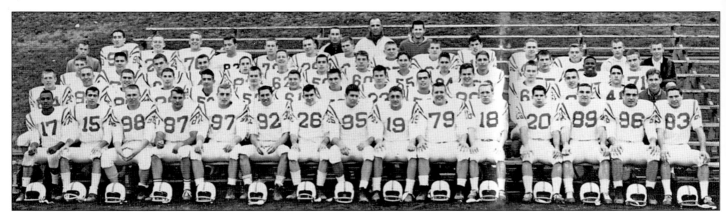

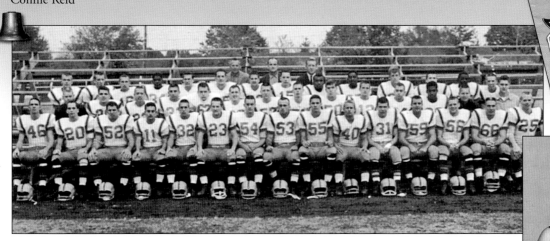

Kirkwood Football (3-4) - Head Coach William T. Lenich

Row 1: West, Clement, Coley, Kinker, Steinkamp, Busbee, Jerrett, Luttbeg, McClanahan, Daniels, Taylor, Wolf, Eddins, Wood, England. Row 2: Heintz, Abbott, Marshall, Holdgraf, McKee, Weisert, Davidson, Dietz, Ross, Koprivica, Baker, Collier, Beyer, McCormick, Manager Saenger. Row 3: Weiss, Velcheck, Seeger, Green, Schleuter, Hope, England, Pohl, Grossman, Hoag, Monolo, Wootten, Reese, Almstedt. Row 4: Manager Grebe, Woodard, Kemple, Schenk, Waldmann, Dunlap, Herndon, Rushing, Croak, Goldwasser, Martines, Wilks, Warmbrodt, Manager Rathert, Manager Sadorf. Row 5: Coach McClanahan, Coach Lenich, Coach Batch.

Football Queen
Connie Reid

Webster Football (5-2) - Head Coach Raymond W. Moss

Row 1: Hale, Best, Hall, Polley, Farmer, Lay, Jennewein, Hartman, Bland, Lansberg, Wagner, Rayburn, Couch, Southworth, Taylor. Row 2: Hopper, Brown, Sprott, Weisenfels, Gibbs, Schroeder, Grant, Wilson, Alt, Robins, LeResche, Fleming, Maurer, Hawkins. Row 3: Fisher, Losse, Mellor, Ernest Reeves, Mautz, Pruege, Scott, Lewis, Cloud, Earl Reeves, Preston, Lantern, Dillon, Seibert. Row 4: Coach Moss, Coach Holmes, Coach Melvin.

Football Queen
Judith Ann Evans

Kirkwood Football (5-4-1) - Head Coach William T. Lenich

Row 1: Ross, Rodwick, Wootten, Goldwasser, Schenk, Kemple, Collier, Baker, Holdgraf, Hoag, Warmbrodt, Croak, Jordan, Rushing, Woodard, Marshall, Abbott. Row 2: Kleinschmidt, Pottgen, Weisert Beyer Douglas, Pohl, Brandenburg, Wainwright, Lang, Chambers, Conway, Sehl, Ferree, Herb, Ziegler, Eberwein. Row 3: Hicks, Burslem, Holley, Mueller, Woodard, Reynolds, Swisher, Phillips, Moon, Forster, Greene, Kunkel, Sehl, Schenk, Grebe. Row 4: Hope, Marshall, Taylor, Hatridge, Weiss, Kavanaugh, Christmann, Velcheck, Dunlap, Hayman, Bailey, Lang, Coach DiGirolamo, Coach Lenich, Coach Stocker.

Football Queen
Judy Nichols

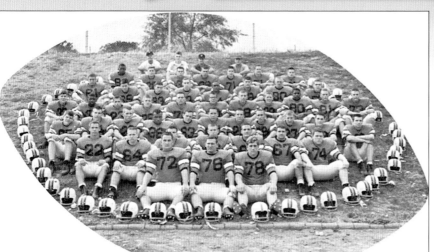

Football Queen
Carol Schacklin

Webster Football (3-4-2) - Head Coach Raymond W. Moss

Row 1: Droege, Mautz, Preston. Row 2: Sprott, Maurer, Rush, Maxwell, Mueller, Scott, Meier. Row 3: Stewart, Stuber, Losse, Cloud, Allin, Lewis Siebert, Mellor, Stocke, Penrod, Lanter. Row 4: Jost, Smallwood, Harrison, Schwendinger, Schroer, Lucco, Vornbrock, Hatfield, Reeves, Dunkman, Anderson. Row 5: Taylor, Dunstan, Crain, Milligan, Thornhill, Frye, Manes, Moss. Row 6: Hollis, Goodin, Willman, Massey, Brandin, Batts, Breckinridge. Row 7: Coach Moss, Hawkins, Coach Jones, Coach Holmes.

Football Queen
Cookie Mason

Kirkwood Football (6-4) - Head Coach William T. Lenich

Row 1: Edwards, Conway, Zimmer, Woodard, Pohl, Ferree, Ziegler, Moon, Pottgen, Burslem, Douglas, Lasadose, Holley, Greene, Mueller, Reynolds, Merkle. Row 2: Hicks, Chambers, McKinney, Garrett, Etter, Lowder, Carlisle, Coley, Craig, Bauer, McCarthy, Weaver, Brinkman, Forster, Herb, Wainwright. Row 3: Swisher, Hardy, Sehl, Kohlmaier, Janders, Sweaney, Taylor, Dick, Brady, Marshall, MacMillan, Campbell, Olson, Scheidt, Whitney, Massler, Bray, Corbet. Row 4: Coach DiGirolamo, Coach Lenich, Coach Stocker, Manager Marting, Manager Schenk, Manager Brus.

Football Queen
Pamela Banks

Webster Football (7-1-1) - Head Coach Raymond W. Moss
Big 10 Conference Champions

Row 1: Weisenfels, Brandin, Massey, Batts, Breckinridge, Smallwood, Dunkman, Willman, Schroer, Crain, Moss, Anderson, Rau. Row 2: Goodin, Patrick, Hollis, Durham, Hatfield, Bennett, Baxley, Epperson, Mickovitch, Landry, Becker, Vornbrock, Thornhill. Row 3: Stromberg, Stuber, Pattillo, Niesen, Dunajick, Curry, Whitener, James, Jones, Knisley, Jost, Harrison. Row 4: Otto, Johnson, Day, Thornton, Meyer, Harrison, Lester, Sparks, Slaten, Sweet, Coach Hoffman, Coach Moss.

KIRKWOOD - 0 | WEBSTER - 9 1965
Thursday, November 25, 2:00 p.m. at Lyons Field

Football Queen
Ann Drochelman

Kirkwood Football (5-5) - Head Coach William T. Lenich

Row 1: Dick, Brinkman, Corbet, MacMillan, Bray, Lowder, Bauer, Mc-Carthy, Solliday, Taylor, Craig, Brady, Sweaney, Whitney. Row 2: Leinicke, Lohse, Brinkman, Kessler, Campbell, Woodard, Hartzog, Evrard, Towns, Hargis, Marting, O'Keefe, Campbell, Carlisle. Row 3: Garrett, Hall, Ray, Hess, Endres, Salivar, Bowers, Shardt, Wallach, Lenich, Markle, Hoag, Olson. Row 4: Marshall, Schmidt, Landry, Jackson, Sohn, Ottofy, Marshall, Butler, Andrews, Knight, Turpin, Robinson. Row 5: Coach Stocker, Coach DiGirolamo, Coach Lenich, Manager Brus, Manager Chrenka, Manager Pebler.

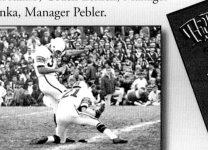

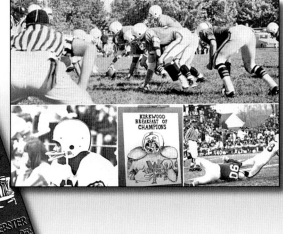

Football Queen
Sue Weber

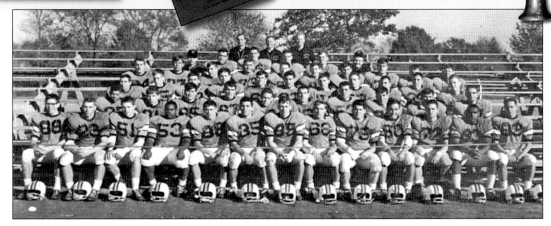

Webster Football (7-1-1) - Head Coach Raymond W. Moss
Big 10 Conference Champions

Row 1: Stuber, Thornton, Meyer, Slaten, Hayward, Lester, Jones, Day, Johnson, Mirkovich, Waters, Thornhill, Knisley. Row 2: Dixon, Taylor, Settlemoir, Davis, Dunkman, Kline, Niesen, Weisenfels, Landry, James. Row 3: Hartung, Defosset, Sleichter, See, Newsom, Walter, Rogue, Gill, Willman, Fleming, McGuire. Row 4: Kraatz, Mollenhoff, Clader, Spathelf, Toma, Sprague, Yeager, Brown, Witler, Rose. Row 5: Niesen, Tillay, Hasselfeld, Fletcher, Peterson, Petersen. Row 6: Coach Jones, Coach Hoffman, Coach Cook.

131

Kirkwood Football (9-1) - Head Coach William T. Lenich
Suburban South Champions
Row 1: Campbell, Kessler, Marting, Handlan, Olson, Brinkman, Lohse, Evrard, Leinicke, Hargis, Hartzog, Knight, Salivar. Row 2: King, Farrel, Ottofy, Lenich, Rychlewski, Bittner, Hanke, Miller, Jackson, Schmidt, Robson, Towns, Dowell, Kiel, Butler. Row 3: French, Hall, Harder, Martines, Hoffman, Ford, Lothman, Ritchey, Stalhuth, Schulz, Fulkerson, Marshall, Thomson, Glusac, Andrews. Row 4: Ray, O'Keefe, Coy, Haley, Marshall, Belcher, Ryan, Fayart, Hovey, Smith, Wallach, Terrell, Carter, Tate, Robinson. Row 5: Manager Williams, Coach Lenich, Coach DiGirolamo, Coach Stocker, Manager Elliott.

Football Queen
Judy Brandau

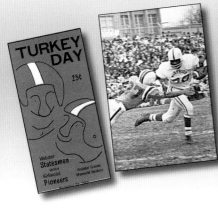

Football Queen
Sue Banker

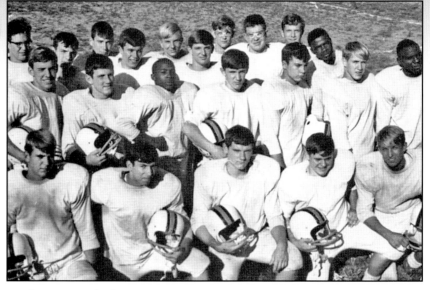

Webster Football (7-2) - Head Coach Jack M. Jones
Sleichter, Rose, Weisenfels, Tillay, DeFosset, Sprague, Davis, Witler, Dixon, Willman, Gill, Fletcher, Hartung, Taylor, Maguire, Dunkman, Settlemoir, Spathelf, Moellenhoff, Hasselfeld, Toma, Kraatz, Clader, Kline, Rogge, Cunningham, Newsom, Brown, Yaeger, Landry, Walther, See.

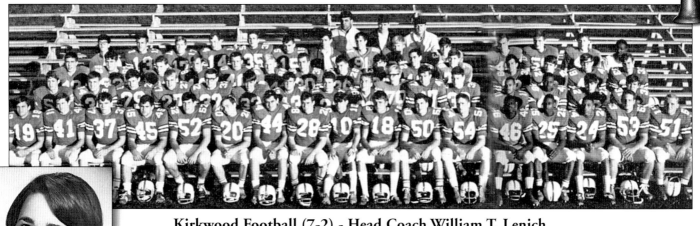

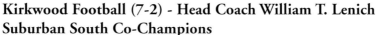

Kirkwood Football (7-2) - Head Coach William T. Lenich
Suburban South Co-Champions

Row 1: Smith, Hall, Farrell, Marshall, Rycklewski, Harder, Coy, Glusac, Harris, Lenich, Wallach. Row 2: Bax, Hawkins, Sikich, Lowder, King, Bray, Stahlhuth, Featherstone, Kessler, Wolling, Terrell, French, Mosley, Thornton, Lapides, Wallace. Row 3: Best, Bennett, Jennings, Hansford, Pepin, Rowles, Fick, Luther, Mohler, Brown, Sparn, Marshall, Temple, Fuhro, Salazar. Row 4: Manager Derryberry, Rockwell, Lothman, Ritchey, Schultz, Fulkerson, Dowell, Brackman, McDonald, Thielmeier, Marshall, Blattner, Murphy, Williams. Row 5: Coach Lenich, Coach DiGirolamo, Coach Stocker.

Football Queen
Abbi Hunt

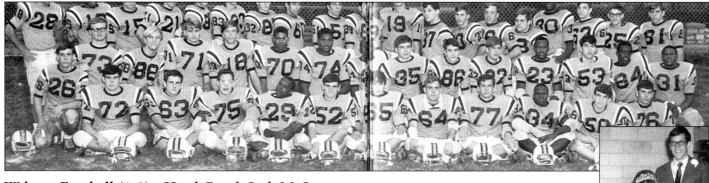

Webster Football (1-9) - Head Coach Jack M. Jones

Row 1: Rush, Gilbert, Mueller, Madsen, Crockett, Schrautemeier. Row 2: Thompson, Marshall, Kling Siler, Goins, Jenkins Young, Bush, Givens, Wehling, Kraatz, Hudgins, Givens, Nichols, Kniffen, Vornbrock, Daniel, Whitner, Hale, Ehret. Row 3: O'Rourke, Coleman, Thompson, O'Rourke, Mancin, Scarato, Perko, Knight, Buchanan, Johnson, Weaver, Stein, Derringer, Hicks, Cabanas, Lewis, Lucco, Hamlin, Donahower.

Football Queen
Jane Schaefer

Kirkwood Football (4-5) - Head Coach William T. Lenich

Row 1: Douglas, Leyhe, Taft, Decker, Morley, Nichols, Trask, Barton, Schneider, Campbell, Wainwright, Nentwig, Wolf, Chiles, Meinhardt Sitting: McNew, Luecke. Row 2: Dailey, Schultz, Saladin, Ross, Williams, Reed, Canda, Sarver, Bywater, Lindberg, Wilhelm, Robinson, Loomis, Mason. Row 3: Coach Batch, Waller, Morelock, Beard, Blackwell, Powell, Pool, Larson, Schmitt, Mueller, Blevins, Sokolsky, Hamilton. Row 4: Coach McClanahan, Ravens, Hobelman, Taylor, Mothersgill, Bond, Skinner, Wendt, Walsch, Williams, Heintz, Wohlgemuth, Tomlin, Coach Lenich.

Football Queen
Julie Smith

Football Queen
Faye DeClue

Webster Football (8-1) - Head Coach Jack M. Jones
Suburban South Champions

Row 1: Cabanas, Nichols, Knight. Row 2: Givens, Derringer, Lucco, Powell, Kling, Hudgins, Thompson, Johnson, Buchanan, Young, Mancin, Goins, O'Rourke, Wehling, Scarato. Row 3: Lake, Stein, Hicks, Siler, Cabanas, Sindel, Weaver, Weisenfels, Bush, Hamlin, Perko, Guenther. Row 4: Anderson, Klein, Hasselfeld, Thomure, Jackson, Terry, DeFosset, Curry, O'Rourke, Maguire, Cob. Row 5: Stocke, Scarato, Goad, Bird Hill, Hamilton, Klinkhardt, Knight.

Football Queen
Debbie Grebe

Kirkwood Football (3-7) - Head Coach William T. Lenich

Row 1: Luecke, Loomis, Ravens, Sarver, Bywater, Williams, Taylor, Leyhe, Wendt, Meinhart, Wilhelm, Ross, Morley, Reed, Taft, Wolf. Row 2: McNew, Douglas, Dailey, Wells, Weatherspoon, Waller, Landis, Frost, Schulz, Fellinger, Austin, Altmansberger, Brock, Canda, Nichols, Decker. Row 3: Coach Lenich, Dorlan, Daviess, Hoeh, Reid, Saladin, Bornemeier, Baker, Larimore, Wirtel, Zeigler, Summers, Lionberger, Edens, Graeler, Coach McClanahan. Row 4: Bond, Coach Baich, Kauflin, Summers, Cannon, McGill, Horn, Smith, Parsonage, Spenser, Reinhart, Hellstern, Knoesel, Dougherty.

Football Queen
Debby Durham

Webster Football (6-3) - Head Coach Jack M. Jones

Stocke, Dahlin, Goad, Ruck, Peet, Dierker, Hall, Givens, Brocks, Morris, Terry, Hill, Inge, McKelvy, Hollandbeck, Maguire, Scarato, DeFosset, Ottolini, Silier, Curry, Thomas, Weisenfels, Peterson, Cobb, Cabanas, Bryant, Jenkins, Hasselfeld, Berri, Musko, Guenther, Preston, Thomure, Bird, Knight, Tetrault, O'Rourke, Holmes, Stokes, Sennewald, Hamilton, Belle, Van Aman, Moore, Jackson, Rogge

TURKEY DAY

Turkey Day is here again, with the cheering fans, bouncing cheerleaders, excitement over the Frisco Bell and the Little Brown Jug, and the anticipation of the annual Friendship Dance. But this isn't just any Turkey Day – today is the Golden Anniversary of the Turkey Day football game. Today marks the fiftieth time in fifty-eight years that Webster Groves and Kirkwood have carried on a tradition which began in 1907. In 1952 the Frisco Railroad unwittingly began a Turkey Day tradition by presenting Kirkwood High School with a large locomotive engine bell to use as the school saw fit. Kirkwood decided to give the bell to the winner of the annual Turkey Day game. The victorious school hauls the bell to all of its football games and rings it vigorously after each touchdown scored by the team.

In this game, the winner does not take all. The Little Brown Jug is presented to the captain of the defeated team each year at the Friendship Dance. The jug is inscribed with the scores of all the games.

The Friendship Dance is held the Saturday following the game. Both schools crown a Football Queen to reign over the dance. The day before the big game, the rival schools hold celebrations.

Tension mounts every year as excited fans view the past records of the schools. Kirkwood has won seventeen of the games, and Webster has claimed victory twenty-seven times. There have been five ties, and eight years when no games were played. Games in 1924, 1925, 1926 and 1927 were forfeited because of a riot which broke out in 1923 after officials recalled Kirkwood's three touchdowns. Webster took the game 7-0. Also cancelled were games in 1909, 1911, 1914, and 1918.

Regardless of which school wins, Turkey Day gives the two communities a wonderful chance to cheer for their team with their friends and practice the good sportsmanship born from mutual respect the two schools hold for each other.

By Pat Corrigan
Webster Alumna 1966
Written for the 1964 Turkey Day Program

SEE YOU AT THE GAME

The highest attendance for a Turkey Day Game was 11,905 in 1965. After this seam-splitting Turkey Day Game, the principals of the high schools agreed that each school would be allotted 5,000 tickets, which students would only be able to purchase in advance of the games. Each school was to determine how many tickets they gave away for free, but both schools agreed that all faculty and even band members must have a ticket for admittance to the games. After this agreement was reached, the attendance stayed near 10,000 attendees until 1970, when the attendance began to again drop.

WALT SMALLWOOD

KAY BARKER
(LIVES IN ATLANTA)

TOM HOLLEY

1967 CROWD

ATTENDANCE FIGURES

1950	6,286	1961	9,715
1951	6,570	1962	11,032
1952	7,178	1963	11,132
1953	7,379	1964	11,653
1954	9,964	1965	11,905
1955	10,047	1966	10,008
1956	8,520	1967	10,390
1957	8,198	1968	
1958	8,398	1969	
1959	8,164	1970	6,329
1960	9,642		

PSYCHO-THERAPY

Lost in the urban sprawl of contemporary America are the twin values of community and tradition. Fortunately, the towns of Kirkwood and Webster Groves, while welcoming multiple Starbucks and a large Wal-Mart, have maintained the type of spirit that celebrates festivals, carnivals, parades and Turkey Day.

My particular experience with Turkey Day was bittersweet. I always envisioned playing in the game, though as I watch the game today, I realize how anonymous I was as a mediocre linebacker/tight end. We were playing a higher-ranked Webster team and were within six points with seconds to go in the game. Coach Lenich, always the master strategist, pulled a triple reverse pass out of his playbook. While I waited undefended in the end zone for the play to develop, Walter Smallwood (a state champion sprinter), caught up with the ball, tipped it out of my grasp (or didn't touch it and I missed it), and preserved the win for the Statesmen. Gone were any delusions I had about being a football hero, getting a date for the Friendship Dance, or ever having a relationship with Kay Barker. Years of psycho-therapy have restored my self-esteem and I am happy to report I have had a moderately successful life and I have been mesmerized by my wife for thirty-four years. Kay Barker lives in Atlanta.

By Tom Holley
Kirkwood Alumnus 1965
Written September 10, 2007

THE 1970S ....

The 1970s were a downturn from previous decades from the 1940s. The United States withdrew its troops from Vietnam unceremoniously and President Richard Nixon would resign from office due to the developing story of the Democratic National Headquarters burglary at the Watergate Hotel. The country would experience its first serious economic recession since the 1930s and an oil crisis would cause hour-long waits in line at the gas station. By 1975 a new filming format known as "Video Home System," commonly known by its acronym "VHS," would be introduced that would later revolutionize the making of home movies. Many factors of style became exaggerated and eccentric as shirt collars became longer, as well as hair, which often appeared disheveled in photographs. A movie named *Saturday Night Fever*, made an icon of a young actor named John Travolta for a new style of music and lifestyle known as "disco." By the end of this decade, disco would be almost immediately reviled and replaced by another youth lifestyle and musical type known as "punk rock."

In the Turkey Day Game, the 1970s were an unbalanced decade favouring Webster seven games to Kirkwood's three. The game would be played at Washington University's Francis Field in 1971 and 1972 because of the building of Interstate Highway 44 and also because of both schools' heavy student populations. In addition to the games being played at Francis Field, the game's starting time began to move to earlier in the day to 1:00 p.m. and noon, so that families could get home earlier to dinner. After the 1972 season ended, Coach Lenich retired, having served longest as Kirkwood's head coach at 24 years. With Coach Lenich retiring, his assistant coach Ron Marler became Kirkwood's new head coach. Ronald Lowell Marler was born September 10, 1935 in Flat River, Missouri. During his tenure, Marler would post a 3-4 Turkey Day Game record, but his career would be cut short in 1980 when he succumbed to cancer. With Ron Marler's passing, Kirkwood would seek a coach outside of the school for the first time in 32 years. In the first year of Ron Marler coaching the Turkey Day Game, a new tradition was made a part of the week long string of activities during Thanksgiving week, which was the playing of the two schools' hockey clubs on the Friday afternoon after the game. Hockey was not at that time an official school sport at either school and they remain unofficial to this day. Despite being private sports clubs, both teams are granted an association with their respective high schools so that they may use the school names and colours.

In many of the years since the game's foundation, there have been many pranks done by students against the other school and sometimes against no one in particular. One of the longest held

pranks was the disappearance of the Little Brown Jug in 1974. At this point in time, the game had its third Little Brown Jug in use. Because the scores are written on the backs of the jugs, approximately every fifteen years a new jug had to be created. As the schools prepared for the 1975 Turkey Day Game, someone noticed that the Little Brown Jug had disappeared. For many years it was rumoured that Jack Jones, whose team had lost in 1974, had taken the jug and hidden it in a closet, because he and every other Turkey Day Game coach since the jug's introduction, hated it so much. It was not until 1996 that the Little Brown Jug No. 3 had reappeared at P. J.'s Tavern, in Kirkwood, that the story of its disappearance was known.

In 1975, a snowstorm caused a two day delay of the Turkey Day Game for the first time since 1928. The game, played at Kirkwood, ended in a one-point victory for the Statesmen, causing the Kirkwood fans to pelt the Webster players with snowballs as they dashed across the field to take possession of the Frisco Bell. Also in 1975, Webster's legendary coach Ray Moss retired, causing the district in 1976 to rededicate Memorial Field as Moss Field, in his honour. One year later in 1977, Moss Field would be just behind Vianney High School in Saint Louis County in installing lights to allow for Friday night games. The lights were financed with the help of the Booster Club, with a special acknowledgement being made to 1954 Webster alumnus Cid Keane, who had a large hand in their support. The lights proved so popular and financially successful for the team that other county schools began also to install them. Kirkwood's Lyons Field had its first game under lights on October 5, 1979 against Parkway West.

As the decade of the seventies wound to a conclusion, something significant happened in 1978 and 1979 for Webster Groves. In 1968, the Missouri State High School Activities Association began to operate a State Championship Tournament, which in 2007 is known as the Show-Me Bowl. Those teams desiring to have the ability to play in the Show-Me Bowl were required to sign a notice to the Missouri State High School Activities Association of their intent at the beginning of the season, agree in writing that they would play no other football game in the season after the Show-Me Bowl was concluded and they would also have to qualify for the Show-Me Bowl based on a point system derived from their conference and season records and the difficulty of their schedule. From the years of the origination of the Show-Me Bowl and until 1978, both school districts opted to play in the Turkey Day Game, neglecting the submission of the application to play in the Show-Me Bowl. After the 1978 football season ended, Webster had a 9-0-1 record with most of its team intact for the 1979 season. This resulted in a lot of community pressure

to have Webster play in the Show-Me Bowl for the 1979 season.

The 1979 Webster football team was packed with very talented players, according to 1979 Webster quarterback Andre Nelson "our team, even if you look at it as a group of individuals, was full of very talented people physically and mentally. We had one of the highest GPAs [grade point averages] of any team to graduate from the school and a significant number of the players have become quite successful and accomplished in their fields of work today." Because the Show-Me Bowl Championship Game was played the Saturday after Thanksgiving, the Webster team had to play five games in fifteen days, in order to play the Turkey Day Game and play in the Show-Me Bowl Championship Game, which was held that year in Saint Louis at Busch Stadium. The 1979 Webster team, having lost only one game in the 1979 season, played the first half of the Turkey Day Game with their starters, leaving the second half of play to their second and third-string players. Webster won the Turkey Day Game 28-6 and two days later became Webster's first football Missouri State High School Activities Association State Champions. The Senior members had a total record over four years of 35-2-1, won two Turkey Day Games, outscoring Kirkwood for a combined total of the two games 76-6 and won one State Championship, refusing an opportunity of possibly winning two, so that they could play the Turkey Day Game instead. They were the Iron Man Team.

1970

KIRKWOOD - 8 | WEBSTER - 22
Thursday, November 26, 12:00 p.m. at Francis Field

Kirkwood Football - Head Coach William T. Lenich
Row 1: Ritchey, Love, Neely, Jackson, Swearingen, Weber, Grant, Roby, Sweet, Royer, Luttbeg, Van Ness, Kay. Row 2: Page, Miller, Weiss, Brunk, Fink, Ward, Milner, Lauber, Wenzel, Lenich, Marting, Harter. Row 3: Nelson, Bohrer, Mason, Bopp, Gamble, Burslem, Glusac, Etter, Teines, Wood, Lothman, Lind. Row 4: Held, Rogers, Stiller, Salisbury, Horn, Woodard, Johnson, Kenan, Whittaker, Peach, Harris, Spence. Row 5: Managers Hodill, Paineten, Kurth, Pennington, Coach Lenich, Coach Shannon, Coach Ehlers, Coach Coombs.

Football Queen
Sue Moreland

Football Queen
Celia Johnson

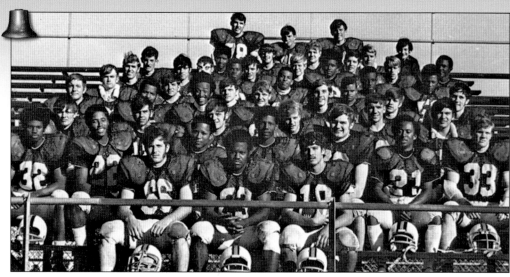

Webster Football (7-2) - Head Coach Jack M. Jones
Suburban South Co-Champions
Row 1: Cobb, Givens, O'Rourke. Row 2: Inge, Brocks, Crosby, Belle, Musko, Hall, McKelvey. Row 3: Bryant, Sennewald, Dierker, Berri, Dahlin, Thomas. Row 4: Roth, Jenkins, Moore, Cunningham, Perko, Holmes, Stedlen. Row 5: Buchanan, Ravensberg, Stay, Dixon. Row 6: Morrow, Smith, Jackson, Alexander, Thornhill, Wilkinson. Row 7: Woodson, Hollanbeck, Fields, Limmie Green, Brown. Row 8: Mitchell, Mohl, Sawner. Row 9: Smith, Brooks, Wyatt, Manager Lynch. Row 10: Rau, Kruse, Southworth. Not Shown: Jacobsmeyer, Siler, Belle.

Football Queen
Carol Schleiffarth

Kirkwood Football (6-3-1) - Head Coach William T. Lenich

Row 1: Lind, Peach, Scott, Lenich, Kenan, Wenzel, Spence, Horn, Harris, Jackson, Lauber, Johnson. Row 2: Dosenbach, Luecke, Reimers, Turner, Zich, Milner, Faver, White, Harter, Durbin, Edwards, Bonner. Row 3: Held, McKinley, Bueler, Page, Carnahan, Toman, Parsonage, Poe, Dowell, Thompson, Hodill, Lumpkin. Row 4: Hunter, Manse, Reese, Tobin, Woodard, Deutsch, Buehler, Maxwell, Brown, Whittaker. Row 5: Dalmer, Moye, Jackson, Grice, Williams, Hughes, Runnels, Angevine, Rogers, Smith, Wood, Lothman. Row 6: Managers Hulsey, Lemmie, Pennington, Kurth, Coach Coombs, Coach Shannon, Coach Ehlers, Coach Cook, Coach Lenich.

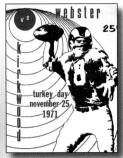

Webster Football (6-2-1) - Head Coach Jack M. Jones
Suburban South Co-Champions

Row 1: Rau, Kruse, McReynolds, Jackson, Cunningham, Buchanan, Morrow, Smith, Ravensberg, Stay, Mohl. Row 2: Fields, Shearman, Jenkens, Roth, Johnson, Wilkinson, Alexander, Crosby, Belle, Brooks, Woodson. Row 3: Southworth, Miller, Joern, Snodgrass, Tillay, Witlock, Tasker, Kohl, Shepherd, Rusan, O'Rourke, Hilliar. Row 4: Florence, Hanser, Schloemann, Krobot, Sloan, Shontz, Jacobsen, Eason, Givens, Ott, Mittler, Ash, Desmond, Stromdahl, Blanchard. Row 5: DeBord, Klinkhardt, Maness, Schulte, Woodring, McDonald, Wandersee, Tisoto, Theis, Barron, Baureis, Kelly, Burt, Frank.

Football Queen
Ann Reed

141

1972
KIRKWOOD - 8 | WEBSTER - 12
Thursday, November 23, 12:00 p.m. at Memorial Field

Kirkwood Football (6-3-1) - Head Coach William T. Lenich

Kirkwood Varsity Backs and Ends: Row 1: Smith, Burtelow, Kyriakos, Harris, Lenich, Woodard, Angevine, Reimers, Bruce. Row 2: Fuszner, Koch, Sethman, Johnson, Moore, Bueler, Harper, Fenton. Row 3: Benson, White, Durbin, Dowell, McHardy, Powell, Angevine, Heyman, Moreland. Row 4: Bertram, Ebinger, LeFort, Jackson, Richey, Burtelow, Maxwell, Williams. Row 5: Coach Lenich, Managers Lemmie & Stiles, Cies.

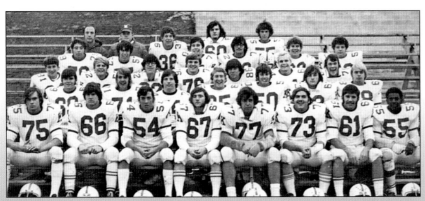

Football Queen
Leslie Kizer

Kirkwood Varsity Interior Linemen: Row 1: Edwards, Bueler, Toman, Held, Lumpkin, Parsonage, Faber, Reese. Row 2: McNamara, Hartwig, Scott, McKinley, Poe, Faggetti, Jacobsmeyer. Row 3: Gibbons, Rasmussen, Higgins, Rau, Branom, Brinkmeyer, Berg. Row 4: Hunter, Nollte, Carnahan, Spence, Bueler, Wilson. Row 5: Coach Coombs, Coach Shannon, Luecke, Horn, Drury.

Football Queen
Carolyn Collins

Webster Football (7-3) - Head Coach Jack M. Jones
Suburban South Co-Champions

Row 1: Barron, Tisoto, Snodgrass, O'Rourke, Tasker, Kohl, Jacobsen, Theis, Hanser. Row 2: McDonald, Southworth, Hilliar, Miller, Krobot, Ott, Woodring, Blanchard, Klinkhardt, Schulte. Row 3: Joern, Wandersee, Sheppard, Tillay, Eason, Stromdahl, Sloan, Baureis, Shontz, Mittler, Taggert. Row 4: Webb, Brown, Schockley, Elsey, Peat, Myrick, Ross, Angrum, Hadley, Oaks. Row 5: O'Neill, Plourde, Leeman, Reynaud, Fletcher, Hunt, Phillips, Smith, Anderson. Row 6: Auinbauh, Sheppard, Williams, Bowers, Carlson.

Kirkwood Football (3-5-1) - Head Coach Ronald L. Marler
Row 1: Schulte, Richey, Lefort, Moreland, Harper, Brown, Harris, Ebinger, Mitchell, Lindberg, Burtelow, Manse, Earl, Berilla, Price, Bruce, McKeague. Row 2: Coleman, Dionne, Wright, Webb, Cies, Russell, Runnels, Jackson, Saunders, Russell, Joseph, Bueler, Wilson, Rasmussen, Ward, Coach Cook. Row 3: Palmer, Grose, Eldridge, Bensinger, Faggetti, Brinkmeyer, Faber, Angevine, Angel, Jacobsmeyer, Corcoran, Corno, Spence, Hartwig, Coach Coombs. Row 4: Barnett, Bonner, Rau, Christmann, Burtelow, Moore, Peppin, Billings, Koch, Williams, Branom, Ford, Managers Styles, Austin, Coach Marler.

Football Queen
Tori Smith

Football Queen
Jane Shutt

Webster Football (5-4-1) - Head Coach Jack M. Jones
Row 1: Goodman, Taggert, Jackson, Oaks, Auinbauh, Phillips, Hadley, Ingram, Reynard, Anderson, Peats. Row 2: Webb, Hilliar, Brown, Hunt, Shocklee, Fletcher, Smith, Glusenkamp, Barnard, Myrick. Row 3: Plourd, Leeman, Carlson, O'Neill, Haney, Bryant, Pfitzinger, Schmidt, Turner, Smith. Row 4: Kotousky, Mahoney, Rogers, Walker, Robnett, Cushshon, Redmond, Gaylor, Harrison, Richie. Row 5: Manager Murray, Zuck, Pike, Watt, Rosemeyer, Ferrenback, Engler, Chollet, Manager Gable. Row 6: Moore, Whittaker, Moore, Manager Keil.

Football Queen
Darcy Howe

Kirkwood Football (6-3-1) - Head Coach Ronald L. Marler
Row 1: Jepsen, Jacobsmeyer, Underwood, Holley, Corcoran, Bentzinger, JosephFaber, Pepin, Smith. Row 2: Jones, Gooch, Becker, Hinkson, Beatty, Wilson, Angel, Hopkins, Steffans, Miller. Row 3: Palmer, Corno, Morris, Mansco, Merriweather, Waier, Buehler, Angevine, Ward, Managers McClug & Edgerly. Row 4: Wright, Ward, Starkey, Gresham, McClure, Musser, Reed, Ford, Quist, Roth. Row 5: Spears, Grose, McKeague, Dixon, Snorton, Manse, Fraser, Dionne, Rogers. Row 6: Ward, Dionne, Harper, Hall, Webb, Jackson, Coleman, LeFort. Row 7: Coach Williams, Coach Marler, Coach Coombs, Coach Cook, Coach Rau.

Football Queen
Linda Crowe

Webster Football (4-6) - Head Coach Jack M. Jones
Row 1: Cooper, Kelly, McBride, Hubbard, Crowe, Fandos, Kellogg, Hinkamp, Wright, White, Forsythe, Hanlon, Dotson, Williams. Row 2: J. Harrison, K. Mahoney, A. Whittaker, P. Zuck, G. Choliet, D. Rogers, G. Robnett, A. Pike, Watt, Engler, Glusenkamp, Coach Jones. Row 3: Redmond, Richie, Cushon, Hayden, Pfitzinger, Smith, Bryant, Schmidt, Barnard, Haney, Ferrenbach. Row 4: Barnard, Weil, Cusan, St. James, Robinson, Jason, Sanders, Ward, Penick, Caruso, Goodman, Coach Hoffman, Coach Miller. Row 5: Crowby, Rabbitt, Jung, Aronoff, Sepe, Appelbaum, Carriker, Rosemeyer. Row 6: Klinkhardt, Fratick, Jennings, Bouchard, Martin, Hougton, Greer, Forest. Row 7: Ravensburg, Sprick, Coons, Kinderfather, Maniaci, Coe, Sherwood, Edwards. Row 8: Keil, Wittenberg, Sanders, Hyde.

Friendship Queen
Linda Bakula

Kirkwood Football (7-2) - Head Coach Ronald L. Marler

Row 1: Miller, Buehler, Merriweather, Angel, Pohle, Becker, Davis, Neely, Stone. Row 2: Dionne, Ward, Waier, Roth, Jacobsmeyer, Broach, Walker, Coleman, Jones. Row 3: Smith, Elliott, Howard, Danna, Ray, Stephens, Hollinshead, Hoekstra, Snorton. Row 4: Harper, Burns, Stamper, Jepsen, Tucker, Taylor, Burns, Ivory, Burns. Row 5: Rogers, Benton, Warrick, Fogerty, Morris, Winston, Barton, Gordon. Row 6: Jones, Ray, Ward, Hoag, Starkey, Musser, Gooch. Row 7: Coach Williams, Coach Coombs, Coach Marler, Coach Cook, Managers Edgerly & McClurg.

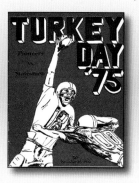

Friendship Queen
Vicki Spanos

Webster Football (7-3) - Head Coach Jack M. Jones

Klinge, Taylor, Jennings, Sprick, McCree, Kinderfather, Grant, Hubbard, Ravensberg, Jason, Coon, Rusan, Robison, White, Temming, Forrest, Smith, Williams, Conerly, Bouchard, Sepe, Kelly, Carriker, Aronoff, Weil, Martin, Davis, Penick, Jones, Hyde, Rabbitt, Sherwood, Wemhoener, Boehmer, Gile, Stepney, Klinkhardt, Crosby, Becker, Edwards, Bielik, Coe, Ward, Caruso, Auinbauh, Sanders, Plourde, Fratick, Farrar, Cook, Wittenberg, Appelbaum, Bowers, Jung.

145

1976

KIRKWOOD - 24 | WEBSTER - 6
Thursday, November 25, 12:00 p.m. at Moss Field

Kirkwood Football (5-5) - Head Coach Ronald L. Marler

Row 1: Manager Ries, Walker, Caruthers, Ritchey, McFarland, Clodfelter, Chapman, Drayton, Djavaherian, Ennis, Newton, Bryan, Manager Hollinshead. Row 2: Manager Blum, Warrick, Williams, Geig, Fogerty, Ferber, Dickherber, Stamper, Howard, Reed, Ivory, Chiaronttino, Coach Marler.
Row 3: Coach Coombs, Coach Cook, Stone, Chambers, Jones, Mackenzie, White, Eldridge, Burns, Danna, Jackson, Ray, Dotta, Warrick, Hurst, Pohle. Row 4: Knight, Gordon, Davis, Neely, Yeast, Miller, Rehnquist, Mueller, Bennett, Neely, Rau, Burnes, Paul. Row 5: Hollinshead, Ray, Forister, Morris, Williams, Albers, Winston, Garrett, Rogers.

Friendship Queen
Andrea Heiss

Friendship
Queen
Mary Kay

Webster Football (5-5) - Head Coach Jack M. Jones

Row 1: Taylor, Davis, Wemhoener, Ploude, Bowers, Sneed, Hubbard, Farrar, Bielik, McCree. Row 2: Andrews, Timmons, Smutz, Maltagliata, Mitchell, White, White, Willis, Wilkinson, Gile. Row 3: Pritzinger, Cook, Gaylor, Williams, Lewis, Gaines, Sargent, Jessup, Bond. Row 4: Felton, O'Reilly, Hogan, McCord, Lewis, Wanner, Brummel, Doder. Row 5: Shelby, Sprague, Stepney, Bennett, Schloemann, Ikemeyer, Applebaum, Barnett. Not Pictured: Andrews, Chenault, Diamond, Fink.

Kirkwood Football - Head Coach Ronald L. Marler

Row 1: McFarland, Richardson, Chapman, Drayton, Funk, Grose, Mackenzie, Clodfelter, Caruthers, Buckner. Row 2: Ferber, Jackson, Dotta, Koch, Dickherber, Eldridge, Bennet, Barnett, Grosberg, Manager Hollinshead. Row 3: Coach Hanna, Bonner, Welter, Moore, White, Reed, Hollinshead, Miller, Gober, Black, Hess, Coach Marler. Row 4: Drew, Wrobel, Evans, Mill, Lemmie, Baker, Rehnquist, Meuller, Coggan. Row 5: Coach Bryant, Yost, Lips, Hawkins, Williams, Forister, Kempf, Yingling, Ogden, Paul.

Friendship Queen
Liz Martin

Friendship Queen
Sally Wolf

Webster Football (5-5) - Head Coach Jack M. Jones

Row 1: Felton, Applebaum, Brummel, Bond, Ikemeyer, Sprague, Gaines, Timmons, McCord, Smith, Maltagliati, Wilkenson. Row 2: Thomas, Barnett, Bennett, Pfitzinger, Hogan, Sullivan, Hoffman, Stamper, Shelby, Cunningham. Row 3: Morris, Etter, Hamilton, Cressler, Welch, Spackler, Hedgepeth, Wittenberg, Jackson, Hinson, Alexander. Row 4: Betts, Jessup, Mercer, Eason, Lewis, Smutz, Acoff, Jessup, Siebert. Row 5: Schloeman, Redmond, Lewis, Trainer Dubuque, Maltagliati. Row 6: Coach Miller, Coach Hoffman, Coach Rau, Coach Jones.

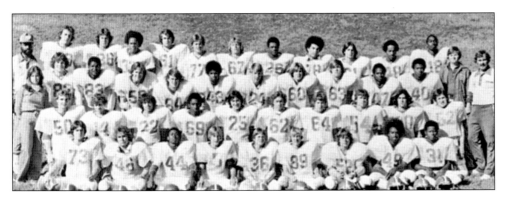

Kirkwood Football - Head Coach Ronald L. Marler
Row 1: Gober, Grose, Stewart, Edmunds, Suarez, Land, Stephens, Manse, Richardson. Row 2: Hesse, Kieffer, Moore, McClelland, Banks, Walter, Weaver, Pohle, Nollman, Drake, Coach Marler. Row 3: Manager Pellegrin, Scott, Hicks, Hollinshead, Crawford, Stanford, Edwards, Mosby, Wrobel, Boyd, Waters, Manager Hollinshead. Row 4: Coach Bryant, Yingling, Ogden, Bonner, Kempf, Mill, Nettles, Shed, Joyce, Vetters, Lemmie, Hawkins Not Pictured: Coach Collier, Coach Miller.

Friendship Queen
Barbara Hershfelt

Friendship Queen
Cheryl Nelson

Webster Football (9-0-1) - Head Coach Jack M. Jones
Suburban South Champions
Row 1: Stamper, Hedgepeth, Laster, Etter, Cunningham, Alexander, Morris, Thomas, Acoff, Hoffman, Wittenberg. Row 2: Sullivan, Queenan, Hamilton, Jessup, Mercer, Welsh, Cressler, Spackler, Grillo, Betts, Eason. Row 3: Brose, Loving, Kramer, Keane, Nelson, Stout, Kelly, Breummer, Roberson. Row 4: Brosie, Mach, Thompson, Morris, Smith, Miserocchi, Buford, Dames, Johnstone. Row 5: Applebaum, Strawbridge, Randle, Jenkins, Ried, Pfitzinger, Blunk, Jackson, Maltagliati.

Friendship Queen
Susan Lumley

Kirkwood Football (1-8) - Head Coach Ronald L. Marler

Row 1: Simmons, Heggie, Lane, Hall, Jaboor, Brown, Belcher, Thode, Drake, White. Row 2: Stewart, Edmunds, Howell, Newton, Weaver, Gegg, Johnson, Zisser, Nollman, Pohle, Moran. Row 3: Banks, Harris, Garn, Terrell, Stevenson, Baker, Watkins, Murphy, Edwards, Smith. Row 4: Pecha, Mosby, Bert, Walter, Crawford, Brogan, McWay, Overby, Cline, Waters. Row 5: Eichoff, Shed, Mc-Clanahan, Parks, Nettles, McKee, Drury, Neuhaus, Perry. Row 6: Coach Marler, Williams, Nappier, Hicks, Smith, Joyce, Coach Miller, Coach Collier, Manager Perkinson.

Friendship Queen
Cheryl Ellis

Webster Football (14-3) - Head Coach Jack M. Jones
Suburban South Champions
Missouri State High School AAAA State Champions

Row 1: Dames, Keane, Brose, Kramer, Morris, Stout, Kelly, Lovin. Row 2: Thomson, George, Maltagliati, Smith, Buford, Nelson. Row 3: Espey, Boing, Shields, Boyd, Speaks, Whittaker, Randle, Stergian. Row 4: Andrews, Robertson, Ball, Blunk, Johnstone, Odom, Mercer, Laher. Row 5: Martin, Brown, Williams, Davis. Row 6: Leonard, Hedgpeth, Cookson, Johnson. Row 7: Jenkins, Jones, Jackson, Tyler.

The Pom Pon Squad! If you've only heard the word and never seen it in print, you might not know that it's actually spelled correctly here . . . with an "m" and then an "n." And I think ours is the only squad which was nicknamed the "Pommies," much cuter than the ordinary "pommers" which is what most other pom squads are called. Franklin McCallie, our Principal and #1 supporter, gave us that name and it stuck for all of my 23 years as coach and choreographer. The pommies' "mission" is to perform unified dances and high kick routines during half-time at home football and basketball games as well as at pep assemblies. Here's how we began:

In 1972, a group of junior girls came to me to ask if they could start a pom pon squad to show the school that black girls and white girls could work together successfully since the cheerleaders were not racially diverse. I was flattered that they knew about my dance background and asked me to assist them since no "clubs" could exist without a faculty sponsor. Once we had tryouts (girls had heard of cheerleaders, of course, but not many had heard of a dance line called "pom pons"), we ended up with nine black girls on the first squad who toughed it out that spring performing only during basketball season. They were completely brave and committed since the audience wasn't expecting anything to be happening at half-time, so most people in the stands left to go buy sodas or popcorn! But "my" girls stayed and danced their hearts out using the worst sound system any gymnasium ever heard!

The girls must have done something right, because our auditions for the following year were stampeded by girls wanting to join the squad, and after eliminating about 20 applicants, we accepted 30 girls for the '73-'74 year: black, white, and even one Asian girl who spoke practically no English but was a lovely dancer. Thrilled with our tasks to entertain at football and basketball games, our next hurdle was getting the marching band to accept us. This was not easy in those early days when they would purposely change the tempo of our songs, because the band members didn't like sharing their half-times with us. Thankfully, we could assuage them by baking brownies for them prior to each game. When Tom Poshak succeeded the previous band director in 1985, we were actually incorporated into the much more elaborate half-time shows. We rehearsed three times a week after school with music that the band taped for us, then had one extra rehearsal with the band as we raced down to the field during "contact period" before facing our audiences on Friday nights (night football under the lights was accomplished in 1979).

Our popularity grew, the squad remained at about 30 girls each year, and we performed at venues as diverse as Powell Symphony Hall for a Pops Concert under the direction of Richard Hayman, the Green Tree parade, a rally in downtown St. Louis for President Ford when he came to town, Busch Stadium several times, and the hot air balloon parade whose pilots marched along with us. We even performed in the late '70s and early '80s with 17 other schools' squads, about 500 girls, at a fantastically coordinated halftime show when the football Cardinals were still in town. Our largest audience was a 4th of July performance in 1988 when we danced on the main stage under the Arch. The performance was televised nationally and, in fact, ABC television purchased red, white, and blue poms for us in keeping with the patriotic theme. It was quite a joy to have not only our on-the-spot home videos of that show, but also taped VCR footage from many "Pom Pon Parents" who were watching us on televisions at home.

And then there is Turkey Day! Even people who know nothing about football know about Turkey Day! Kirkwood High School's traditions leading up to the big day itself include each

POMMIES ...

By Penny Stein
Director and Coach 1972-1995
Written July 19, 2007

club in the school and each graduating class decorating one hall creating a theme to be carried out with tons of poster paper, crepe paper, paint, tape etc. It's a tremendous competition (Senior hallway almost always wins!) and very time consuming. There's a "tacky day" during the week, and for Kirkwood, "tacky" means dressing in orange and black which are Webster's colors. There are also not one but two pep assemblies: one during the Wednesday school day before the game and the other on Wednesday night so that all the returning pom alumnae can participate, and participate they did!

One of our most memorable years was 1982 when the skies let loose just before half-time. The band was ordered to take their instruments inside, a command which they reluctantly obeyed. They returned when the rains stopped, the pommies were soaked through, but "the show must go on," so the band played and the girls' tears turned to smiles while they performed their routine on the cinder track since the rain-soaked field had to be saved for the second half of the actual game.

For the pep assemblies prior to Turkey Day, the pom pon girls always wore red tights with football players' shirts over them (getting the "right" player's number was treacherous), and the girls danced as a squad alone as well as with alums who always remembered one of our routines that was a yearly tradition to perform during pep assemblies; we brought extra pairs of poms for the graduates, let the older girls squeeze into the line wearing just their street clothes (sometimes as many as 60 girls covered the gymnasium floor), and the year I retired from coaching the pommies, even I performed with them during "Get It On."

Faculty and community members who never attend sporting events frequently

choose to be part of Turkey Day in some capacity. As years go by, some traditions may be altered, the costumes the pommies wear may change with the styles of the day, the music may become more contemporary than "Stars and Stripes Forever," but the excitement, adrenalin rush, increased blood pressure, and nervous energy will always be present on Turkey Day for audience, athletes, and performers alike. "And the beat goes on!"

THE KIRKWOOD CHAIN GANG

My name is Gregory Filley. I am the head of what is known as the "Kirkwood Chain Gang." In 1972, I was asked by a neighbor of mine, whose son Rick Smith was a running back and kicker for Kirkwood at the time, if I would like to participate in holding the down markers for the Kirkwood football team. Not really thinking, I said sure. After all, I was only going to be holding part-time and never intended to do it longer than a season. However, Kirkwood had other plans. At the end of the '73 season, I took over the chains full time. So, when the 1974 season came around, I decided to put a permanent crew together. I enlisted the help of my current neighbor, Bill Macy, who has faithfully held the chains with me for 31 years; my sister, Donna Filley, who has held chains with me for 27 years; and my high school classmate, Allen Reichardt, who's been holding the chains for 15 years;. As I understand, we are the longest running chain gang west of the Mississippi, totaling over 100 years of combined experience. We got so well known over the years that Coach Collier and some players began calling us "Greg Filley and the Grungy Bunch." The name has stuck ever since.

One of the greatest times on field holding the chains is during the annual football game that we call "Turkey Day." The

was hurt. There were also times that we would accidentally get caught up in the cords of the coaches head sets and drag them down the field behind us.

We always have to be very aware of where the football is and going, lest we get tackled on the sidelines by a player chasing the ball carrier. That has happened more than once and it is always painful when it does. We also need to pay close attention to the refs in case they need us on the field to do first down measurements. We must make sure to pay close attention to penalty flags thrown, that way we don't move and cause confusion on the field.

Being on the Kirkwood Chain Gang or Greg Filley and the Grungy Bunch, as some call us; have given me some great memories. One of these memories happened on first Turkey Day that I took over the chains in 1974. My wife, Maxine, who was nine months pregnant at the time wanted to be part of the Turkey Day experience, so she had signed up to sell tickets. At that time, the tickets were sold in these tiny little booths at the entrance to the field. Somehow she managed to get into the booth to do her job but when time came for her to get out she got stuck in the door because of how big she was. The

best part is the fact that we get to stand on the visitors side and listen to them comment on plays that Kirkwood has made. It is also rather dangerous though because when they get mad, they have a tendency to forget that we are standing there. I have been run over a few times, during that particular game, by an upset coach. Matter of fact, I think just about everyone has.

Trying to maneuver the chains is a scary task at times. I remember one Turkey Day Game, my daughter was helping us and a coach got excited and jumped in her path while we were moving the chains down field and collided with her. Nobody

booth had to be taken completely apart so that she could get out. Needless to say, she never sold tickets in a booth again.

Another memory from Turkey Day that I've held onto took place in the 1973. It was late in the fourth quarter and Kirkwood had to punt. The coach, Ron Marler, called, "Punt right." Rick Smith, kicking at the time, thought Marler said "Run right," so he did. He was downed just short of the first, giving Webster prime field position to score, and they did, winning the game.

My favorite memory of Turkey Day was a game played in the early '90s. It was early in the fourth quarter; Kirkwood had the ball on third and goal. They scored. A Webster coach, realizing that the touchdown was the winning score, started jumping up and down. Well, the ground was wet where he was bouncing and he slipped and fell in a mud hole.

Well, those are my memories of Turkey Day from the sidelines. I have really enjoyed my time on the chain gang and feel honored to be able to share my story. Here's to many more years of great Turkey Day Games. On behalf of Greg Filley and the Grungy Bunch, good luck to both Kirkwood and Webster.

By Gregory Filley
Kirkwood Chain Gang Member
1973 – Present
Written August 3, 2007

DONNA FILLEY, BILL MACY, GREG FILLEY AND ALLEN REICHARDT (GREG FILLEY AND THE GRUNGY BUNCH)

WE'VE GOT SPIRIT, YES WE DO!

We're from Kirkwood, couldn't be prouder. If you can't hear us now, we'll yell a little louder!

For the past 100 years the cheerleading squads from both Kirkwood and Webster have worked hard to turn up the volume and spirit from the fans in the stands - and the stands are never fuller than on Turkey Day.

As a Red Pepper for Kirkwood back in '73, I got to be on the front line for all the excitement. Although being a cheerleader gets you closer to the action, you actually have the worst seat in the stadium since the giant players stand along the sidelines blocking the view. Often we had to rely on the crowd's reaction to know what was going on in the game! But being close to the field did give us the advantage of a head start to run across the field to claim The Bell.

Preparations for T-Day began in the summer when we'd have practices early in the morning in front of the windows of the auditorium so we could be sure our jumps were synchronized and lines were straight. Knowing that 10,000 spectators would be at the game made us want to be sure our jumps were high, toes were pointed and that we got all the way down in the splits. (The Bell didn't ring in Kirkwood much in the late '60s and early '70s, but every year the anticipation for the game was just as exciting.)

During regular season games, the crowd barely responded to the cheerleaders, except for their favorites: "Battle Cry," which pitted the classes to out-cheer each other; "Gimme a K"; and "Down to the River" led by the Boys' Pep Club who came out of the stands to work the crowd into a frenzy shouting "Yeah, Man!" No one even knew what the words meant, but it always got the fans on their feet and chanting before the fourth quarter.

The week of Thanksgiving we got very little sleep, emotions ran high, and there were so many festivities going on that we barely had voices left to cheer with. Every day had a special theme and activity. On Tacky Day, everyone dressed up in goofy, tattered costumes. (Today's KHS kids define Tacky as being anything black and orange, and vice versa in Webster.) For Red and White Day the halls were plastered with banners and crepe paper and we wore dresses with hula hoops in the hems to swing like Bells. We delivered Special K cereal to the players to give them pep and made mischievous midnight raids into Webster doing the Kirkwood Honk. (Have you ever heard of any other schools having a HONK?!?) There were pep rallies,

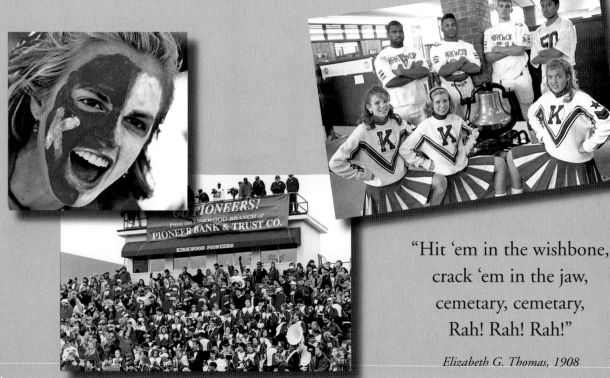

"Hit 'em in the wishbone,
crack 'em in the jaw,
cemetary, cemetary,
Rah! Rah! Rah!"

Elizabeth G. Thomas, 1908

a parade, the bonfire, and a slumber party where we all slept in our white V-neck sweaters with the red K for good luck. We had breakfast and exchanged gifts with the Webster cheerleaders and then, FINALLY, the game.

Unlike many of the players, I may not remember every detail from that 7-6 victory (except that Tom Ebinger stopped Jeff Hilliar from making a 2-point conversion in the final seconds of the game), but I'll never forget my Pioneer Pride and joy while honking That Honk and ringing That Bell.

By Cindy Jones Coombs
Kirkwood Alumna 1974
August 17, 2007

HAVE YOU EVER HEARD OF ANY OTHER SCHOOLS HAVING A HONK?!

THREE GENERATIONS OF TURKEY DAY IN WEBSTER GROVES AND KIRKWOOD

Turkey Day has always been a great memory for our family. My Dad, Wilfred "Willie" Robert Winters played right end for Webster Groves High School in 1936, 1937 and 1938. He wore number 44 on his football jersey. I, Sally Winters McNeill, went to Webster Groves High School in 1971, 1972 and 1973. I have moved to Kirkwood to raise my family. Our Turkey Day dinner growing up was always geared around the game. My son, Michael Robert McNeill played tight end for Kirkwood High School in 2002, 2003, 2004 and 2005. He wore number 44 on his football jersey. The Turkey Day game meant everything to my Dad. He said it was the whole season. Winning was everything. My son liked that it was the longest rivalry west of the Mississippi, it had a lot of tradition behind it and it was the coolest game of the year. Dad's most vivid memory of the 1938 game was that the caught a pass for a touchdown. Mike's memory of the 2004 game was that they won with 18 seconds left with a field goal and it was an awesome victory. Dad always thought the Turkey Day game was everything, but Mike would have loved to play in a state championship, given the choice, because Kirkwood had never

done that before. When Mike asked his coaches if he could have the number 44, he was told tight ends don't wear that number. When he said it was his grandpa's number at Webster, they said okay. My Dad was so proud Mike chose to wear his number. He thought it was just terrific, he felt honored.

On Turkey Day we have dinner at our house in Kirkwood. Dinner is always eventful. Dad and Mike always razz each other. They give each other trouble that their school is better and that they are the better athlete. My Dad always said to Mike "you'll never be as good as I am big boy!" They had so much fun going back and forth. My Dad rooted for Mike except for Turkey Day. He sat on the Webster side, wore orange & black and rooted for his alma mater. After high school Dad went to Central Methodist College in Missouri on a football scholarship. Michael is at the University of Nebraska on a football scholarship. Time will tell who was the best athlete. All three of us will look back at this great tradition of the Turkey Day Game and how lucky we were to be a part of it.

By Sally Winters McNeill
Webster Alumna 1971
Written June 20, 2007

THE DREAM WAS REALIZED

In a word, one might describe the Webster Groves/Kirkwood Thanksgiving Day game as "unique."

The game has its roots deep in the history of the communities of the two school districts. For the past 99 years the competing teams have battled for the pride of their respective school districts. Through various weather conditions and with some notable interruptions due to the events surrounding the First World War and a brief pause because of some bad blood between the two schools, the game continues. Overall, the communities have been in lockstep with their undying commitment to this highly traditional contest.

Although there remain a few games played on Thanksgiving Day in other sections of the country, most of these types of contest have been eliminated due to the development of a state championship series in football. Through most the 1960s and '70s, Webster Groves and Kirkwood chose to forego participation in the Missouri Football Playoffs, so as to maintain their annual T-Day Game. This situation was dramatically altered prior to the 1979 football season.

In 1978 the Webster Groves football team completed an undefeated season. Led by a great group of senior athletes, the team also featured a large number of talented juniors. During the spring of 1979 there was much discussion regarding the potential of the two school districts applying to participate in the football playoffs while at the same time continuing to plan for the traditional Thanksgiving Day game. The decision was made to enter the playoff structure, well knowing that the qualifying for the playoffs was a dream.

As luck would have it, the dream was realized by Webster Groves. The Statesmen qualified for and subsequently won the Missouri Class 4-A State Football Championship. The road to the championship and a successful win on Thanksgiving Day required the Statesmen to play five games in sixteen days.

The joy and goodwill that was created as a result of the Webster Groves team winning both a Sate Championship and being victorious on Thanksgiving Day was in sharp contrast to the events that transpired in 1988. In that year, another talented Statesmen team won the Missouri Class 4-A State Championship. That was the good news. The bad news was revealed when it was realized that the State Championship Game was scheduled to be played the Friday after Thanksgiving Day at a site 125 miles from St. Louis; Columbia, Missouri. This obviously created a conflict that could only be resolved by cancellation of the Thanksgiving Day game. It was a bittersweet pill for many loyal supporters of both Kirkwood and Webster Groves to realize that "their game" was not to be played and in serious jeopardy of being eliminated as a scheduled contest in the future.

During the following few weeks there was much discussion between the two administrations of the school districts and it was decided that in some manner there would always be a Thanksgiving Day game.

During the past nineteen years there have been three other occasions when either Kirkwood or Webster Groves has been involved in the State Championship Football Game. On those occasions, and when the varsity teams have not been available to participate on Thanksgiving Day, the game was played and featured the junior varsity squads from each school.

So, the annual battle for the Frisco Bell continues.

By Jack M. Jones
Webster Head Coach 1965-1989
Written September 6, 2007

1976 PEP ASSEMBLY
COACHES VIC MILLER, TERRY RAU,
BOB HOFFMAN AND JACK JONES

A Historic Season

It was a typical steamy St. Louis August day when we heard the familiar two whistles followed by "everybody up." This meant Coach Jones wanted the entire team to assemble around him. Unlike most of his normal addresses to the team, this one took on a whole new direction. This day marked the beginning of a whole new path for our team. For the first time the State final football game would be held after Thanksgiving, which meant that if we declared we wanted to participate in the State Football Championship, we could. On that day, we set out to 1) win all home games, 2) win the Suburban South Conference Championship, 3) go undefeated and 4) win the Missouri State Class 4A State Championship.

Pound for pound, man for man, skill level, speed, quickness and depth, I have to admit our 1978 team was a better squad. The senior class coming into this year did have some good experiences. Up to now, our overall record was 21-1-1 and we were coming off a 9-0-1, Suburban South Conference Championship season.

It seemed like a daunting task to replace the players that graduated the year prior, but Coach Jones knew exactly how to fit the pieces of the puzzle perfectly. Originally, I scoffed, but what did I know. He moved Tracey Mack from defensive tackle to fullback, John Keane from offensive tackle to tight end, replaced Johnny Mercer with Kurt Mercer at offensive end and added a few more changes and tweaks here and there. I don't remember them all but I do remember to insure everyone jelled we practiced three times each day during that steamy August.

We won our first game against Parkway South 56-6 but as the season progressed, some interesting things happened. Half way thru the season, two of our goals were shattered. We lost to Lafayette High School 12-7 on our home field. Don't ask how, but it happened, but quite frankly I believe it was the best

thing that ever happened to us. The rest of the regular season was a blur. Some games were stopped due to the point margin and one of their players being injured. The referees saw no use to resume play after such long delays. We also had a controversial overtime victory against Parkway Central, but we finished the regular season 9-1 and still needed Northwest House Springs to beat CBC so we could slide into the playoffs.

First stop…a long trip to Cape Girardeau to play a very tough Cape Central team on a Wednesday afternoon. I don't recall, but I think everyone got out of school that day because we had an entourage of chartered buses that showed up at the stadium. This game started with one of our best players and leaders "Brick" Johnstone suffering an injury on the opening kickoff. Cape had a defensive player by the name of Solo Dupree, who yelled repeatedly while Brick was lying on the field, "…get up, get up, we came to play, we came to play." Let's just say that Solo did not get to play this entire day. I often wonder where Solo is playing now and how his broken leg is doing. As the day developed, we had lots of stars that shined. Actually, too many to mention, but they know who they are. It was a fantastic team effort, offense, defense and special teams! We beat Cape 33-26 but we were wounded, especially on defense.

No time to heal… three days later we hosted the undefeated Sumner Bulldogs who up to now averaged 60 points a game. I remember getting to the field early that Saturday morning and the Sumner team and their fans already there and thinking these guys are pretty bold coming out here to try to intimidate us. I'm sure they thought they could but they did not overhear John Keane, Mike Kelly and Brad Stout say "…we are goin' to kick their [expletive] all over this field today, this is our field…" That was all I needed to hear since these three guys anchored the strong side of the offensive line. We beat Sumner 14-12. To slow down their offense, Coach Jones had Tracey Mack play defensive tackle and Tracey sacked the quarterback three times in row for total losses of about 40 yards to seal the victory.

Next up… Kirkwood on Thursday and defending State Champion Jefferson City on Saturday night. If you are keeping track, that's 4 games in 11 days. Game plan for Kirkwood was to have the starters play the first half or so and then have the reserves including some sophomores finish up. Don't get me wrong, we did not take Kirkwood lightly. Turkey Day your senior year is what you grow up hoping to have a chance to be a part of. Win or lose, memories you will long share with your children and hopefully your children's children. I never knew Thanksgiving without this game. Our entire day centered around this day and I assume everyone else in the two communities enjoyed football at noon and turkey at four also.

In 1978 we beat Kirkwood 48-0 on our home field and there was no way we could lose to them in 1979. A few things happened that day. Mark Loving set the stage for the most momentous occasion in Webster Groves football history as he scored a very long touchdown run on a play called "21" and he also caught a touchdown pass. As the clock wound down on the first half, we had a lead of 14-0 when I pitched the ball to Joel Blunk and he headed around the left end. The goal was to simply run the clock out but Joel thought differently. He broke one tackle and ran down the sideline and to encounter another Kirkwood defender and then it happened… the Blunk stop and go move. I'd seen that move fool would be tacklers for four years now and this guy was no different. Joel put on the brakes, stepped aside and then turned on the jets and headed to pay dirt. Not sure if Joel can still do that move, but if you ever meet my Dad, ask him, he still does it pretty well. Final score Turkey Day 1979, Webster wins 21-6.

So here we are at the Stadium Club for pre-game meal at the Show-Me-Bowl prior to facing Jefferson City. John Keane's dad and a few other great team supporters asked how I was doing. Not sure what they where expecting to hear from me, but I told them I was nervous. Sure, our offense was in good shape physi-

cally, but the real backbone of our team was our defense. Seriously, our offense had two 1,000 yard rushers, a receiver who caught 1,000 yards in passes and quarterback that passed for 1,000 yards, but the defense set school records and they were a mean bunch. Ken Buford, Kurt Pfitzinzer, Brian Dames, Jack Kramer, Brick Johnstone, Tim Smith and Phil Davis provided the senior leadership while a few juniors provided great toughness and skills throughout the year. At this time Dan Speaks and Terry Jones were on the shelf but other Juniors as I recall lifted everyone up; Chris Ball, Kevin Espey and Curt Randle to name a few. All season long this bunch rose to the occasion and I hoped they had one more in 'em.

Jeff City scored first and missed the extra point, buy my worries were beginning to materialize. As the game progressed, unsung heroes stepped up their game. Guys like John George making a timely tackle or Scott Jackson pulling in an errant pass began to add to my confidence. It wasn't until the waning moments of the first half that I saw the light at the end of the tunnel. The defense caused a fumble in Jeff City territory. We took possession and on the first play, Mark Loving broke loose across the middle and made a catch on a wobbly pass then scurried to the end zone. Game tied 6-6. We celebrated so much we got a delay of game penalty. Snap back, ball down, kick is up, kick is good… we went in at halftime leading 7-6.

The second half of this game proved to be an unbelievable display of defensive football. Every play, any play could be the game winning score. However, our defense prevailed and the offense and special teams held true and the Webster Groves Statesmen won the 1979 Missouri State High School Championship 7-6.

My Mom and Dad always told me to complete my education because no matter what, that can never be taken away from you. As my Dad knows, even though that may be true, winning a State Championship is a memory that can never be erased. Here's to great memories and thanks to everyone in the Webster Groves community that has contributed to these memories…a season of hope, a season of growth, a season of community and most of all… a season that made history.

By Andre K. Nelson
Webster Alumnus 1980
Writen June 4, 2007

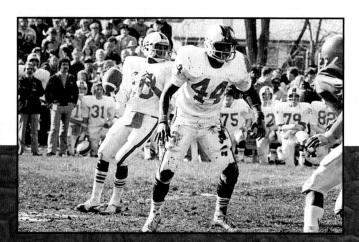

THE 1980S

The 1980s was referred to as "The Decade of Greed" both with revile and jubilation. In essence, greed became good, at least by those who could obtain wealth. President Ronald Reagan had overwhelming popular support in the United States, but he was restrained by a Democratic Congress. The Cold War with the Soviet Union was reaching its finale as the United States declared victory as the Berlin Wall fell in 1989. Everywhere in America appeared a new type of person known as a "yuppie," which was taken from the term "young urban professional preppies," and their counterculture counterparts known as "burnouts." Webster Groves would begin to foster music bands, such as The Painkillers, A Perfect Fit and The Urge and by the end of the decade Kirkwood graduates would start appearing on television, such as Scott Bakula in *Quantum Leap* and Dustin Nguyen, born Nguyen Xuan Tri, in *21 Jump Street*. The popular trends in music at this time were known as "pop," "ska-reggae," and "heavy metal" and vinyl audio records would be replaced by a new digital format, known as a "Compact Disk" or "CD."

Needing to find a new coach for their team, Kirkwood hired Ladue assistant coach Dale Collier. Dale L. Collier was born September 23, 1941 in Saint Louis, Missouri. He attended Northeast Missouri State Teachers College and, although two years younger, played on the same team ranked first in the State of Missouri with Jack Jones.

With the acquisition of Dale Collier as head coach, the balance of Turkey Day Game power shifted immediately to Kirkwood, in that they would lead the Turkey Day Game series this decade 7-2, 8-2 including a playoff game, with one game cancelled. The decade of the 1980s is fraught with first time occurrences, controversy, phenomenal athletes, disappointment and the biggest tragedy to befall a player...

In 1980, Dale Collier's first year as Kirkwood's head coach, he was awake in bed at 5 a.m., not having slept much the night before his first Turkey Day Game, when the phone rang. "Hello?" he answered. "What do you want to do?" Jack Jones asked. "What do you mean, what do I want to do?" Collier asked surprised. "Look outside your window, it snowed 18 inches [46 centimetres]." Thus would begin Coach Collier's Turkey Day Game quest, a two-day postponement of the game until Saturday at Webster Groves, so that they could clear the field. Kirkwood would win the game 28-7, with quarterback Scott Brogan completing 13 of 18 passes for a total of 193 yards.

1982 was the senior year of Kirkwood's All-Star athlete Alvin Miller. Miller was, as Coach Collier was quoted, "the best athlete of all the great kids it was my pleasure to coach. He had great

speed and could catch anything thrown in his direction." Miller led the team in receptions with 23 for a total of 432 yards his senior year. While his statistics do not nearly reflect the talent of this player, it should be known that the reason for this was his limited time with the football. Miller's opportunities with the football were nothing short of spectacular and it seemed that he scored nearly every time he was given the ball, despite being frequently covered by two opponents on the field. Due to these circumstances, opposing teams began kicking the ball far from him, or even to the sidelines, just to avoid getting the ball close to Miller. As a wide-end on the team, Miller was also restricted greatly from possession of the ball. In other sports, Miller scored a school season record of 1,606 points in basketball and through his individual performance of 44 points, single-handedly won the state championship for Kirkwood High School in track & field. Kirkwood beat Webster in football in 1982 for the third straight year under Coach Collier's leadership, with Miller's role in the game being nothing more than an insurance policy against an assumed victory.

In 1983, for the first time in 75 years, Kirkwood and Webster would play twice in one season, to Webster's detriment. In the first game on November 14 an 8-2 Kirkwood team would meet an undefeated Webster team at the Show-Me Bowl quarterfinals at Busch Stadium, home of Major League Baseball's Saint Louis Cardinals and, at that time, home of the National Football League's Saint Louis Cardinals. Kirkwood would win the game 14-0 and hold Statesman star running back and *Saint Louis Globe-Democrat* newspaper's High School Football Player of the Year, Keith Jones, to only 60 yards. Before their second meeting with Webster, Kirkwood would lose to Hazelwood Central in the Show-Me Bowl semifinals. On November 24, Kirkwood met Webster again at Lyons Field and beat Webster for a second time and fifth overall for Coach Collier against Webster. At five straight, uninterrupted wins, Kirkwood tied its longest football winning streak against Webster, which had occurred with five straight wins in the 1907 and 1908 seasons, and Coach Collier remained unbeaten by Webster since taking command of Pioneer football. At the end of the season, Kirkwood had a 10-3 record and Webster a 10-2 record, having lost both of its games to Kirkwood.

In 1984, Kirkwood's winning streak would be broken and in 1985 the teams would play at Busch Stadium for its second time, giving Coach Collier his second loss to Webster. Prior to this year's Turkey Day Game, it rained for three days prior to the game and the water then froze, making Lyons Field unplayable.

FORMER TEAMMATES MAKE GREAT RIVALS

Because Busch Stadium was being used for the Show-Me Bowl, the Missouri State High School Activities Association officials allowed Kirkwood and Webster to use the stadium the Friday morning after Thanksgiving for the game.

In 1986, the Turkey Day Game was played in overtime for the very first time after the game ended in a 13-13 tie. In 1979, the Missouri State High School Activities Association established the rules for overtime, allowing each team to have four chances to score from the 10-yard line. Webster was given the first series with the ball. After three attempts at scoring a touchdown, Sophomore Matt Arrandale kicked a field goal. Next, Kirkwood had its series. Despite fumbling the ball on the first play, Kirkwood recovered and later on fourth down, with three yards to the end zone, Dale Collier called timeout and asked his players if they wanted to kick a field goal and go to double overtime. In an indelible moment, team captain and right guard Jay Leeuwenburg, who would later have a nine-year National Football League career, said to Collier, "Give it to [linebacker Clever] Taylor and run it right up my butt, and we'll score." In a chaotic scene at the line, reminiscent of game held eighty years earlier, the officials declared a touchdown, Kirkwood winning the game, 19-16.

1986 was also the first year that the Friendship Dance moved from the Saturday after the game to a Saturday before the game. The first year that it was moved, it was moved to the Saturday just preceding the Turkey Day Game, but in later years it was moved as early as the last Saturday of October. The initial reason for the move was that it was simply too difficult to conduct all of the Turkey Day week activities and then have a big formal dance at the end of the week. Moving the Friendship Dance to an earlier date relieved school administrators from a great deal of pressure that the dance was causing, but it was also discovered that attendance increased with the move because no team had yet lost the game.

The 1986 game, in addition to ending in such chaotic fashion which caused Webster players and coaches to question whether Kirkwood had actually scored or if the officials just wanted to go home, also had an additional controversy when it was thought that a Kirkwood player was ineligible. The controversy was unfair to the player as it involved a misstatement on his school record by his old school when he transferred to Kirkwood from a school outside of Missouri. The Missouri State High School Activities Association later absolved Kirkwood and the player from doing anything wrong, but nonetheless the damage had been done to both the school's and player's reputations.

The next year, in 1987, the greatest tragedy to befall a player

at the Turkey Day Game would occur. Many tragedies had been endured over the years, a player being shot the morning of the game in 1913 and the 1923 riot are but two examples; however they do not compare to the event known as "The Snap." In 1987 neither Kirkwood nor Webster had stellar teams, both schools' records being 4-5. The entire game both teams seemed determined not to win the game, both failing to capitalize on several scoring opportunities. On fourth down, with 50 seconds left in a 0-0 game the Webster center snapped the ball over the head of the punter and past the end zone causing a two-point safety. The game ended 2-0.

Until 1981 the Missouri State High School Activities Association was divided into four sizes of schools, with the largest schools being labeled AAAA, commonly shortened and known as 4A. In 1982 the Missouri State High School Activities Association added an additional class, making the largest class 5A. In all of the years since the creation of the size classes, Webster and Kirkwood were always in the largest class. In 1988, Webster was lowered to Class 4A, while Kirkwood remained a Class 5A school. With the class change, Webster's football team achieved a 6-3 regular season record, losing three of their first four games. Despite their Class 4A change, Webster continued to play a Class 5A school schedule, better preparing them for the Class 4A playoff series. Having won all of their games in the Class 4A playoff series, Webster needed to decide if they could play the Turkey Day Game and then one day later play in the Class 4A Show-Me Bowl Championship Game at Faurot Field, at the University of Missouri, in Columbia. The decision was made and Webster cancelled the game, but won their second State Championship on Saturday, November 26, 1988, much to the disappointment of fans of the Turkey Day Game. In the *Echo* yearbook, a black page was printed with a white banner reading "Turkey Day, 1988 - Cancelled - Seniors, and alums mourn loss of Turkey Day - Superintendents vow to save future games."

Responding to the outcry from the communities, both school districts' coaches, principals and superintendents gathered in February, 1989 and devised a contingency plan to continue the Turkey Day Game if one of the teams was playing in the Show-Me Bowl Championship Game. According to the plan, everything about the game would remain as normal, however the first string players on both teams would be limited to the amount of time that they could compete, which the coaches would decide before the game.

Friendship Queen
Robyn Booker

Kirkwood Football (6-4) – Head Coach Dale L. Collier

Row 1: Moran, Watkins, McClanahan, Simmons, Terrell, Schamel, Waters, Brogan, Williams, Jaboor, Smith, Gregg. Row 2: Kramer, McWay, Blair, Smith, Harris, Murphy, Pecha, Dryry, Simmons, Neuhaus, Heggie. Row 3: Greenwald, Ingle, Torrence, Haddock, Curry, Hudgins, Procter, Baxter, DuPree, Cooper, Pence. Row 4: Harrison, Travis, Campbell, Berthold, Greenweghe, Childers, Berilla, Breslo, Lemp, Cooper, Witcher. Row 5: Magers Pennington, Katzenberger & Stewart, Brogan, Lips, Ferber, Miller, Boyd, Williams, Williams. Row 6: Coach Collier, Coach Warren, Coach Miller, Coach Fraser, Coach Collier, Coach Williams.

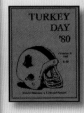

Friendship Queen
Jill Carlton

Webster Football (4-6) – Head Coach Jack M. Jones

Row 1: Loher, Ball, Andrews, Shields, Randle, McCree, Johnson, Thomson, Farwell. Row 2: Wilson, Boing, Wicks, Hooker, Maltagliati, Sandbach, Wedekind, Stofer, Martin. Row 3: Jackson, Booker, Nelson, Brown, Snyder, Jenkins, Auble, Sellers, Mercer. Row 4: Stanfield, Whittaker, Brown, Etheridge, Redmond, Crenshaw, Stepany. Row 5: Reichardt, Cooke, Stergion, Buss, Peterson, Hedgepath. Row 6: Coach Jones, Lemmie, Bennett, Stewart, Serati, Cardinali, Sullivan.

Friendship Queen
Sherry Fantroy

Kirkwood Football (8-2) – Head Coach Dale L. Collier

Row 1: Coach Collier , Coach Miller, Baxter, Curry, Thornton, Spears, Patterson, Miller, Lips, Ferber, Bulard, Blassingame, Carlson, Madison. Row 2: Managers Pennington & Fischer, Coach Warren, Hutchinson, Barrett, Boyd, Proctor, DuPree, Ingle, Williams, Williams, Mosley, Blair, Cooper. Row 3: Coach Cadwallader, Coach Williams, Bruce, Thompson, Mather, Size, Faber, Collins, Travis, Freise, Mayfield, Haddock, Burgess, Blair. Row 4: Coach Kurtz, Coach Sneed, Jordon, Schwartz, Drake, Shirley, Simms, Brogan, Groenweghe, Berilla, Clouse, Lemp, Jacobsmeyer. Row 5: Manager Steward, Coach Thornburg, Coach Bryant, Hanley, Newcomb, Webb, Childers, Breslo, Witte, Campbell, Witcher, Teter, Gegg, Berthold, Campbell.

Friendship Queen
Mary Ann Calhoon

Webster Football (4-5) – Head Coach Jack M. Jones

Row 1: Bennett, Wilson, Stanfield, Kemper, Cooke, Buss, Leonard, Gilliam, Durns, Bloemke, McGee. Row 2: Brose, Berra, Serati, Nelson, Hooker, Stewart, Crenshaw, Lemmie, Hansel, Maltagliati. Row 3: Wright, Etheredge, Nathan, Redmond, Farwell, Jones, Drier, Odem, Stofer. Row 4: Lowell, Johnstone, Sullivan, Snyder, Wedikind, Sandbach, Hunt, Stepney.

1982

KIRKWOOD - 14 | WEBSTER - 7
Thursday, November 25, 12:00 p.m. at Moss Field

Friendship Queen
Stephanie Adams

Kirkwood Football (7-3) – Head Coach Dale L. Collier

Row 1: Manager Pennington, Trainer Fraser, Size, Blair, Jacobsmeyer, Moye, Breslo, Brogan, Miller, Thomas, Blair, Collins, Coach Cadwallader. Row 2: Coach Miller, Faber, Burgess, Bulard, Burns, Barrett, Clouse, Witte, Campbell, Jackson, Hopper, Patterson, Coach Williams, Coach Warren. Row 3: McBrayer, Thornton, Hauck, Ming, Madison, Mather, Carlson, Mayfield, Gegg, Merriweather, Newcomb, Bruce, Mueller, Coach Thornburg. Row 4: Coach Yarborough, Blackwell, Zimmerman, Breslo, Miller, Mosley, Tyler, Sheppard, Morgan, Travis, Shaw, Harris, Weeks, Coach Bryant. Row 5: Coach Kurtz, Cole, Khahil, Chatfield, Ulz, Guirl, Jones, McKinney, Blassingame, Hilderbrand, James, Gorman, Stout, Young, Coach Collier.

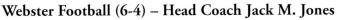

Webster Football (6-4) – Head Coach Jack M. Jones

Jones, Brown, Wilson, Biggs, Cazer, Leonard, Lemmie, Hunt, Mrazek, Gilliam, Robinson, Brose, Bennett, Edwards, Durns, Fritz, Bloemke, Johnson, Kemper, Minney, McCormack, Young, McGee, Jones, Drier, Hunt, Bloemke, Yokley, Hunt, Parker, Hansell, Black, Roberts.

Friendship Queen
Terri Malone

MSHSAA Show-Me Bowl
Quarterfinal

KIRKWOOD - 14 | WEBSTER - 0
Monday, November 14, 7:00 p.m. at Busch Stadium

KIRKWOOD - 17 | WEBSTER - 12
Thursday, November 24, 12:00 p.m. at Lyons Field

Turkey Day Game

1983

Friendship Queen
Tootie Grone

Kirkwood Football (10-3) – Head Coach Dale L. Collier
MSHSAA Show-Me Bowl Quarterfinal Winner

Row 1: Gorman, Harris, Guirl, Shawn, Ulz, Skinner, Mosley, Cole, Chatfield, James, Young, Weeks, Hauck, McKinney. Row 2: Blackwell, Harris, Corley, Ulz, Froman, Khalil, Stout, Breslo, Mueller, Miller, McBrayer, Cannon, Ming. Row 3: Miller, Mohler, Isselhardt, Nolan, Leeuwenberg, Lopez, Custer, Pollman, Smith, Weber, Tyler, Jones. Row 4: Vaughn, Hicks, Poholsky, Bryan, Tennent, Rice, Manse, Coach Curry, Trainer Fraser, Coach Warren, Coach Collier.

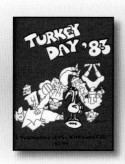

Friendship Queen
Leslie McMillan

Webster Football (9-2) – Head Coach Jack M. Jones – Suburban South Champions

Row 1: Hunt, Etheredge, Johnson, Minney, Saylor, Jones, Mrazek, Fritz. Row 2: Redmond, Snyder, Cazer, Roberts, Young, Yokley, Bloemke, McCormack, Edwards. Row 3: Marsh, Johnson, Alexander, McIntosh, Johnson, Keane, Buss, Salsich, Mitchell, Pankoff. Row 4: Spring, Coburn, Smith, Randle, Beckman, Powers, Yarbrough, Gann, Eason, Lavender, Jones, Thomson, Harris, Cotta, Heimann, Brown, Smith, Adorjan, Matagliati, Campbell.

1984

KIRKWOOD - 14 | WEBSTER - 27
Thursday, November 22, 12:00 p.m. at Moss Field

Friendship Queen
Anna Dodson

Kirkwood Football (9-4) – Head Coach Dale L. Collier
Row 1: Hritz, Hurst, Simmons, Bryan, Poholsky, Vaughn, Leeuwenburg, Lopez, Pollman, Rice. Row 2: Custer, Mohler, Nolan, Manse, Jordan, Isselhardt, Hicks, Weber, Deutschmann, Miller. Row 3: True, Jaboor, Atkins, Thompson, Caswell, Scott, Stecina, Macvittie, McCullough. Row 4: Paulsen, Miller, Dark, McLaughlin, Schwarz, Vespa, Mohler, Graf, Patterson. Row 5: Scheidt, White, Brown, Williams, Powell, Duggan, Leeuwenburg, Graf. Row 6: Brown, Eames, Keller, Hughes, Spraggins, Hale, Manager Fearheily. Row 7: Coach Bryant, Trainer Fraser, Coach Curry, Coach Warren, Coach Collier, Coach Washington.

Friendship Queen
Kathy Bentley

Webster Football (8-2) – Head Coach Jack M. Jones – Suburban South Champions
Row 1: Marsh, Ponkoff, Thomson, Johnson, Maltagliati, Alexander, Brown, Heimann, Yarbrough, Lavender, McIntosh, Buss. Row 2: Distler, Thomas, Mitchell, Spring, Wenell, Cotta, Adorjan, Campbell, Smith, Enyard, Randle, Salsich. Row 3: Buss, Henderson, Peacock, Patrick, Morrissey, Parker, Briggs, Smith, Cardinal, Meriweather, Wilson, Harkin, Powers, Nelson. Row 4: Johnson, Coleman, Jeanly, Edmonds, Cloud, Johnson, Sheppard, Scharf, Oliphant.

Row 1: Keller, Atkins, Graf, Duggan, Simmons, Jaboor, True, Riegelsberger, Logan.
Row 2: Bailey, Conklin, Keiser, Rice, Bickel, Scott, Young, Chambers. Row 3: Caswell, Smith, Nelson, Hines, Warren, Schoch, Hinrichs, Hosto, Edwards. Row 4: Thompson, Dark, Breeding, White, Quevreaux, Todd, Kelly, Miller. Row 5: McLaughlin, Schwarz, Kniffen, Willis, Paulsen, Toombs, Mohler, Graf, Lechner. Row 6: Haas, Patterson, Stevenson, Dyess, Miller, Eames, Mather, Randell. Row 7: Zinn, Hamilton, Finley, Brown, Scheidt, Jochens, McGinty, Bonner, Allen. Row 8: Coleman, Powell, Cook, Brown, Crump, Spraggins, Morris, Hughes. Row 9: Fisher, Hamlett, Leeuwenberg, Drexler, Ingle, Manager Wicker. Row 10: Coach Warren, Coach Curry, Coach Thornburg, Coach Horton, Coach Collier, Coach Williams, Trainer Fraser, Ingerson.

**Kirkwood Football (4-6) –
Head Coach Dale L. Collier**

Friendship Queen
Laz Miller

Friendship Queen
Tammy English

**Webster Football (11-2) – Head Coach Jack M. Jones Suburban South Champions
MSHSAA Show-Me Bowl Quarterfinal Winner**

Coleman, Stephens, Jackson, Sheppard, Parker, Edmonds, Evans, Gilmore, Johnson, Jeanty, Farrar, Bryant, Cloud, Eggers, Banks, McIntosh, Johnson, Stephens, Morrissey, Oliphant, Buss, Cookson, Wilder, Ford, Greene, McDowell, Peacock, Cardinali, Jones, Kwentus, Rhodes, Moulton, Brown, Williams, Thomas, Harkins, Davis, Gray, Patrick, St. James, Stanfield, Boerner, Meriwether, Greenwood, Pankoff, Nordman.

1986

KIRKWOOD - 19 | WEBSTER - 16
Thursday, November 27, 12:00 p.m. at Moss Field

Friendship Queen
Shari Borella

Kirkwood Football (10-3) – Head Coach Dale L. Collier
Row 1: Elking, Conklin, Leeuwenburg, Cook, Riegelsberger, Rice, Henrichs. Row 2: Bickel, Schoch, Hosto, Scott, Edwards, Todd, Willis, Quevreaux. Row 3: Toombs, Lechner, Finley, Hamilton, Mather, Stevenson, McGinty. Row 4: Powell, Atkins, Allen, Keiser, Fisher, Morris, Drexler, Manager Bulard. Row 5: Simmons, Smith, Nelson, Bopp, Johnson, Young, Wise, Cheatham. Row 6: Young, McMiller, Chambers, Taylor, Buchannan, Allen, Waskow, Ingle. Row 7: Smith, Godi, Nolen, Smith, Moore, Williams, Wagner, Gardner. Row 8: Coach Williams, Coach Curry, Couch Washington, Coach Ingerson, Coach Collier, Coach Bryant, Coach Kurtz, Coach Thornburg, Trainer Fraser.

Friendship Queen
Nicole Tucker

Webster Football (5-4) – Head Coach Jack M. Jones
Row 1: Smith, Best, Ragland, Jackson, Stephens, Egger, Stephens, Hoyle. Row 2: McIntosh, Mohan, Jackson, St. James, Davis, Hoffman, Blaney. Row 3: Greene, Kwentus, Mooney, Moulton, Carstens, Hawksley. Row 4: Dames, Cazer, Thornhill, Booth, Greenwood, Boerner. Row 5: McGuire, Alt, Beuc, Reeves. Row 6: Rhodes, Ford, Jones, Jackson. Row 7: Williams, Alexander. Row 8: Brown, Cookson, Robinson.

Friendship Queen
Sara Miller

Kirkwood Football (5-5) – Head Coach Dale L. Collier

Row 1: Smith, Ventimiglia, Bucannon, Bopp, Nelson, Ingle, Young, Johnson, McMiller. Row 2: Simmons, Chambers, Young, Lambert, Williams, Waskow, Hodges, Cordes. Row 3: Potthoff, Sugrue, Moore, Nolan, Allen, Wagner, Hapke, Cooper, Standard, Whittaker, Jamison, Graham, Whittaker, Thornhill. Row 4: Smith, Thomson, Kennedy, Hirschbeck, Jackson, Wise, M. Losse, Baldridge, Bert. Row 5: Lane, Payne, Lay, Smith, Noot, Smith, Rice, Beyer, Nicolson. Row 6: Bates, Taylor, Lane, Hammerschmidt, Godi, McFall, Chung, Hull, Parham, Denby. Row 7: Manager Wicker, Poholsky, Manager Pitts. Row 8: Coach Dostal, Coach Kurtz, Coach Curry, Coach Ray, Coach Washington, Coach Collier, Coach Miller, Coach Bryant, Coach Thornburg, Coach Pittman, Coach Williams, Trainer Fraser.

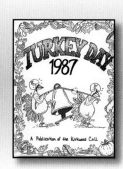

Football Queen
Tracy Tarpley

Webster Football (4-6) – Head Coach Jack M. Jones

Row 1: Abbott, Williams, Magill, Watson, Best, Booth, Mohan, Arrandale. Row 2: Hennkens, Daniels, Whinery, Thomas, Love, Washington, Calvin, Belt, Van Leunen. Row 3: Hoffman, Benz, Herman, McGuire, Alt, Rhodes, Oliphant, Schrijver. Row 4: Swenson, McMillan, Hawksley, Dames, Carstens, Blaney, Hannigan, Hoyle, Fugate.

1988 CANCELLED

Kirkwood Football (9-1) – Head Coach Dale L. Collier

Row 1: Lane, Bert, Smith, Jackson, Godi, Wise, Peal, Cooper, Hirschbeck. Row 2: Payne, Noot, Beyer, Rice, Hammerschmidt, Bates, Lee, Taylor. Row 3: Hull, Parham, Nicolson, McFall, Chung, Baldridge, Denby, Poholsky. Row 4: Allen, Whittaker, Thornhill, Allen, Losse, Whittaker, Chambers, Graham, Dolan. Row 5: Avis, Wills, Woods, Mottl, Abounader, Hogan, Tucci, Lechner. Row 6: Reim, Thiel, Woodard, Becchetti, Bone, Brown, Morris, Lischer. Row 7: Trainer Hageman, Coach Fraser, Coach Washington, Coach Ray, Coach Collier, Coach Bryant, Coach Thornburg, Coach Kurtz, Coach Williams.

Friendship Queen
Julie Fay

TURKEY DAY, 1988

CANCELLED

Seniors, and alums mourn loss of Turkey Day
Superintendents vow to save future games.

Friendship Queen
Holly Sheffler

Webster Football (9-3) – Head Coach Jack M. Jones
Missouri State High School AAAA Champions

Arrandale, Bourne, Bryant, Daniels, Davis, Dixon, Fugate, Hannigan, Henkens, Herrman, Hoag, House, Jackson, Jenkins, Kenney, Lang, Love, Magre, Mann, McGuire, McLaughlin, Oliphant, Pace, Ha Rhodes, Ho Rhodes, Robinson, Ryan, Serfas, Swenson, Trevino, Van Leunen, Washington, Watkins, Watson, Works, Washington, Williams, Whinery, Coach Jones, Coach Miller, Coach Manwarring, Coach Hoffman, Coach Gillan.

Kirkwood Football (4-6) – Head Coach Dale L. Collier

Row 1: Allen, Whittaker. Row 2: Ross, Whittaker, Thornhill, Graham, Jackson, Chambers, Moore. Row 3: Dickson, Lechner, Tucci, Robinson, Whisenhunt, Ming, Gatwood, Callion. Row 4: Manager Thornburg, Losse, Wills, Mungo, George, Mottl, Brown, Morris, Manager Morrison. Row 5: Manager Bopp, Avis, Abounader, Becchetti, Stewart, Reim, Woodard, Manager Thompson. Row 6: Hull, Mohler, Howard, Gutchewsky, Drexler, Drews, Ramsey, Henderson, Landry. Row 7: Trainer Pflug, Coach Williams, Coach Gilkey, Coach Kurtz, Coach Ray, Coach Bryant, Coach Wade, Coach Collier, Coach Thornburg, Coach Meyer, Coach Weld.

Friendship Queen
Sally Roever

Webster Football (9-3) – Head Coach Jack M. Jones Suburban South Champions

Row 1: Ragland, Bourne, Mann, Williams, Washington, Cloud, Pace. Row 2: Walters, Magre, Mulholland, Serfas, Domino, Ewing, Brown, Ryan. Row 3: Griffin, McCain, Grant, Beckman, Bryant, Washington, Jones, House, Hathaway, Eberhardt. Row 4: Watkins, Hoag, Mera, Greene, McLaughlin, Patterson, Gilliam, Hornberger. Row 5: Randolph, Ottofy, Moeller, King, Kwentus, Rutledge, Lang.

Friendship Queen
Karen Swain

TURKEY DAY Traditions

Webster Groves Principal Jerry Knight called when I arrived at Kirkwood in June, 1979: "We have important issues to discuss." At lunch, Jerry made a pronouncement. "You don't have to worry about the Turkey Day Game. We'll play Kirkwood and win; then on Saturday, we'll win the state championship." I had not heard of the "Turkey Day Game" or the state championship series, but his prophecies would prove true.

Jerry invited me to Webster's library to see "the Frisco Bell." "This is what you want," he

said, "and what we won't let you have." But we won the Bell the next year, and I learned that winning brings pride, but can also cause problems. As that 1980 game came to a close, I moved with Associate Principal Rick Burns and a *Webster-Kirkwood Times* photographer to the Webster side of the field to be ready for the onslaught of Kirkwood students and football players to claim the bell. Dr. Burns and the photographer made the mistake of standing on the side of the bell closest to the Kirkwood crowd. When the final buzzer sounded, I shouted a warning, but too late. Kirkwood players and students moved completely over them, and I knew they must be hurt. Amazingly, they both popped up safe. That incident should have been the impetus for action we did not take until some years later.

In 1991, we were back at Kirkwood, seeking to regain the bell again. Before the final buzzer, Kirkwood administrators took the traditional walk to the Webster side. We positioned ourselves more appropriately this time, and the first person to reach the bell was powerful guard, Joe Groves. Within seconds, he disappeared under 25 fans and fellow players. Simultaneously, I heard a terrible scream of pain from the bottom of the pile, and as I and others dove in to pull bodies off the bell, we found Joe with his leg bent back over the iron casing. A little more time and his leg certainly would have broken.

We decided immediately to confer with our Webster colleagues about a plan to have both teams meet at the center of the field, as is traditional at the end of all other football games, while our fans remained on the sidelines. The winning players would then move to the bell and hoist the 400 pound [182 kilograms] casing and bell onto their shoulders, avoiding disastrous accidents. Both schools agreed to the plan. While some fans were not happy, staff supervision and the understanding by most students of possible tragic consequences have kept this tradition viable for subsequent Turkey Day Games.

By Franklin McCallie
Kirkwood Principal 1979 – 2001
Written August 25, 2007

The day I was hired as Kirkwood's football coach, I was told "Turkey Day is bigger than life itself!" It is and more! The Game is not just a contest between the two schools but a reunion of families and friends from both communities. While the competition is always fierce, the atmosphere of respect and camaraderie between the teams and their fans is unmatched.

Thanksgiving 1980 as I lay tossing and turning, there was a phone call before dawn from Webster coach Jack Jones asking what I thought we should do. Since Jack was an old teammate of mine, I thought he was trying to get in my head until he said to look out the window. Well, there was about 10 inches [25 centimetres] of snow on the ground and we had to wait until Saturday to play the game. The added delay made me a nervous wreck before my first Turkey Day Game. But it was worth the wait! We won the game and the Frisco Bell and paraded the Bell through the streets of Kirkwood. It may have been the longest parade in Kirkwood's history.

I remember also a game when we were losing and had a fourth and two at the end of the game. I called time out and asked our guys in the huddle if they wanted to kick a field goal and tie or go for the win. Without hesitation, they said go for it and Jay Leeuwenburg said "run it over me." Jay made a great block with the other guys and we won the game.

Just one other was when the Webster center snapped a punt attempt out of their end zone for a safety giving us a 2-0 win. I saw how devastated he was and understood his feeling having played center throughout my career. We walked off the field together and though we won, I have never felt so bad for a player.

But win or lose, Turkey Day is special for all those who are playing or have played before. The memories, friendships, and lessons learned by all those young people remain with them through life. Each year families arrange their individual celebration around the game. We share a common bond unmatched by other communities. The stories get better and scores may be forgotten but each year the Turkey Day Game brings families together at 12:00 noon at one of the school's fields to continue the tradition.

So many players and fans… So many memories… I cherish them all.

By Dale L. Collier
Kirkwood Football Head Coach 1980-1992
Written June 21, 2007

> # "TURKEY DAY IS BIGGER THAN LIFE ITSELF!"
>
> Dave Holley, 1980

GANG GREENE'S GANG

One thing that puts a smile on my face when researching the Webster-Kirkwood rivalry is the reoccurrence of family names over the years. It fills me with the truest feelings of community and continuity. What kind of place would Kirkwood be without its generations of Mudds, Coggans, Jones, Woodards and Holleys and Webster without its Keefers, Keanes, Alts, Dames, Thornhills and Clouds?

My family, while not one of the original families to settle the area, located here in its early years. My grandfather, John "Gang" Greene was a star Webster athlete in football, basketball, baseball and track & field. As a sophomore, he split time as starting quarterback for the 1923 team and became the full time starting quarterback in the years 1924 and 1925. In 1926, he was moved to the backfield and became Webster's highest scorer that year with 44 points, ahead of famed athlete Bud Sample. After high school, my grandfather settled in Kirkwood, as one uncle stated to me, "just to get away from all of the celebrity of his high school achievements." My grandmother, Helen Buchanan, also came from a family that moved to Webster in its early years. Little did I know until I started doing research on the Turkey Day Game that Uncle "Buck," George Buchanan Junior, had a state record in long-distance running in the early 1920s. Unfortunately, further details were not disclosed in the 1924 *Echo* yearbook.

My father, Phil Greene, was a starting fullback at Kirkwood until his team, which started the season with a 6-1, 4-0 conference record, fell to a "pretty good" McCluer team. In that game, every backfield player fumbled the ball, everyone except for my father. Regardless, Coach Lenich demoted the entire starting backfield to backup positions, including my father. By Thanksgiving, everyone had earned their starting positions back, except for my father, which I think still leaves a bitter taste in his mouth because he didn't even fumble the ball!

In 1963, when my father was just a sophomore in high school, my grandfather died of a stroke. Having never known him, I never put much thought into when exactly he died, but it struck me horribly coincidental that, while again doing research for this book, I discovered that my father, brother and I all carried the same number on our jerseys in football… "63." Not one of us was aware that the other wore the number and none of us recall how or why we got the number. Maybe, now I do know.

So, to all families that have spent generations wearing the uniform on one or both sides of the line of scrimmage, I wish you all a fond and memorable Thanksgiving and Centennial Turkey Day Game. To my own family who played in the game; George Buchanan Junior, Chester Greene, John Greene, Roy Greene, George Buchanan III, Bob Greene, Jon Greene, Norm Greene and Phil Greene, I look forward to your presence at the Turkey Day Centennial Alumni Game, either in body or in spirit.

By Shawn Buchanan Greene
Webster Alumnus 1987
Written August 13, 2007

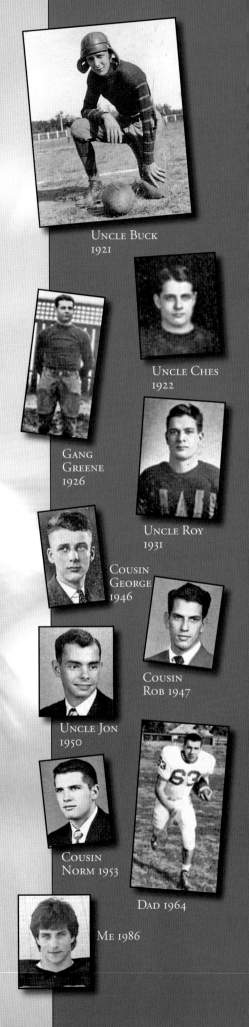

UNCLE BUCK
1921

UNCLE CHES
1922

GANG GREENE
1926

UNCLE ROY
1931

COUSIN GEORGE
1946

COUSIN ROB 1947

UNCLE JON
1950

COUSIN NORM 1953

DAD 1964

ME 1986

TWO GREAT TOWNS, ONE GREAT GAME

When the words Turkey Day are spoken, so many different things come to mind. I have had so many experiences because of Turkey Day. I met my wife, a science teacher at Kirkwood at the time, while showing my niece Bianca the traditional hallway decorations Wednesday morning. This was one of many memories that I carry due to this great event. The earlier memories are those of teammates making predictions on the radio. The traditions were plentiful and many are still in place.

I had a friend named Wayne Cooper who lived for the Turkey Day festivities. He made sure we had a new "Lil' Red Rag," the towel we tucked in the front of our football pants. The seniors were allowed to go to lunch off campus. Since we were a team, the Wednesday before Thanksgiving we would go out to lunch together. Many were dressed like it was Easter or an uncle's wedding. We had teammates sometimes helping each other tie a tie a certain way. Wednesday night was like the night before Christmas. There was such anticipation of what the next day would bring. Late that night, the girls pep club and cheerleaders arrive at your home and tape a sign on your door with the help of your parents. I never heard these young ladies arrive. I just know that for four years my mom would say every Thanksgiving morning, "go open the door." One morning, she said "go open the door" and there not only was a nice sign encouraging me to beat the Statesmen, but about nine inches of show on the ground. This caused the Turkey Day Game of 1980 to be rescheduled for Saturday.

I remember going to Turkey Day Games, then coming home to mom's greatest meal of the year. To me, playing in the game meant that I was delayed getting to that meal. The meal always tasted better when you had the Frisco Bell. The 1980 game was so memorable because we hadn't had the bell for a while. We won 28-14, and ran across the field to get to the bell and ring it. That was the goal. Once, I was traveling in Europe and a man found out where I was from and asked me who had the bell. After my last Turkey Day Game in 1982, my father celebrated with me after the game and each sister thought he caught a ride with the other sister. Needless to say, my dad caught a ride back to Kirkwood on the team bus. (We did not have cell phones back then.) The best thing about the Kirkwood-Webster tradition is that every former player at each school has some type of bond with a player at the other school.

Going on to play at Notre Dame led me to be involved in many traditions. I will always treasure my time with Touchdown Jesus, Number One Moses and ND vs. USC; but there is nothing like the Battle for the Bell. Two great towns, one great game.

By Alvin Miller
Kirkwood Alumnus 1983
Written August 31, 2007

No. 17 Alvin Miller

175

In 6th grade I was elected as a student council proxy and found myself sitting at a meeting regarding upcoming school holidays for North Kirkwood Middle School. There was Red-and-White Day, our school colors and there was Tacky Day. "Tacky Day… what's that?" I asked. The response was "Everyone wears orange & black, like Webster."

Of course they do. Having an older brother in high school and being the son of a Kirkwood graduate, I felt a little silly having asked the question in the first place. I was already aware of the rivalry. I guess I didn't realize I was supposed to participate prior to high school. But it makes sense… I mean we are in the same school district, right?

So a few years later, as a member of the freshman football team, I was as excited as the other several hundred people when we rushed across Moss field to snatch the Frisco Bell away from the Statesmen. My brother was a senior, and we had just won the game in overtime. Later on, during Thanksgiving dinner, my brother & I, along with our cousins, aunts, uncles, and of course mom and dad, huddled around the TV to catch the evening news coverage of the game. No DVRs back then… so we tried to watch the channel whose sports begins first, then as soon as the story is over you switch to the other channel to see if they have better footage. Occasionally, even the national news would include coverage of the game.

My brother was a starting offensive lineman. I was smaller, probably too small to play, really, but I wanted to play football, even if I only played on special teams. My junior year, we had a really good team. The seniors were talented, plus we had a few underclassmen starters. We went undefeated in the regular season, 9-0. It was the first time a Kirkwood team had done that and we were feeling strong. Webster was having a good year, too. Since Webster was Class 4A, and we were Class 5A, we both had a decent shot at a state title. But MSHSAA rules dictated a certain number of days rest between games, and with Thanksgiving falling only 2 days before the state championships, each team was faced with a decision: if it comes down to it, would we play the Turkey Day Game, or the State Championship?

So, before the playoffs began, we met for a team meeting in the weight room. Coach Collier explained the situation to us. Each team was to take a vote: play Turkey Day, or go to State. I don't remember how close the vote was, but I do remember thinking that it seemed like Coach really wanted us to play the Turkey Day Game. I mean, anybody can play for a state championship, but only two teams are privileged enough to play for the Frisco Bell. We voted to play on Thanksgiving.

Then we marched right out and lost our first playoff game, 10-2 to Parkway South. It rained so hard you could barely see the other side of the field. Our season was over. The bright side was that we still had a couple of weeks to practice and prepare for Turkey Day.

But, the week before, Webster had chosen to play for the state title. We wait-

TO PRODUCER

ed and watched as they made their way through the playoffs, eventually winning the semifinal game, qualifying for State, and snuffing out the 1988 Turkey Day Game. Our season was over... again.

It was a strange holiday that year. There was all this extra time sitting around the house waiting for our extended family to arrive. Mom didn't have to wonder if she was burning the house down, because she was at home while the turkey was cooking. No need to sit around the TV to see highlights of the game. We watched anyway, to see the report about the cancellation.

The next year we were an average team. We didn't make the playoffs, and after not being allowed to play our junior year, I was excited for Thanksgiving. Before the game some of the '89 graduates were in the locker room to remind us that they didn't get to play either. Coach Collier really drove it home when he said that for almost all of us, this would be the last time in our lives that we would play organized football. It hadn't occurred to me until then, and when I think back on the game, I think about that moment. How fortunate we were to know that this would be our last game.

Coach always made sure the seniors got to play, and I played in the 4th quarter. I gave up a TD because I took a bad pursuit angle. It didn't matter, though. The starters had given us a cushion and we won 16-14. Thankfully they did not include my mistake in the highlights that night.

Fast forward 10 years or so; like many St. Louisans, I had moved back home after college. I had a degree in TV pro-

duction, and a friend of the family landed me a job working for Charter Communications in their programming department, where I produced shows for CCIN, the local cable channel. Before I knew it, I was producing *High School Football* on CCIN. Not exactly big time television, but when I produced my first Turkey Day Game, it occurred to me how big time it was for the kids. The whole game will be on TV when they get home. It's a good feeling to be involved with the game again, this time perhaps in a more effective role that when I was on the field.

This year I will have produced seven Turkey Day Games on CCIN, and although we aren't playing, there are 22 people on the crew... all of us working together towards the same goal, anticipating the next play, planning ahead, synchronizing our actions and having fun doing it. It's the last football game of our TV season... everyone knows it and we want to finish the year with a strong telecast. My brother comes out in the morning and barbecues turkey legs for the crew, and after the game we head home to our families for Thanksgiving dinner. I get to answer the question "Who won?" when I walk in the door, and of course, turn on the TV in the evening to see the game.

By Brad Lechner
Kirkwood Alumnus 1990
CCIN Turkey Day Game Broadcast Producer 2000 – Present
Written August 9, 2007

aRt
AND THE TURKEY DAY PROGRAM

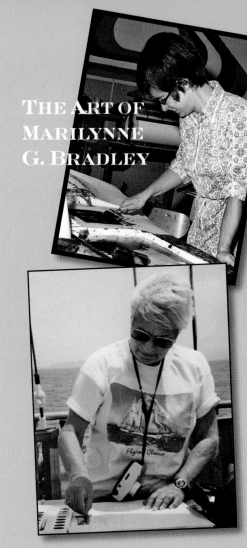

Every other year Webster Groves High School was responsible for printing the Turkey Day program. Usually this project was delegated to the Journalism Department which in turn asked for help from the Art Department. When I began teaching in the high school, I was asked to add to my curriculum the lesson of designing a cover for the program. My previous years in the advertising business helped with a reference morgue or files of pictures of subject matter. I hunted through the files for action shots of football games and passed out the references to my classes. The students were required to design a black and white drawing of something interesting for the cover, the finished work was hung on the wall and all classes voted for the best ones. These winners were given to the Echo staff and they picked the cover design.

Throughout my years of teaching I never gave up the practice of designing and painting for the commercial world. I moonlighted composing paintings and drawings for book covers. My watercolor paintings provided me with an opportunity to sell my work in galleries and exhibits. These experiences were carried over to my presentations in the classroom. I proved that one could make a career in the art world.

Curiosity of the world around me is reflected in my paintings. I love architecture. St. Louis landmarks and homes in the area are my primary source of subject matter Who's Who in American Women Artists, World's Who's Who of Women and Who's Who in the World have acknowledged my work. I am a signature artist member in the Southern Watercolor Society, Transparent Watercolor Society, Georgia Watercolor Society, Kansas Watercolor Society, Kentucky Watercolor Society, Oklahoma Watercolor Society, Watercolor Society of Alabama and a Distinguished Member of the St. Louis Artists Guild. I have had over 150 one person exhibits and received over 75 awards. My work is recognized in museum exhibitions, accepted in major national juried competitions and included in many major corporate collections in United States, France, Switzerland, Germany, Poland, Korea, Australia, Tahiti and China.

By Marilynne Bradley
Webster Teacher 1969-1998
Written July 13, 2007

Marilynne Bradley has produced numerous series of paintings including the Katy Trail, Santa Fe Trail, Paris, Tahiti, and St. Louis Landmarks. She is always working on a new body of work and experimenting with color. Design and vibrant colors dominate the perception of her compositions. To her, painting requires endless change, experimentation, and variation both in content and technique. Each painting is an effort to explore the subject from a different viewpoint, allowing a personal statement for each work of art.

To obtain more information, please visit www.MGBrad.com.

MSHSAA QUARTERFINAL

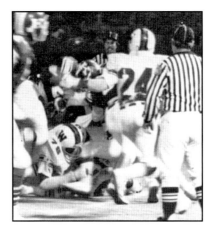

"IN 1983, FOR THE FIRST TIME
IN 75 YEARS, KIRKWOOD
AND WEBSTER WOULD PLAY TWICE
IN ONE SEASON."

TURKEY DAY GAME

THE 1990S............................

The 1990s ushered in the information and digital age and a great time of prolonged economic prosperity. In the early nineties, a recession ended that had begun in the late eighties. The Internet became widely accessible to people allowing them to connect to people from around the world at a fraction of the cost of previous methods. Cellular phones continued to get smaller and were able to hold charges for longer times. Globalization and global capitalism were under way and the North American Free Trade Agreement (NAFTA) would be ratified. In the early 1990s, a Seattle, Washington based band, Nirvana, would usher in the age of "grunge rock." "Rap" and "hip-hop" music, once considered on the fringe of the music industry, would become the new "pop" music of the nineties. By the end of the decade home movie VHS tapes would be replaced by a new digital device known as a "Digital Versatile Disk," or "DVD."

With the exciting and turbulent years of the 1980s finished, and with the acceptance of the Turkey Day Game Proposal resulting from the 1988 cancellation, the 1990s began and ended with no interruption and little controversy, save that of the developing strength of the Missouri State High School Activities Association, the importance of the Show-Me Bowl to the players and the spec-

tre that further league and size separation between the schools would finish the competitiveness of the Turkey Day Game. In retrospect, the balance of wins and losses remained almost even, Kirkwood leading the series this decade 6-4. Never was the Turkey Day Game Proposal used, as neither team advanced to the Championship Game of the Show-Me Bowl.

At the end of the 1989 season, Jack Jones left his role as Webster football's head coach after 25 years, but remained the athletic director. Jack Jones humbly believed and desired that

he not beat Ray Moss' record as longest serving football coach, which he believed was the longest in the school's history. However, due to a miscalculation on his part, he actually beat Moss by one year. Also, unknown to him, was that Charley Roberts was the previous record holder at 25 seasons. Despite the additional game that Roberts coached in the 1932 season, Jones tied Roberts' record for total number of seasons as head coach. With Jack Jones stepping down as Webster's head coach, assistant coach Ken Manwarring took charge of the Webster team at a time of great transition due to the school's shrinking population and the Missouri State High School Activities Association class separation from Kirkwood's and Webster's other traditional rivals. Kenneth Wayne Manwarring was born May 2, 1959 in Bonne Terre, Missouri. His wife is a 1984 Webster alumna and, like many of those who marry Kirkwood and Webster alumnae and alumni, is now a lifetime member of his spouse's community.

In 1991 a first time event occurred at the Friendship Dance, in that Kirkwood elected two queens that year because of a tie in voting. In Kirkwood the election of the maids and the queen, who must be nominated from a fall sports team or from any club that supports sports, is done as a campus election, making a tie unlikely. In this particular year, however, both April Schenk and Beth Giuntoli were elected as queens for Kirkwood, which was actually great news to the two friends. In the Turkey Day Game, Manwarring won his first Turkey Day Game this year and after a 3-6 record in 1990, reversed the program, so that his teams in 1991 and 1992 had season records of 8-3 and 9-1.

Four years after Jack Jones left his job as head coach, so did Dale Collier at the end of the 1993 season. The game at this time was amidst change, as some of the older and time-endured remnants were leaving the game and being replaced by those that were new to the tradition and the towns. As a result, the traditions grew grander than in previous years and made more formal. Like most instances of change, alumni began to worry that the "true" spirit of the Turkey Day Game was being lost and the traditions were being changed for the worse. These sentiments were only reinforced when a shooting occurred at the end of the 1992 game. Although the shooting was not related to the Turkey Day Game, it did occur in the parking lot of Moss Field shortly after the conclusion of the game, making it a Turkey Day Game incident. The fact that it was a Webster student that had fired the weapon and that two Kirkwood citizens were hit by bullets only compounded speculation as to why the shooting occurred.

THE BEGINNING OF THE END?

Some of the changes that were occurring in the game were things such as the "peaceful" transfer of the Frisco Bell initiated by Franklin McCallie in 1992. Prior to the "peaceful" transfer, immediately upon conclusion of the game, the team that had won the Turkey Day Game ran wildly to the Frisco Bell, along with fans from the bleachers, to grab and hoist the Frisco Bell in jubilation, clanging its chime and carrying it across the field. McCallie, who says that he had witnessed life endangering moments in previous years, in 1991 watched as a Kirkwood student fell to the ground and had his leg bent around the base of the bell and nearly broken. Because of this final, near calamitous incident, McCallie determined that some type of peaceful transfer should occur with the bell that would also afford the players an opportunity to shake hands after the game, which they had never done before that time. From the 1992 game until now, at the conclusion of the game a presentation of the bell is made to the victorious team.

In 1994, Mike Wade took charge of the Kirkwood football team in Dale Collier's stead. Michael David Wade was born August 18, 1960 in Duluth, Minnesota and graduated college from Southwest Missouri State University, now Missouri State University, with a Bachelors degree in Education. He also received a Masters degree in Education from Lindenwood College. He would win his first two Turkey Day Games, lose two more, and then win his next three. It is during the span of these three victories that some controversy began to develop about the disparity between the teams. Webster's program seemed to be affected negatively by its shrinking student population and it was believed by people in Webster that Mike Wade was allowing his teams to needlessly "run-up" the games' scores. The idea of "running-up" the score has been an intermittent contention between coaches over the years. Coach Lenich was displeased with Webster after the 1954 Turkey Day Game and Webster had beaten Kirkwood 48-0 in 1978. Mike Wade's 1997 Turkey Day Game team scored 35 points against a scoreless Webster team and he also beat Webster 43-14 in 1998. The 1997 win was the largest point difference favouring Kirkwood in a Turkey Day Game, which had many Webster alumni unhappy. Within the context of this game's history, however, that point difference is not higher than the games favouring Webster in 1978 and 1954, saying nothing of the 1917 76-0 Webster victory.

In 1998, Mike Wade fielded his best team since taking charge of the Pioneers. The team advanced to the semifinals of the Missouri State High School Activities Association 4A Show-Me Bowl. At the Trans World Dome, home of the National League Football's Saint Louis Rams, the team lost in the semifinals to Riverview Gardens, blemishing their near-perfect season record, 12-1.

That year, at the 1998 Friendship Dance, there was controversy when Kirkwood High School required any Webster student who brought a guest from outside of the two schools to write an application form and also obtain the signature of the guest student's school principal before they were sold a ticket to the dance. If the guest was not in high school, then a work supervisor's signature was required with a verifiable phone number. In years past, students were also able to buy tickets for the dance at the door, but this policy also changed in 1998. The reason for requiring the signatures was that similar practices were becoming common practice at other schools and it seemed logical for Kirkwood to do the same. The Friendship Dance attendance was also reaching capacity, with as many as 2,000 students at one of the dances. In order to better regulate the attendance and to allot tickets to students more interested in the dance, rather than those that came on a whim, the practice of pre-selling tickets held firm.

After the 1998 season, Ken Manwarring resigned as Webster football's head coach, but continued coaching other Webster sports, while also providing occasional help to the new football coach. The school hired former Hazelwood Central High School assistant coach, Cliff Ice. Clifford Wayne Ice was born September 16, 1964 in Thomas, Oklahoma. Cliff Ice had two goals as Webster football's new head coach; be the first Webster coach to never lose a Turkey Day Game and to never have a losing season. In a 2006 interview, Coach Ice laughed, "After my first year, I failed both of my goals." Coach Wade would win his third straight victory against the Statesmen in 1999, but would soon see the competitiveness of the rivalry reborn under the guidance of Cliff Ice.

Friendship Queen
Gretchen Splinter

Kirkwood Football Head Coach: William T. Lenich (Record W-6 L-4)

Row 1: Gutchewsky, Watts, Callion, Mohler, Drexler, Landry, Friar, Clark. Row 2: Hull, Allen, Hulsey, Ramsey, Smith, Moore, Navarrette, Moore. Row 3: Nickells, Zeigler, Macon, Reynolds, Cothrine, Power, Jeffries, Johnson. Row 4: Ziegenfuss, Landsbaum, Tart, Gaal, Conway, Gibney, Boyd, Groves, Ratican. Row 5: Bates, Schoemehl, Maurer, Smith, Parks, Smith, Jackson, Ruiz, Hahn.

Row 6: Clawson, Jackson, Phillips, Bush, Johnson, Walsh, Allen, Rolfes, Corley, Austin. Row 7: Blank, Schleiffarth, Hahs, Ennis, Hodo, Donnell. Row 8: Coach Fraser, Coach Bass, Coach Meyer, Coach Wade, Coach Collier, Coach Bryant, Coach Thornburg, Coach Weld, Coach Gilkey, Trainer Watson, Manager Thompson.

TURKEY DAY '90
$1
A Publication Of
The Webster Echo Newspaper

Friendship Queen
Alice Thomas
with Dr. Dan
Edwards
and Tony Domino

Webster Football Squad - Head Coach: Ray Moss - Record W-5 L-5

Row 1: Johann, Ryan, Ottofy, House, Patterson, Bill, Domino, Regans, Greenbury, Hancock, Baarnes. Row 2: Augustine, Carstons, Roberts, Rutledge, Jayne, Gill, Griffin, McCain, Strickland, Jones, Walters. Row 3: Coach Hoffman, Coach Manwarring, Coach Gillian, Coach Mahoney, Coach Harder, Teague, Meara, Hill, Myerscough, Gibbs, Parsons, Grant, Roberts, Swapshire, Cannon, Rothery, Smith, James, Schuman, Thomas, Davis, Whitehead, Coach Abegg, Coach Coffman, Coach Dutcher.

Friendship Queen
Beth Giuntoli

Friendship Queen
April Schenk

Kirkwood Footbal Head Coach: William T. Lenich (Record W-6 L-4)

Row 1: Groves, Ratican, Donnell, Ennis-Inge, Drexler, Hull, Young, Flynn. Row 2: Blank, Parks, Jackson, Campbell, Navarrette, Jones, Ashford, Allen, Hodo. Row 3: Bates, Hammond, Bush, Allen, Walsh, Clawson, Cole, Sharpe. Row 4: Landsbaum, McMiller, Boyd, Fair, Kelley, Maurer, Schoemehl. Row 5: Smith, Fifita, Moore, Moore, Phillips, Fields, Washington, Ali. Row 6: Conlon, Carl, Hahs, Schleiffarth, Wilkins, Johnson, Manager Hope. Row 7: Coach Fraser, Coach Arico, Coach Smith, Coach Bryant, Coach Collier, Coach Wade, Coach Thornburg, Coach Bass.

Friendship Queen Danan McSellers

Webster Footbal Head Coach: Ray Moss - Record W-5 L-5

Row 1: Walters, Westfall, Grant, Gill, Carstens, Roberts, Davis, Parsons. Row 2: Jones, Strickland, Gast, Butler, Young, Nordmann, Cummings, Young. Row 3: Brown, Gibbs, Ragland, Griffin, Meara, Elliot, Chapman, Domino, Patton. Row 4: Koenig, Hill, Oberkrom, Holland, Burns, Jory, Lister, Thompson, Yarbrough, Thomas. Row 5: Ganahl, Leffel, Chappell, Kuhn, Rayon, Roberts, Jayne, Myerscough, Smith, O'Gorman, Rutledge.

183

Friendship Queen
NOT AVAILABLE

Kirkwood Football Head Coach: William T. Lenich

Row 1: Pullum, Martin, Gillespie, Derenski, Brady, Givens, Coultrip, Rains. Row 2: Nardie, Jones, Hardesty, Grus, Beuncamino, McCain, Walls. Row 3: Hall, Rutledge, Drummond, Telfair, Harris, Shepard, Smith, Darr. Row 4: Blicharz, Corbett, Stevener, Bell, Wagener, Eaton, Koenker, Longnecker, Schleiffarth. Row 5: Wroughton, Phillips, Wilson, Canatsey, Frost, Buford, Schindler, Thomas. Row 6: Miller, Green, McClendon, Dabler, Olssen, Taylor, Eversgerd, Souhrada, Brown. Row 7: Spoto, Coach Pitman.

Friendship Queen
Tawama Reeves

Webster Football Head Coach: Ray Moss

Row 1: Roberts, Parsons, Gill, Canon, Roberts, Carstens, Myerscough, Teague. Row 2: Schuman, Davis, Chapman, Cummings, Gibbs, Leffel, Ryan. Row 3: Thomas, Kim, Smith, Holland, Brown, Ganahl, Kuhn, Gast. Row 4: Burns, Kooning, Fore, Cook, Condra, Hill, Hill. Row 5: Riley, Knichel, Williams, Fountain, Porchia, Hauser, Neimyer.

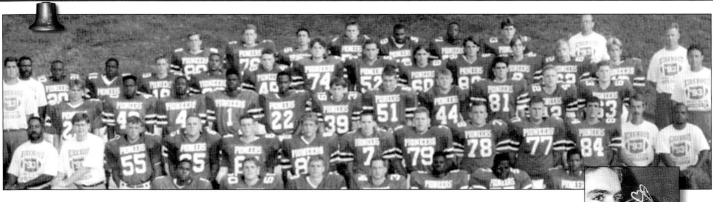

Kirkwood Football Head Coach: William T. Lenich

Row 1: Cothrine, Trask, Layman, Nauman, Dixon, Murff, Sharpe. Row 2: Coach Bass, Manager Derenski, Hoffman, Miltenberger, Losse, Norris, Kennedy, McKamy, Wood, Rosenberg, Smith, Coach Thornburg, Coach Jeffery. Row 3: Coach Irvin, Sowell, Ward, Macon, Dixon, Perry, Casey, Cook, Smith, Rooney, Waltz, Westbrook. Row 4: Coach Bryant, McCain, Walls, Stevener, Drummond, Hults, Donnell, Johnson, Wroughton, Nardie, Longnecker, Hardesty, Coultrip, Coach Wade, Coach Arico. Row 5: Canatsey, Dabler, Wilson, Schleiffarth, Green, Handley, Corbett, Coach Collier.

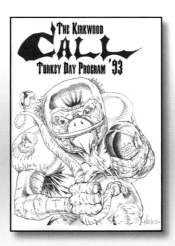

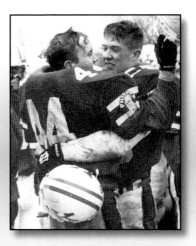

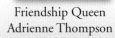

Friendship Queen
Adrienne Thompson

Friendship Queen
Megan McLlroy

Webster Football Head Coach: Ray Moss

Row 1: Manager Pollock, Carothers, Hanson, DeLong, Mueller, Greene, O'Kelley, Stauber, Braun, Dring, Zeis, Kirby, Ramming. Row 2: Dames, Von Hoffman, Kropp, Brown, Schwarz, Patterson, Fowler, Schute, Madole, Knickman, Fitzgerald, Odor, Cliff. Row 3: Lippincott, Bruno, Marshall, Cooper, Peterson, Rogers, Bobbitt, Burton, Crigler, Wade, James, Sydow, Kuhlman. Row 4: Coach Moss, Hellmich, Bingham, Noonan, Detjen, Cox, Altenhofer, Link, Swartz, Ward, Nolan, Euhler, Coach Bryant.

Friendship Queen
Libby McCormac

Kirkwood Footbal Head Coach: William T. Lenich

Row 1: Macon, Layman, Johnson, Smith. Row 2: Ward, Dixon, Damerall, Casey, Cook, Schuster, Waltz. Row 3: Drummond, Stevener, Donnell, Rooney, Westbrook, Denham, Enos, Walls. Row 4: Givens, Wroughton, Coultrip, Berry, Bell, Canatsey, Handley, Nardie, Phillips. Row 5: Dabler, Caffey, Rebstock, Corbett, Souhrada, Morrow, Schleiffarth, T, McMillen. Row 6: Manager Donnell, Mallroy, Hizer, Taylor, Brown, Reger, Whitehorn, Dickinson, Shakofsky, Brown, Manager Stopple. Row 7: Devres, Crissman, Kochera, Miller, Joseph, Kuhlman, Faron, Jones, DeLargy, Grayson. Row 8: Coach Gilkey, Coach Havener, Coach Arico, Coach Olderman, Coach Irvin, Coach Wade, Coach Bryant, Coach Smedra, Coach Bass, Coach Curry, Coach Thornburg.

Friendship Queen
Candice Yoder

Webster Footbal Head Coach: Ray Moss

Row 1: Worley, Johnson, Fountain, Kim, Cook, Sinclair, Korte, Davis. Row 2: Toughey, Condra, Powell, Bond, Futrell, Oliphant, Lovan. Row 3: Delaney, Niemeyer, Lay, Evans, Simon, Brader, Schook. Row 4: Taylor, Irwin, Gilbert, Taylor, Kuhn, Nehemiah, Taff, Cowan, Whittaker, Williams. Row 5: Jones, Hamilton, Tipp, Frigerio, Bates, McConnell, Kramer, Jones, Bach. Row 6: Wright, White, Green, Rhodes, Yancey, Davis, Hayden, Rideout, Young, Schiller.

Friendship Queen
Allison Bell

Kirkwood Footbal Head Coach: William T. Lenich

Row 1: Walls, Drummond, Souhrada, Schleiffarth, Phillips, Stevener. Row 2: Brody, McCain, Harris, Garner, Berry, Cleckner, Bennett. Row 3: Wroughton, Grayson, Green, Nardie, Canatsey, Rebstock, Dabler, Muhlenkamp. Row 4: Walker, Brown, Corbett, Brubaker, McMillen, Taylor, Sanders. Row 5: Kochera, Miller, Baker, Sgarlata, Landry, Fletcher, Shakofsky, Devres, Whitehorn. Row 6: Bonds, Houston, Benton, Hemmenway, Joseph, Caffey, Sleight, Holtgrieve. Row 7: Faron, Crissman, Delargy, Miller, Jones, Morrow. Row 8: Coach Strader, Coach Havener, Coach Arico, Coach Irvin, Coach Wade, Coach Bryant, Coach Thornburg.

Friendship Queen
Jocelyn Grant

Webster Footbal Head Coach: Ray Moss

Rhodes, Woodson, Lay, Kuhn, Lavender, McCowan, Yancey, Randoolph, Stanfield, Budzinski, Lawrence, Wright, Davis, Rackley, Bankhead, Hayden, Rideout, Johnson, Evans, Joerling, Landa, Campbell, Nixon, Crawford, Frigerio, Taylor, Lauder, Lewis, Sinclair, Morris, Russell, Foder, Lovan, Gist, Schook, Walker, Gilbert, Brader.

1996

KIRKWOOD - 12 | WEBSTER - 33
Thursday, November 28, 12:00 p.m. at Moss Field

Friendship Queen
Markeisha Henderson

Kirkwood Footbal Head Coach: William T. Lenich

Row 1: Taylor, Devres, Morrow, Caffey, Whitehorn. Row 2: Walker, Crissman, Bonds, Kochera, Davis, Miller, Shakofsky, Faron, Jennings, Brown. Row 3: DeLargy. Row 4: Caffey, Manager Hoeninger, Manager Deckard, Trainer Bruce, Dr Bill Stetson, Coach Olderman, Coach Havener, Coach Wade, Coach Irvin, Coach Bryant, Coach Strader, Coach Velton, Manager Donnell. Row 5: Whitfield, Spivey, McDaniel, Devres, Porter, Curry, Brown, Saitta, Lewis, Mason, Brubaker. Row 6: Hammond, Sgarlata, Sanders, Nickerson, Whitehead, Taylor, Brown, Ratliff, Benton, Shcleiffarth. Row 7: Blanner, Fletcher, Jones, Lindler, Krapfl, Burgett, Brockhouse, McClelland, Williams, Barnett, Powell. Row 8: Sleight, Schmitt, Cox, Komerous, Schoenbauer, Ortmann, Groth, Dabler.

Friendship Queen
Hannah Stevenss

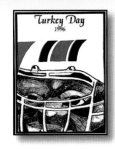

Webster Footbal Head Coach: Ray Moss

Row 1: Davis, Rhodes, Yancey. Row 2: Saitta, Lovan, Landa, Taylor, Rideout, Gilbert, Hubbard, Foder, H h Stevens. Row 3: Kachulis, Woodson, Nixon, Gordon, Bankhead, Rhodes, Wright, Bohn, Lavender, Anson, Sindel. Row 4: Harmon, Dyson, Edwards, Rideout, Robinson, Lay, Cannon, Browne, Cannon, Yarbrough, Weisenfels. Row 5: Cumming, Peterson, Shearburn, Thomas, Hood, Campbell, Joerling, Hildebrandt, Moppert, Stamps, L Jacobs. Row 6: Demotte, Epps, Bartels, Erdman, Strawbridge, Cole, Simmons, Hazel, Little, Flemming.

Friendship Queen
Julie Lapides

Kirkwood Footbal Head Coach: William T. Lenich

Row 1: Fletcher, Krapfl, Freeman, Sleight, Dabler, Powell, Glover, Jones. Row 2: Sgarlata, Baker, Taylor, Taylor, Brubaker, Allen, Mason, McDaniel, Landry. Row 3: Manager Flynn, Reed, Linnihan, Lee, Williams, Hardesty, Stemmermann, Sciacia, Groth, Manager Price. Row 4: Osterholt, Whitfield, Stephey, Spivey, Newstrom, Freeman, Latimore, Taylor. Row 5: Hoff, Whitehead, Brown, Blan- ner, Hoffmann, LaMartina, Beecher, Schleiffarth, Burgun, Porter. Row 6: Anderson, Maclin, Hammond, Manager Hoeninger, Coach Strader, Coach Havener, Coach Wade, Coach Merritt, Coach Olderman, Porter, Watkins, Manager Caffey. Row 7: Brown, Whiteside, Schneider, Brown, Saitta, Brown, Haynes, Rau, Tillman, Curry, Merriweather.

Friendship Queen

Webster Footbal Head Coach: Ray Moss

Row 1: Stanfield, Rhodes, Bankhead, Nixon, Lay, Robinson, Bond, Gordon, Lavendar. Row 2: Anson, Yabrough, Woodson, Erdman, Campbell, Joerling, Shearbaum, Rideout, Hood, Strawbridge. Row 3: Granderson, Haessig, McCormick, Hittler, Hllwig, Ostman, Adams, Ramey, Stamps, Sims. Row 4: Ming, Wail, Smith, Hildebrandt, Gewinner, Blanchard, Gluesenkamp, Goldsby. Row 5: Wiliams, Schlegel, Harden, Gillilan, Cannon, Manwarring.

1998

KIRKWOOD - 43 | WEBSTER - 14
Thursday, November 26, 12:00 p.m. at Moss Field

Friendship Queen
Desiree Mitchell

Kirkwood Footbal Head Coach: William T. Lenich

Row 1: Curry, Porter, Whitehead, Blanner, Groth, Burgun, Brown, Maclin. Row 2: Manager Flynn, Porter, Venneman, Williams II, Brown, Schleiffarth, Stemmermann, Burgett, Hammond, Devres, Manager Krapfl. Row 3: Ragland, Watkins, Woolf, Tillman, Taylor, Hurst, Haynes, Whitfield. Row 4: Manager Olderman, Merriweather, Spivey, Stephey, Osterholt, Cooley, Cooper, Rockel, Neustrom, Wagner, Manager Krapfl. Row 5: Fleming, Hardesty, Reed, Sciacia, Lee, Hoggmann, Worrall, Linnihan, Ward, Coombs, Manager Crenshan. Row 6: Whiteside, Marlock, LaMartina, Brown, Lawler, Beecher, Tau, Donnell, Watkins. Row 7: Coach Merritt, Coach Olderman, Coach Fletcher, Coach Zemke, Coach Wade, Coach Heinemann, Coach Velten, Coach Havener, Trainer Russell.

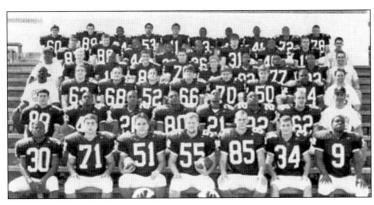

Friendship Queen
Courtney Smoot

Turkey Day 1998

Statesmen vs. Pioneers
Thursday, November 26

Webster Footbal Head Coach: Ray Moss

Row 1: Strawbridge, Erdman, Yarbrough, Joerling, Peterson, Rideout, Cole. Row 2: Hood, Smtih, Stamps, Granderson, Trevino, Walker, Anson, Coach Ken Manwarring. Row 3: Coach Williams, Hildebrandt, Hittler, Velten, Adams, Ostman, Ramey, Simmons, Coach Schlegel. Row 4: Coach Hardin, Gewinner, Bass, Linhorst, Sullivan, Gaffney, Washington, McDowell, McCall, Coach Gillian. Row 5: Hagley, Downs, Grandberry, Eason, Whittaker, Koch, Ming, Oldenwald, Shipp. Row 6: Brauer, Gewinner, Simms, Hill, Warner, Baily, Bowie, Frasier, Beard, Harrison.

KIRKWOOD - 14 | WEBSTER - 6
Thursday, November 25, 12:00 p.m. at Lyons Field

Friendship Queen
Keisha Moody

Kirkwood Footbal Head Coach: William T. Lenich

Row 1: Waters, Spivey, Woolf, Maclin, Jackson, Watkins, Brown, Osterholt. Row 2: Moody, Pauly, Brown, Schneider, Winters, Saunders, Tillman, Watkins, Levy. Row 3: Haynes, Rau, Marlock, Taylor, Dillon-Fish, Nigh, Krisman, Schleiffarth. Row 4: Cooley, Clark, Rockel, Cooper, Spivey, Wolfe, Pott, Stephey, Merriweather, Manager Nieman. Row 5: Fleming, Hardesty, Williams, Sciacia, Smith, Lee, Worrall, Smith, Ward, Linnihan. Row 6: Manager Watkins, Lawler, Moynihan, Freeman, Emas, Tyler, Whiteside, Stott, Presberry, Pratt, Manager Krapfl. Row 7: Manager Krapfl, Coach Fletcher, Coach Merritt, Coach Braudrick, Coach Heinemann, Coach Zemke, LaMartina, Brown, Reed, Coach Wade, Coach Velten, Coach Olderman, Trainer Russell.

Friendship Queen
Jasmun Norful

Webster Footbal Head Coach: Ray Moss

Row 1: Gewinner, Simmons, McCormick, Hildebrandt, Walker, Trevino, Smith, Osuegbu. Row 2: Shipp, Velten, Haessig, Granderson, Hittler, Fagnani, Linhorst, Bailey, Grandberry. Row 3: Burnett, Holmes, Downs, Frasie, Eason, Washington, Ming, Whittaker, Odenwald. Row 4: Harrison, Beard, Koch, Givens, Smith, Michael, Ranciville, Jessups. Row 5: Sullivan, Jenkins, Worth, Sheppard, Armstead, Ebberson, Jones, Bennett, Nea, Coach Tomko, Coach Hardin, Coach Cannon, Coach Sunderland, Coach Ice, Coach Gillian, Coach Lieberoff, Coach Yarmon, Coach Kirksey
Not Pictured: Sims, Howard, Butler, Stamps, Granderson, Hayes, Luster, Roberts, McDowell, Thompson, Harper, West.

I REMEMBER THE CHILLS

Turkey Day is more than a football game. It is 100 years of tradition that goes far beyond the game. There are the bonfires, pep rallies, chili cookoffs, and the Turkey Day Run that winds its way through the streets of Kirkwood, Glendale, and Webster Groves. Class reunions and alumni games from other sports are even scheduled to coincide with the Turkey Day game.

To be a spectator at the Turkey Day game is one thing. But to have the opportunity to participate as a coach or player in the oldest continuous high school rivalry west of the Mississippi is something that is very difficult to describe. The feeling that comes with participating is something you have to experience to understand. I remember the chills in my spine during my first Turkey Day game in 1989 and having that same feeling each year thereafter. I used to get great pleasure from watching some of the players on the field playing at a level I didn't think they were capable of simply because it was Thanksgiving. And the tears. There were always tears; either of joy or sorrow, depending on how the game turned out.

I felt extremely honored to be able to carry on the tradition of Turkey Day that had been set before me by the great players and coaches who had competed against each other at Moss Field and at Lyons Field. Although I am no longer coaching football, I still get great pleasure from being able to experience the game as a spectator and fan.

By Kenneth W. Manwarring
Webster Football Head Coach 1990-1998
Written July 27, 2007

" THERE WERE **ALWAYS TEARS**; EITHER OF **JOY** OR **SORROW** "

"My first year as Head Coach we were fourth and one on our twenty-yard line. The game was 17-13 with us winning with less than a minute to play. We had two punts already blocked and I thought 'how can they stop my fullback?' On the play, the fullback never got the ball and the quarterback was sacked. Webster had four plays to score, but didn't... I was almost a one-year coach."

— Michael D. Wade, 2007

Turkey Day to me is tradition, a way of life for two communities. I remember watching the movie *Hoosiers* for the first time. It recounts the Indiana State Championship basketball game in the 1950s and how the small town of Hickory shut down for the game. Kirkwood is like that. Thanksgiving Day means the Turkey Day Game. Very quickly in my career, I understood it was so much more than the "game." It is the connection and the reconnection of generations of people through the game of football. It is the story of games past. It is seeing fathers and sons and, yes, even fathers and daughters, walking into the Turkey Day Breakfast together. During my years as coach, our team won more than we lost, but when I think of Turkey Day, I really don't think of the scores, I think of the faces, the traditions, and all our shared memories.

By Michael D. Wade
Kirkwood Football Head Coach 1994 – 2003
Written September 7, 2007

THE GOOD, THE BAD AND THE UGLY

When reading such a wonderful story with so many great people and events attached to it, I increasingly had to ask myself on which negative events I should dwell and for what duration of time should there be spent on such negativity. From a writer's perspective, controversy is good for generating interest and it provides balance for the story. I would be remiss if I did not offer some explanation to the negative events over the years, so I have chosen to address them in this article, so as to not leave the instances ignored and to give the details that I believe people desire to know and state their relevance or irrelevance to the game.

The first controversial events of the book I believe are suitably addressed; the accidental shooting of a Webster player by a hunter in 1913, the morning of the Turkey Day Game, the background and unfolding of events for the 1923 riot and the near riot of 1938 and its positive aftermath.

In the modern era, there are three other events that have cast shadows on the game; a Kirkwood player thought to be ineligible in 1985 and 1986, a shooting that occurred in the parking lot of Moss Field after the 1992 Turkey Day Game and the conviction of a Webster player for the repeated sexual assault of a minor.

In regards to the Kirkwood player who was thought to be playing ineligibly, this is an instance in which the school administrators and the player were deemed to be not at fault by the Missouri State High School Activities Association. Rumours have persisted that Kirkwood forfeited games in which the player had played in the 1985 season, which are also baseless. It is unfortunate that the player has had to endure such rumours and have his reputation besmirched.

The shooting that occurred in 1992 is a very sensitive topic, as several people have mentioned that the shooting was not motivated by the Turkey Day Game or any animosity between Webster and Kirkwood students. The circumstances of this incident involve a Webster student, whose brother lost a fist-fight to another adolescent that morning. The fact that one of the adolescents was from Kirkwood and the other from Webster had little to do with the fight. The adolescent, who fired the weapon, first attempted to find his brother's assailant at the Turkey Day Game and then, after being ejected from the game, retrieved the gun from home and hid near the parking lot waiting for the game to end to settle the matter. Upon locating the Kirkwood student, the assailant sprang from the bushes and fired the weapon, wounding his intended target in the leg, while also misfiring and wounding a Kirkwood woman walking with her young niece. The woman was injured severely and spent many months in the hospital recuperating. The senselessness of the incident requires no other comment or explanation and everyone is relieved to know that there were no fatalities involved with the incident, the perpetrator spending time in prison.

Finally, after showing much promise for a professional football career, a Webster player was indicted in 2004 for sexually molesting a 10-year old girl over a two year period of time. The player was convicted of a sexual crime and ordered not to play collegiate football, causing him to lose his scholarship. Because Webster's teams in 2002 and 2003 played in the Show-Me Bowl Championship Game, this player does not have a strong connection to the Turkey Day Game and its story.

So stated, are the darkest times between the two schools. It is sad that such events stand to cast shadows on so many wonderful moments and heroes that have existed over the years for this game and rivalry. It is my hope that now that you have read this article, it is one which you will never again read as there are so many other better and more interesting stories.

Shawn Buchanan Greene
Webster Alumnus, 1987
Written July 12, 2007

THE 2000S...........

Although incomplete, it can be said that the first decade of the new millennium was heavily influenced by the attack on the World Trade Center. Hip-Hop was now the most popular music of the time and a University City High School graduate, Nelly, had a string of hits being played on radios around the world. Having learned from previous wars, Republicans and Democrats struggled to find a way to debate aspects in favour and in opposition to the war, without undermining the troops that were bringing the President's policy to action. Mathematicians lamented the celebration of the new millennium on the eve of December 31, 1999, knowing that there was no such thing as a year "0," and therefore also knowing that the new millennium would start in 2001.

Just before the new millennium, Coach Ice would win his first Turkey Day Game in 2000 and then the next year he would be the first coach to win a Turkey Day Game in the new millennium in 2001. Coach Wade would win Kirkwood's first Turkey Day Game of the new millennium in 2002 at Webster.

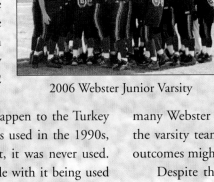

2006 Webster Junior Varsity

Despite the paranoia of what might happen to the Turkey Day Game if the Turkey Day Proposal was used in the 1990s, now known as the Turkey Day Agreement, it was never used. The new Millennium started its first decade with it being used three times, much to the dismay of the alumni of the game. In 2002, the Missouri State High School Activities Association changed the sizing system, eliminating the "As" and replaced the system with straight numbers, also adding an additional division. The sizes of the school divisions now ran from Classes 1-6, with Webster assigned to Class 5 and Kirkwood assigned to Class 6. In its first year as a Class 5 school, Cliff Ice fielded Webster's third State Championship team, causing the Turkey Day Agreement to be used for the first time.

There is much contention as to how the Turkey Day Agreement was used in 2002 and again in 2003, as Webster again went to, but lost, the Missouri State High School Activities Association Class 5 Championship Game. While the Turkey Day Agreement permits the use of varsity players for any duration of time agreed to by the coaches prior to the game, the fact remains that no coach wants to needlessly risk injuring a varsity player two or three days prior to a State Championship Game and as a result, the agreement that was reached was that only freshmen and sophomores would play the Turkey Day Game, ostensibly making it a junior varsity game. Some alumni were upset by this decision and felt both that a time-honoured tradition was being forsaken and that they were being shown below average football. Reinforcing their belief was that while Webster went to the State Championship Game two years in a row, winning one of them, the Turkey Day Game records show Webster with defeats for those two years in the Turkey Day Game. It is still believed by many Webster alumni that if the junior and senior members of the varsity team had any time to play in the games, then their outcomes might have been different.

Despite the varsity teams not playing in the 2002 Turkey Day Game, Mark Bowden was hired by *Sports Illustrated* as a freelance writer to write an article regarding the Turkey Day Game between Kirkwood and Webster Groves, which appeared in the December 9 issue of that year. Bowden is connected to Webster Groves through his mother, who is a 1942 alumna. Bowden, who works for the *Philadelphia Inquirer*, wrote a well known book titled *Black Hawk Down*, which was subsequently made into a movie, for which he also wrote the screenplay.

The 1943 teams reunited at Turkey Day 2003. Ed Carmody (K), Jimmy Allen (W), Carl Deutch (W), Paul Richter (K), Bud Reifsteck (W), Bud Stein (W), Bob Harper (K), Jack Frier (W), Dick Koch (W), Dan Croghan (W).

FOR WHOM THE FRISCO BELL TOLLS

At the end of the 2003 season, Mike Wade resigned as Kirkwood's head coach, so that he could become a school class principal. A school class principal's job is to manage the students of a particular age group throughout their yearly advancement through the school. The idea is for the class principals to get to know the students in their charge very well over their four-year advancement through the school. His resignation was a result of a long-standing Kirkwood School District policy that before any person could accept a job as a school administrator they would have to resign any coaching duties that they had.

In 2004, Larry Frost would become Kirkwood's new football head coach. Lawrence Paul Frost was born January 28, 1951 in Saint Louis, Missouri. He graduated from Normandy High School and was an All-Metro player in football. Frost graduated from the University of Missouri in 1974 with a degree in Special Education and played in the Fiesta Bowl with their team in 1972. After graduation, Frost became a member of the National Football League Saint Louis Cardinals, but was released before the start of the season. Frost then attended Northeast Missouri State University and earned a Master's degree in Health and Physical Education.

In his first year as head coach in 2004, Larry Frost would win the Turkey Day Game in one of the most exciting games in two decades, by the score of 24-23. In 2005, both Kirkwood's and Webster's freshman teams from 2002, were now poised to possibly play the Turkey Day Game for four years in a row for the first time in history. Kirkwood's team in 2005 was an exceptional group, who seemed likely to go to the State Championship Game. To the elation of Webster and Turkey Day Game fans, Kirkwood lost to Hazelwood Central 36-28 in the semifinal game. The teams would play for a record fourth time in the Turkey Day Game, with Webster winning 20-19.

There was no doubt amongst the players at that time, which game the Kirkwood players would have wanted to play. In an interview conducted with Kirkwood tight-end and team co-captain Mike McNeill in 2005, which was indicative of most if not all of the Kirkwood players, McNeill stated that his team would rather play and win a State Championship Game than play in the Turkey Day Game. The players' desire to win a State Championship in football for the first time in Kirkwood's history is quite understandable, yet it still contrasts sharply with how important the Turkey Day Game was to players in 1979 that, with a 9-1 season record, elected to play both the Turkey Day Game and two days later play in the Show-Me Bowl and the 1945 Webster team which elected to not play the best City of Saint Louis team, so that they also could play the Turkey Day Game.

The next year in 2006, the Friendship Dance started a new tradition when both schools elected Friendship Dance Kings; Scott Jones from Kirkwood and Ned Stevens from Webster. Although 2005 was expected to be Kirkwood's first Missouri State High School Activities Association football championship season, it actually almost became a reality in 2006, as Kirkwood did make it that year to their newly assigned Class 5 Championship Game. Unfortunately, Kirkwood lost that game to Raymore-Peculiar by the score of 42-32. The 2006 Turkey Day Game was therefore for the third time played under the Turkey Day Agreement, and as had been the case in the previous two uses of the Turkey Day Agreement, although Kirkwood's varsity team went to the Championship Game, its junior varsity team lost the Turkey Day Game, this time by the score of 28-12, ironically and for a third time recording a loss in the Turkey Day Game for the school that went to the State Championship Game. So, in what was supposed to be the hundredth Turkey Day Game, it was concluded as what many considered an exhibition game.

2002 State Class 5
Champions

Friendship Queen
Adrian Drummond

Kirkwood Football (6-5) - Head Coach Michael D. Wade

Row 1: Saunders, Woolf, Watkins, Brown, Pauly, Schleiffarth, Rockel, Pott, Wolfe, Fleming. Row 2: Ruck, Marlock, Rogers, Moynihan, Lawler, Stott, Emas, Presberry, Brown, Nigh. Row 3: Manager Pauly, Deckard, Jackson, Maclin, Durham, Donald, Levy, Jackson, Clark, Williams, Ming, Manager Nieman. Row 4: Man- ager Peterson, Reed, Smith, Williams, Nigh, Poole, Cutelli, Smith, Smith. Row 5: Favel, Pittman, Marlock, Susman, Moody, Marlow, Loyd, Kundert, Fumo, Longnecker, Heintz, Spigzza. Row 6: Coach Stevener, Coach Merritt, Coach Olderman, Coach Zemke, Coach Wade, Coach Heineman, Coach Havener, Trainer Russel.

Friendship Queen
Karen Jones

Webster Football (7-3) - Head Coach Clifford W. Ice

Row 1: Ming, Eason, Shearburn, Smith, Ranciville, Watts, Baile, Buchanan, West, Frazier, Neely. Row 2: Cook, Speth, Muller, Ebberson, Bri Beard, Nea, Cook, Jenkins, McCall. Row 3: Luster, Moore, Kraft, McDowell, Washington, Shute, Bennett, Wall, Hagely, Roberts. Row 4: Koch, Whittaker, Grandberry, Harrison, Jones, Wilks, Burtnett, Lange, Odenwald. Row 5: Adams, Sullivan, Fabio, Gold, Linhorst, Granderson, Bry, Toney, Beard.

KIRKWOOD - 33 | WEBSTER - 0

Thursday, November 29, 12:00 p.m. at Lyons Field

2001

Friendship Queen
Laura Davis

Kirkwood Football (4-6) - Head Coach Michael D. Wade

Row 1: Clark, Wells, Deckard, Macklin, Jackson, Donald, Lockhart, Williams. Row 2: Manager Pauly, Pittman, Moody, Susman, Lloyd, Favell, Durham, Fumo, Johnson, Levy. Row 3: Johnson, Nigh, Jones, Ko. Smith, Smith, Williams, Cutelli, Clasen, Cronin. Row 4: Baker, Watts, Ming, Jackson, Krafft, Brown, Carr, Washington, Drummond, Dickinson, Czerniejewski. Row 5: Earnhart, Wing, Marlock, Schleiffarth, Moon, Hille, Caffey, Miller, Franks. Row 6: Manager Patterson, Turner, Hardesty, Pauley, Spiguzza, Skinner, Willis, Hartweck, Heints, Waters, Burgett. Row 7: Coach Townsend, Coach Heinemann, Coach Heinemann, Coach Velten, Coach Wade, Coach Havener, Coach Brown, Coach Brown, Coach Stevener.

Friendship Queen
Susan Barr

Webster Football (10-2) - Head Coach Clifford W. Ice

Row 1: Givens, James, Adams, Roberts, Ebberson, Jenkins, Luster, Ranciville, Williams, Jessup, Sullivan. Row 2: Hayes, Gold, Schute, West, Granderson, Kibby, Thompson, Nesbitt, Neely, Shepperd. Row 3: Tullmann, Moore, Kraft, Toney, Newman, Cook, Wilson, Fulton, Schauman. Row 4: Trainer Collins, Coach Ice, Trainer Thompson, Bennett, Beard, Smith, Helle, Coach Gillian, Coach Lieberoff, Coach Hefner.

197

Friendship Queen
Rachel Gaglio

Kirkwood Football (7-4)- Head Coach Michael D. Wade
Missouri State High School Activities Association District Champions
Row 1: Johnson, Robertson, Malnassy, Eisenbeis, Drummond, Carr, Allen, Jackson, Zofness, LaGrone, Baker, White, Czerniejewski, Herbster, Watts. Row 2: Kennedy, Pennington, Pauly, Blake, Grotha, DeBord, Kopp, Krapfl, Spencer, Lewis, McCrary, Ming, Pittman, Johnson, Kramer, Watkins. Row 3: Manager Pauly, Dickinson, Wing, Jones, Johnson, Earnhart, Hille, Krapfl, Harris, Earl, Schleiffarth, Moon, Vernon, Spiguzza, Dorsey, Krafft. Row 4: Heintz, Wood, Marlock, Dyson, Mopkins, Miller, Burgett, Nigh, Cronin, Rekart, Cejka, Skinner, Franks, Waters. Row 5: Trainer Brown, Coach Townsend, Coach Brown, Coach Hagerty, Coach Wade, Coach Havener, Coach Stevener, Coach Parini, Coach Gillespie.

.Turkey Day.
.2002.

Webster vs Kirkwood

$2.00

Friendship Queen
Karen Jones

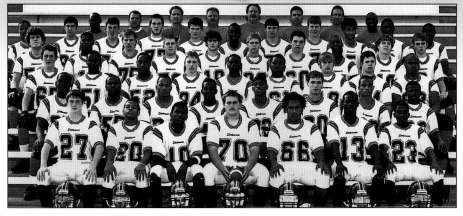

Webster Football (10-3) - Head Coach Clifford W. Ice
Missouri State High School Class 5 Champions
Row 1: Rogan, Jackson, Brotherton, Wilson, Webster, McClean, Neely, Gold. Row 2: Murray, Schauman, Aubuchon, Koscielniak, King, Campbell, Nesbitt. Row 3: Nesbitt, Patterson, Beard, Coleman, May, Stokes, T Sutherlin, Johnson. Row 4: Tullmann, Cook, Kibby, Bohannon, Kraft, Ivy, Diederichsen. Row 5: Runyon, Duke, Odman, Loudill, Boyd, Whitledge, Helle, Neunreiter. Row 6: Coach Ice, Thompson, Clayborn, Adams, Wilson, Brehmer, Jackson, Maher, Coach Kirksey. Row 7: Coach Lieberoff, Coach Broadnax, Coach Gillian, Coach Abegg, Coach Cartier, Coach Manwarring, Coach Roach, Coach Gray.

Friendship Queen
Kristin Heitz

Kirkwood Football (8-3) - Head Coach Michael D. Wade

Row 1: Kotovsky, Johnson, Lewis, Dorsey, Jones, Norman, Cronin, Caffey, Mopkins, Zofness, McCrary, George. Row 2: Athletic Director Velten, Fechter, Jones, Skinner, La Grone, Harris, DeBord, Hille, Vernon, Miller, Dickinson, Waters, Wing, Eisenbeis, Pennington, Coach McGee. Row 3: Coach Napoli, Underwood, Pryce, Lakey, Johnson, Drummond, Baker, Chapman, Rice, Broeder, Garey, Hurst, Williams, Wagner, Gray, Coach Clark. Row 4: Shih, Krapfl, Hadler, Eckwood, Grotha, Braddy, Baldenweck, McNeill, Lothman, Dyson, Nieman, Kramer, Maclin, Lockhart-Korris. Row 5: Coach Woolf, Coach Bensinger, Coach Townsend, Coach Hagerty, Coach Wade, Coach Havener, Coach Stevener, Coach Taylor, Coach Davis, Coach Parini.

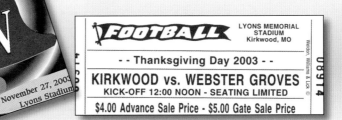

LYONS MEMORIAL STADIUM
Kirkwood, MO

FOOTBALL

- - Thanksgiving Day 2003 - -

KIRKWOOD vs. WEBSTER GROVES
KICK-OFF 12:00 NOON - SEATING LIMITED
$4.00 Advance Sale Price - $5.00 Gate Sale Price

08914

Friendship Queen
Susan Barr

Webster Football 10-3)- Head Coach Clifford W. Ice
Missouri State High School Activities Association Class 5 Second Place

Row 1: Walker, King, JSchute, Murray, Wilson, McLean, Brotherton, Jackson. Row 2: Sutherlin, Brehmer, Johnson, Nesbitt, McGraw, Webster, Aubuchon, Schauman, Rogan. Row 3: Runyon, Williams, Bohannon, Williams, Stokes, Carlson, Patterson, Nixon, Lashmett. Row 4: Jackson, Neunreiter, Odman, McClure, Loudill, Duke, Fitzgerald, Whitledge, Ivy, Banks. Row 5: Coach Liberoff, Coach Gray, Coach Kirksey, Coach Thomas, Coach Abegg, Coach Nicastro, Coach Manwarring, Coach Broadnax, Coach Gillilan. Row 6: Coach Collins, Coach Ice, Coach Kirksey.

2004

KIRKWOOD - 24 | WEBSTER - 23
Thursday, November 25, 12:00 p.m. at Moss Field

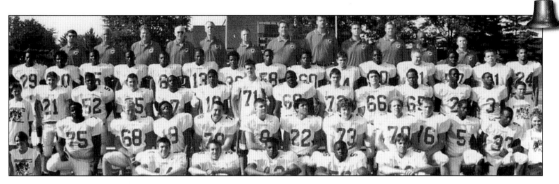

Friendship Queen
Kendra Murray

Kirkwood Football (10-2) - Head Coach Lawrence P. Frost
Row 1: McNeill, Hadler, Lyn, Dyson, Lothman. Row 2: Manager Adams, Manager Barrett, Underwood, Kotovsky, Powell, Fechter, Krapfl, Nieman, Wroughton, Pott, Grotha, Jones, Drummond, Managers Welborn & Webb. Row 3: Lakey, Collins, Schleiffarth, Garey, Harris, Haring, Turner, Pryce, Steffen, Banks, Maclin, Baker. Row 4: Cooper, Cannon, Adams, Williams, Wagner, Johnson, Williams, Lewis, McCray, Gray, Jones, Chapman, Rice, Bommarito, Lockhart-Korris. Row 5: Coach Ball, Coach Weissman, Coach O'Neal, Coach Woolf, Coach Hagerty, Coach Stevener, Coach Frost, Coach Brown, Coach Bensinger, Coach Clark, Coach Davis, Coach McGee.

Friendship Queen
Karen Jones

Webster Football (6-4) - Head Coach Clifford W. Ice
Row 1: Coach Ice, McElrath, Hill, Hull, Patterson, Barksdale, Swapshire, Farrar-Childs, Rogan, Coach Gray. Row 2: Coach Lieberoff, King, Bennett, Walker, Dixon, Owensby, Robertson, Madden, Aubuchon, Jackson, Bartley, Coach Coffman. Row 3: Coach Gillian, Schauman, Stokes, Wallace, Saleh, McCoy, Bohannon, Taylor, Hope, McLean, Coach Kirksey, Trainer Collins. Row 4: Coach Woodson, Smith, Banks, Francis, Patterson, McClure, Clayborn, Davis, Sutherlin, Conners, Ingram, Coach Abegg.

Friendship Queen
Caitlin Roth

Kirkwood Football (9-2) - Head Coach Lawrence P. Frost

Row 1: Bommarito, Williams, Lewis, Trotman, Williams, Hurst, Neealy, Wagner, Cannon, Lighten, Johnson, Adams, Yaw. Row 2: Managers Niehuas &, Brecklin, Drummond, Barker, Collins, Haynes, Barry, Jones, Steffen, Schleiffarth, Managers Pauly & Brecklin. Row 3: Coach Fischer, Coach McGee, Coach Bensinger, Coach Brown, Coach O'Neal, Coach Nixon, Coach Frost, Coach Woolf, Coach Hagerty, Coach Weissman, Coach Stevener, Coach Davis, Coach Boddy. Row 4: Brown, Pope, MacKenzie, Maclin, Harris, Powell, Kimple, Ron Taylor, Rob Taylor, Thomas, Weathers, Shepard. Row 5: White, Schaefer, Dyson, Wroughton, Grumke, Fields, Turner, Weyerich, White, Evans, Jones. Row 6: Holmes, Adzick, Korte, Haring, Graham, McNeill, Lyn.

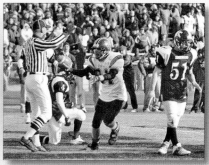

Courtesy Nordmann
Sports

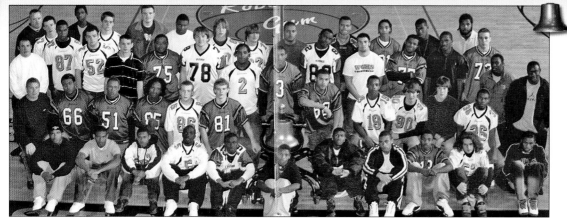

Friendship Queen
Susan Barr

Webster Football (10-1) - Head Coach Clifford W. Ice

Farrar-Childs, Swapshire, Hull, Barnett, Dace, Wrickerson, Taylor, Bowie, Michaelree, Hill, Coleman, Whittier, Morris, Watson, Mitchell, Ford, Sharp, Moss, Perry, Clayborn, Geraci, Thomas, Dixon, Davis, Madden, Bond, Menzel, Cressler, Gaikins, Bennett, Bartley, Harrell, Schute, Roberts, Wallace, Davis, Barksdale, Saleh, Stevens, Smith, Arnold, McElrath, Francis, McBride, Richards, Bennett, Boney, Conners, Robertson, Battle, Wallace, McCoy, Coach Ice, Coach Abegg, Coach Gillilan, Coach Gray, Coach Kirksey, Coach Kirksey, Coach Kirksey, Coach Lieberoff, Coach Mack, Coach Stallcup, Coach Thomas, Trainer Wright.

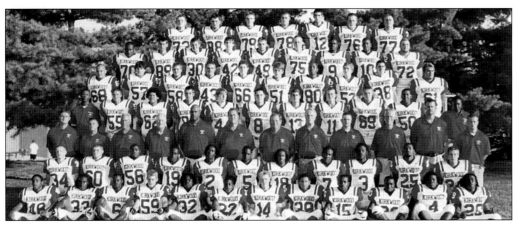

Friendship Queen & King
Jennifer Barrett
and Scott Jones

Kirkwood Football (10-2) - Head Coach Lawrence P. Frost
Missouri State High School Activities Association Class 5 Second Place

Row 1: Lewis, J Price-Cohen, Cooper, Ablin, Keller, Proctor, Turek, Terry, Trotman, Cannon, Adams, Williams. Row 2: Yaw, Yaw, Williams, Johnson, Granderson, Austin, Davis, Williams, Stingfellow, Hopfer. Row 3: Coach Bensinger, Coach McGee, Coach Weissman Coach Woolf, Coach Nixon, Coach Frost, Coach O'Neal, Coach Hagerty, Coach Stevener, Coach Yarborough, Coach Brown, Coach Fisher. Row 4: Thomas, Goeke, Merriweather, Brennan, Staten, Backer, Harris, Broeder, Albrecht, Jones, Neely. Row 5: Pauly, Weyerich, Bussman, Preston, Mackenzie, Haynes, Brown, Clemins, Boyer, Watson. Row 6: Fields, Dalgaard, Drochelman, Duggan, Grumke, White, Evans, Harris, Barker. Row 7: Schleiffarth, Adzick, Graham, Haring, Homeyer, White, Schaefer.

Friendship Queen
& King
Karen Jones and
Ned Stevens

Webster Football (4-6) - Head Coach Clifford W. Ice

Whittier, Mitchell, Ingram, Barnett, Dace, Wrickerson, Eason, Davidson, Wilson-Topps, Menzel, Stricland, Morris, Watson, Bowie, Times, Moye, Carr, Perry, Thomas, Booker, McMiller, Davis, Wadley, Moss, Gaikins, Binder, Lyles, Cressler, Wallace, Edwards, Sullivan, Hadley, Barksdale, Stevens, Sandefur, Arnold, Burley, Williams, Richards, Bennett, Boney, Michaelree, Olateru, Toney, Sherril, McCoy, Coach Ice, Coach Kirksey, Coach Lieberroff, Coach Gray, Coach Mack, Coach Abegg, Coach Stallcup, Coach Dwi. Kirksey, Coach Dwa. Kirksey, Trainer Wright.

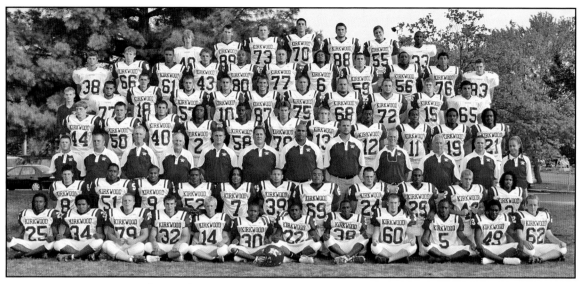

Kirkwood Football - Head Coach Lawrence P. Frost

Webster Football - Head Coach Clifford W. Ice

2007 WEBSTER

What is an All-Star? It is an opinionated designation that states that a player is best of all others under consideration in a category. While this author felt that such designations are superfluous and often times politically motivated, it was too great a temptation to not design an All-Centennial team for this book. The All-Centennial team is not to be confused with the All-Century teams being selected by the high schools, but rather it is only the opinion of the Turkey Day Game Book Committee. We have chosen to evaluate the best player of each decade as they competed against their peers, otherwise the list would be too heavily weighted with players who have played recently. With no further ado, here are the Turkey Day Game All-Centennial Teams:

WEBSTER ALL-CENTENNIAL TEAM	
DECADE	PLAYER
1900s	Fred Heath
1910s	Al Lincoln
1920s	Joe Lintzenich
1930s	Gale Keane
1940s	Jack Frier
1950s	Hank Kuhlman
1960s	Bill Southworth
1970s	Joel Blunk
1980s	Keith Jones
1990s	Antwian Davis
2000s	Mike Whittier
Coach	Charles A. Roberts

Webster Cheerleaders

Moss Field 2007

KIRKWOOD ALL-CENTENNIAL TEAM	
DECADE	**PLAYER**
1900s	Oscar Mudd
1910s	Maitland McKee
1920s	George Harsh
1930s	Malcolm Patrick
1940s	Henry Christmann
1950s	Alan Coggan
1960s	Phil Landis
1970s	Steve Powell
1980s	Alvin Miller
1990s	Alvin Morrow
2000s	Jeremy Maclin
Coach	Dale L. Collier

Kirkwood Cheerleaders

Kirkwood
Dance Squad

Lyons Field 2007

HISTORY OF THE TURKEY DAY BREAKFAST

The first gathering on Turkey Day by a bunch of former Kirkwood High Football players wasn't as you might think. In fact, it's best to call it a merger of several different groups.

First to the mid 1950s... Seven or eight friends from the classes of 1948-1950, including David Lee Jones, Jr. and Carroll Mace, began getting together on Thanksgiving evening. No one can remember with any degree of accuracy just why they got together or what they talked about. None can even remember where they met. This is surprising to the author, because these guys really aren't that old yet to be losing their marbles.

Sometime around 1963, another group of alumni football players from the late 1930s and early 1940s started gathering at the Geyer Inn on Thanksgiving morning before the Turkey Day Game. The Geyer Inn at that time was owned and operated by a former KHS football quarterback by the name of Karl Degley. The group was composed of Karl, Kay Felker, Bob Mika, Bob Hizing, Walter Goeggle, Fred Kinyon and John Williams.

In 1968, an individual by the name of King Martin (Class of '45) thought it would be good to get all the separate groups together and have a breakfast of Thanksgiving morning to honor the long tradition of Kirkwood football and the Turkey Day Game. King was the only 4-year varsity football letterman Kirkwood ever had and the Captain of the 1944 football team, and he was appointed by the group to officially run the breakfast. King Martin did so for 32 consecutive years until 1995.

By the mid 1970s, the attendance had now surpassed 70 people, and this prompted a move to a larger banquet room at the Howard Jonson's on South Kirkwood Road. It met there until the crowd again outgrew the space, and in 1989 the group met at the Loop Lounge where former St. Louis football tight end Jackie Smith was the speaker.

Just one year later, in 1990, the Kirkwood Football Alumni & Friends Turkey Day Breakfast, as it is now known, began meeting in the cafeteria at Kirkwood High School at the invitation of high school principal Franklin McCallie. The first breakfast held at the high school had over 150 people in attendance, had at least 10 father-son alumni present, and over 40 graduates of various classes before 1945. The oldest attendees were Eddie Mack of the class of 1919 and Harlan Gould of the class of 1920.

King Martin retired in 1995 and died a year later, but the Thanksgiving morning breakfast continues on in his honor. Year 2000 was the 33rd breakfast anniversary (officially) of the group. The oldest members in attendance were Harry J. Kaufmann (class of 1936) and Sherwood Hughes (class of 1937). We invite you to join us. Come have breakfast with your classmates and fellow team members each Thanksgiving morning at 8:00 a.m. Participate in the festivities of Turkey Day football. Keep the tradition alive.

By Charles Fuszner
Kirkwood Alumnus 1973
Written for the Kirkwood Football
Alumni Association in 2005

The Kirkwood Football Alumni Association

King Martin (right, facing camera) at the 1941 game

WINNING PHOTO

I photographed my first Turkey Day in 1991 when I was contemplating a career in photography. My son Paul was playing in the game for Webster Groves and I remember being nervous and excited on that particular day. My turkey was in the oven, family in tow and I forged ahead to the field. I had three rolls of film in my camera bag, one lens and one camera. I was nervous being on the field with all of the players and coaches. There were also a lot of alumni football players on the field. I remember the excitement on the field as well as in the stands. It was electric. I shot my few rolls of film and got a few good shots. By the way, the only points scored by Webster Groves that day were by my son Paul with a field goal.

The next year my son Timothy started shooting by my side and, later, on assignment for the Suburban Journals and St. Louis Post-Dispatch. It was so exciting to be on the field with all of the press photographers. All the photographers were jockeying for position to capture the best image. When a catch was made or a touchdown scored, we would all eye each other to see who may have gotten the award winning image.

Our company has come a long way since that first very cold Turkey Day. We have photographed every game since producing thousands of images. We no longer use film and always come to the game with several cameras and lenses. My son Paul in 1999 took over the sporting events and created a separate company now called Nordmann Sports Photography. My other son, Kevin, took over in 2005 and is now the owner of Nordmann Sports Photography. My husband John joined us in 2004 and Timothy now has his own videography company called Nordmann Productions. We have grown our family business with two business' under one umbrella. Nordmann Photography, which specializes in high school seniors portraits and weddings and Nordmann Sports Photography, which is the premier sports photography business in the St. Louis region.

We have photographed on Thanksgivings when it has been so cold you could not feel your fingers and others when you could be wearing shorts. But we always looked forward to that one special day. It was always a day for Webster Groves High School to shine and for the Nordmann family to be an integral part of the Webster Groves community.

Lisa Nordmann
Owner, Nordmann Photography
Written September 28, 2007
Visit Nordmann Photography at:
www.NordmannPhoto.com
www.NordmannSports.com

BROADCAST HISTORY

The Thanksgiving Day Game has been heard on several radio stations over the past few decades and now has gained a local television outlet to replay form, Charter Cable. On radio, little WGNU Radio aired the Turkey Day Game on and off for years at 960 AM.

In the '80s, my new regional and national radio-television syndication company, SNI Sports Network, began producing the game as well. The SNI outlets bounced between the old 550 AM KSD Radio and 1460 AM WIL Radio. Those stations vastly improved the radio audience reach of the game to the entire metropolitan St. Louis region.

Then, in 1998, I purchased the city's top all-sports radio station, 590 AM KFNS Radio, and soon after added 100.7 FM KFNS to both simulcast the AM programming and reach to almost mid-Missouri with a solid signal. They became the new home of the Turkey Day broadcasts with a three-man broadcast crew, Dave Greene in the press box and my son, John Marecek on the sideline microphone. That first season, KFNS also arranged for a Wednesday night, pre-Thanksgiving private dinner for the Webster team and the Kirkwood team already had one in place, which allowed KFNS to broadcast "live" from both restaurants with an one-hour Turkey Day Game Special, featuring players and coaches.

At this printing, KFNS Radio is set to enter their 10th broadcasting of the game and 1120 AM KMOX Radio has been added to the local radio coverage of the 100th year anniversary game.

While in earlier years the Turkey Day Game was not broadcast on live radio, it had gained national recognition on National Football League telecasts. For years, CBS Television would broadcast a Thanksgiving Day NFL doubleheader and the game announcers would always graciously acknowledge the nation's oldest high school football traditions by giving updated scores – including Webster and Kirkwood.

The addition of local cable television coverage on tape delay is a major growth for the game in allowing the participants and fans to relive each year's classic at home for days after the game.

By Greg Marecek
Webster Alumnus 1967
Written October 7, 2007

Turkey Day 1998 - Keith Costas, Bob Costas, John Marecek and Chris Nupert

MORE THAN JUST A GAME

Four years ago, after being hired as the head football coach at Kirkwood High School, I was extremely excited about the new challenge I was about to undertake. The new administration and teaching staff I would get to know, the new coaching staff and players that I would get to lead and the new game rivalry that I would have the opportunity to coach were challenges that I had not experienced since my first year coaching at Clayton High School, over thirty years ago. Being a lifelong St. Louis resident, I thought that I had a pretty good idea what the Turkey Day Game was all about – I soon found out that I really had no idea what the Turkey Day Game means to the people that live in, or that have ties to, the two high schools and communities of Webster Groves and Kirkwood. After getting to meet many of the students, parents and residents of both communities, I realized that the game that has been played for the past ninety-nine years was not just a game, but rather a major unifying event in which both communities not only look forward to, but take a great sense of pride in being a part of. I really believe that it is this unification and pride that makes these two communities what they are.

After being involved in this event the past three years, I feel like I have gone back in time to the 1950s or '60s. Kirkwood is a school and community that possess many of the same values of that era. We have pep rallies, parades, chili cook-offs, a marching band and church services devoted to our team and the Turkey Day Game. Our Friday night football games (except for the Turkey Day Game) are attended by the whole community and our school has a superintendent that is from Texas, where they believe that football is an extremely important extra curricular activity. The entire community is interested in and follows our football program very religiously. What football coach would not want to coach here?

My first Turkey Day Game coaching experience was a memorable one. I will need to give you a little family background before getting into the game itself. My daughter Andrea is married to Christian Ryan, who is Webster Groves High School graduate and football alum, and his mother is Flo Ryan, who was the Athletic Director's assistant at Webster for a number of years (she recently retired.) We were scheduled to have Thanksgiving dinner at Christian's uncle's house… on neutral turf. The game was close, with both teams sharing the lead during the first three quarters. We were losing by two points with about 1:36 left in the game and Webster had the ball. A lot of people left before the game was over, including my family, to prepare for the Thanksgiving meal and assuming the outcome of the game was well in hand for Webster. However, on fourth down, Willie Dyson blocked their punt and we took over on about Webster's thirty-four yard-line with one time out left. We moved the ball to the eleven yard line, and on fourth and one we called time out and decided to kick a field goal with 32 seconds left in the game. The field conditions were very muddy and wet. The field had frozen with a little snow and ice over night, and was thawing during the game. It was a very difficult 28 yard kick, to say the least, under those conditions. Our field goal team went out and everyone did their job. Rob Grotha snapped, Matt Krapfle held and Jimmy Dickson kicked it through for a 24-23 victory. It was one of the most exciting finishes I have been associated with in my entire coaching career – one that I will never forget. Upon arriving at Christian's uncle's home I was greeted by my wife and daughter, who both told me that they loved me and that it was OK. I asked "You did not stay for the whole game… did you?" They both replied that they had left with about two minutes remaining. I then asked, "You don't know that we won the game in the last thirty-four seconds on a field

I remember before dinner thanking God for my family, our food, the wonderful young men that allowed me to coach them and the great football game and tradition that I got to be a part of. It just doesn't get any better than that.

goal?" They were very surprised and happy. Andrea immediately turned to her husband Christian with a funny grin and began to tease him about the outcome of the game. I found out later that Christian and his mom and dad sat on the Webster side for part of the game and on the Kirkwood side for part of the game before leaving early. The turkey tasted great, but I was too exhausted and excited to eat very much. I remember before dinner thanking God for my family, our food, the wonderful young men that allowed me to coach them and the great football game and tradition that I got to be a part of. It just doesn't get any better than that.

I have just a few closing thoughts; upon returning to school after the Thanksgiving break, my captains and I were allowed to roll the Frisco Bell through the halls, ringing it as we went for about twenty minutes of the first hour, before it was returned to its place of honor in our library. For me, it was like being a teenager in high school again. The other thought is how difficult it was, especially for our players, after losing to Hazelwood East in the semifinal game of the 2005 state playoffs, and then having to practice for the Turkey Day Game. It was one of the most difficult tasks I have had to endure as a coach.

By Lawrence P. Frost
Kirkwood Football Head Coach 2003-Present
Written July 31, 2007

DEFINING FABRIC

Turkey Day is quintessential high school football at its finest. There is nothing else like it in the St. Louis area. This event is much more than a football game; it is a family, school, and community celebration.

Cliff Ice in 1999

Turkey Day is part of family tradition and the defining fabric of two communities. Until I went through the week of hype leading up to Thanksgiving, and then stepped onto the field for my first Turkey Day; I did not understand the magnitude of the game. It is akin to a college football bowl game. The pomp and circumstance leading up to the game, you feel the sense of anticipation building throughout the week. There is a whirlwind of school and community events leading up to and surrounding the game. All of the ancillary activities of cheerleading, band, student government, friendship dance, reunions, bonfires… It is a special experience for players and coaches. There is nothing like walking onto the field and sensing the pride of two communities, hearing the roar of the crowd at kick off, and feeling the rush of victory towards the Frisco Bell.

By Clifford W. Ice
Webster Football Head Coach 1999-Present
Written August 28, 2007

TURKEY DAY 2007

In the course of writing this book and filming a documentary, I have been asked by many people what this game is in the context of history. Is it the oldest rivalry west of the Mississippi River? Is it the oldest Turkey Day Game west of the Mississippi River? Technically stated, this game is the oldest high school Turkey Day rivalry west of the Mississippi River, the oldest current Turkey Day rivalry west of the Mississippi River and the oldest high school rivalry west of the Mississippi River. When reading those words and acclaims, the game really does not seem to be that important. After all, Saint Louis being just next to the Mississippi River seems to make it virtually the first in anything just west of the Mississippi River. It should be noted that based on some limited research, some of the high school rivalries that are west of the Mississippi River that are claimants to being longer held rivalries, really are not. The three contested rivalries are those of Abilene-Chapman, in Kansas, Pueblo Central-Pueblo Centennial, in Colorado and Saint Ignatius-Sacred Heart, in San Francisco, California. The San Francisco rivalry claims its start in 1893, while the other two claim 1892. In the case of the schools claiming their rivalries began in 1892, none of them have

documented evidence of the series, making their claims suspect. The San Francisco claimants began playing continuously starting around 1920 and played perhaps two games between 1893 and 1920. Does the playing of two games in 27 years constitute a rivalry? If so, then every single game that a school played would constitute a rivalry. In effect, unless a rivalry is continuous, which has been the Webster-Kirkwood claim, a game is not a rivalry. I rivalry must be continuous, not dating from the first time that the teams played, but rather from the time that it became a consistent, and heated, affair.

The research done for this book now dates the Webster-Kirkwood rivalry to 1901, when the first documented score between the two schools has been found. Further evidence suggests that there may be scores dating to 1899 and perhaps earlier. If these scores can be found, then this rivalry will continue to move up the oldest high school football rivalries list. Presently, the Webster-Kirkwood rivalry shares the twenty-fourth position with the Woodberry Forest School-Episcopal High School rivalry in Virginia. In regards to the first Turkey Day Game, that unfortunately was started in 1907 and nothing can be done to move that

Tom Gibson
1903-1903

Charlie Roberts
1907-1931

Froebel Gaines
1932-1934

John McArtor
1935-1940

Ray Moss
1941-1964

Jack Jones
1965-1989

Ken Manwarring
1990-1998

Cliff Ice
1999-Present

tradition earlier. However, the only older Turkey Day Game that has been found west of the Mississippi River than Webster-Kirkwood is the game that was held between the University of Kansas and the University of Missouri. Their Turkey Day Game started in 1891 but was switched to a game the week of Thanksgiving in the early 1950s.

Another issue commonly mentioned is that there have not been 100 games between the two schools. Actually, there probably have been more than 100 games. There were definitely games in 1901, 1902, 1903, 1906, 1909 and 1911 and likely games in 1904 and 1905. Combine those games with the additional games played in 1907, 1908 and 1983 and you have an additional twelve games to add to the record, which more than offset the seven games that are listed as having been cancelled.

Depending upon how you count the series, 2007 is a significant year. Due to the confusion of counting an anniversary versus counting games played between the schools, some people have difficulty in knowing what to call the game in 2007. Is 2007 the 100th Anniversary Game or is it the Centennial Game, despite that this year should be the 101st Turkey Day Game

between the two schools? In my opinion, a rivalry does not exist until you play for a second time, but truthfully there is no easy answer other than to say that it is a deserved celebration no matter what you call it. This book exists not just to satiate the curiosity of those that buy the book in 2007, but in effect to document for posterity a history whose earliest materials will have vanished by 2107. There are many that are fighting to keep this tradition alive and they know that their fight is not in vain. With the observance of this milestone event, administrators from both schools are examining the Turkey Day Agreement to find a way to allow the Turkey Day Game to be played by the schools' best squads, while simultaneously being able to participate in the Show-Me Bowl. The message for those of 2107, the year of the Bicentennial Game, is that if this game does not exist for you, then shame on you that allowed it to die, for you have failed not just the communities of Kirkwood and Webster Groves, but our nation because it is a nation's honouring of its traditions that define its character.

W. C. Ashley
1913-1915

Ed Beumer
1916-1918

Hap Bernard
1919-1922

Ernie Lyons
1928-1948

Bill Lenich
1949-1972

Ron Marler
1973-1979

Dale Collier
1980-1993

Mike Wade
1994-2003

Larry Frost
2004-Present

GAME RECORDS AND STATISTICS

Webster-Kirkwood Football Rivalry Record 1901-2006   WG 59 – KW 42 – 5 Tied

Webster-Kirkwood Turkey Day Game Record 1907-2006   WG 48 – KW 37 – 5 Tied

DATE	TIME	DAY	FIELD	WG	KW
1901-10-12		Saturday		22	0
1902-10-11	3:00 p.m.	Saturday	KHS Athletic Field	16	0
1903-00-00			cow pasture	25	14
1904-00-00					
1905-00-00					
1906-09-00	3:00 p.m.		WHS Athletic Field	6	0
1907-10-05	3:00 p.m.	Saturday	The Stadium	0	5
1907-11-04	3:00 p.m.	Monday	WHS Athletic Field	0	6
1907-11-28	**3:00 p.m.**	**Thursday**	**KHS Athletic Field**	**0**	**5**
1908-11-07	3:00 p.m.	Saturday	The Stadium	12	17
1908-11-26	**3:00 p.m.**	**Thursday**	**WHS Athletic Field**	**0**	**5**
1909-10-30	3:00 p.m.	Saturday	The Stadium	23	0
1910-11-24	**3:00 p.m.**	**Thursday**	**WHS Athletic Field**	**13**	**10**
1911-11-29	3:00 p.m.	Friday	Francis Field	14	12
1912-11-28	**3:00 p.m.**	**Thursday**	**Francis Field**	**13**	**12**
1913-11-27	**3:00 p.m.**	**Thursday**	**Francis Field**	**5**	**9**
1914-11-26					
1915-11-25	**3:00 p.m.**	**Thursday**	**Francis Field**	**19**	**6**
1916-11-03	3:00 p.m.	Saturday	Francis Field	6	0
1917-11-22	**3:00 p.m.**	**Thursday**	**Francis Field**	**76**	**0**
1918-11-28					
1919-11-21	3:00 p.m.	Friday	KHS Athletic Field	7	0
1920-11-25	**3:00 p.m.**	**Thursday**	**Kopplin Field**	**7**	**0**
1921-11-18		Friday	KHS Athletic Field	7	6
1922-11-23		**Thursday**	**Kopplin Field**	**7**	**6**
1923-11-22		**Thursday**	**KHS Athletic Field**	**7**	**0**
1924-11-27					
1925-11-26					
1926-11-25					
1927-11-24					
1928-11-22	**2:00 p.m.**	**Thursday**	**Kopplin Field**	**6**	**0**
1929-11-28	**2:00 p.m.**	**Thursday**	**KHS Athletic Field**	**14**	**0**
1930-11-27	**2:00 p.m.**	**Thursday**	**Kopplin Field**	**6**	**8**
1931-11-26	**2:00 p.m.**	**Thursday**	**KHS Athletic Field**	**0**	**0**
1932-11-24	**2:00 p.m.**	**Thursday**	**Kopplin Field**	**0**	**6**
1933-11-23	**2:00 p.m.**	**Thursday**	**KHS Athletic Field**	**0**	**7**
1934-11-22	**2:00 p.m.**	**Thursday**	**Kopplin Field**	**12**	**6**
1935-11-28	**2:00 p.m.**	**Thursday**	**KHS Athletic Field**	**7**	**0**
1936-11-26	**2:00 p.m.**	**Thursday**	**Kopplin Field**	**14**	**0**
1937-11-25	**2:00 p.m.**	**Thursday**	**KHS Athletic Field**	**28**	**0**
1938-11-24	**2:00 p.m.**	**Thursday**	**Kopplin Field**	**13**	**6**
1939-11-23	**2:00 p.m.**	**Thursday**	**KHS Athletic Field**	**0**	**6**
1940-11-28	**2:00 p.m.**	**Thursday**	**Kopplin Field**	**6**	**12**

DATE	TIME	DAY	FIELD	WG	KW
1941-11-20	2:00 p.m.	Thursday	KHS Athletic Field	19	13
1942-11-26	2:00 p.m.	Thursday	Kopplin Field	12	12
1943-11-25	2:00 p.m.	Thursday	KHS Athletic Field	14	20
1944-11-23	2:00 p.m.	Thursday	Kopplin Field	0	0
1945-11-22	2:00 p.m.	Thursday	KHS Athletic Field	12	0
1946-11-28	2:00 p.m.	Thursday	KHS Athletic Field	7	6
1947-11-27	2:00 p.m.	Thursday	KHS Athletic Field	0	14
1948-11-25	2:00 p.m.	Thursday	Memorial Field	7	14
1949-11-24	2:00 p.m.	Thursday	Memorial Field	6	0
1950-11-23	2:00 p.m.	Thursday	Memorial Field	37	0
1951-11-22	2:00 p.m.	Thursday	Memorial Field	0	33
1952-11-27	2:00 p.m.	Thursday	Memorial Field	0	0
1953-11-26	2:00 p.m.	Thursday	Memorial Field	33	13
1954-11-25	2:00 p.m.	Thursday	Memorial Field	46	7
1955-11-24	2:00 p.m.	Thursday	Memorial Field	7	25
1956-11-22	2:00 p.m.	Thursday	Memorial Field	7	0
1957-11-28	2:00 p.m.	Thursday	Lyons Field	13	27
1958-11-27	2:00 p.m.	Thursday	Memorial Field	13	0
1959-11-26	2:00 p.m.	Thursday	Lyons Field	13	14
1960-11-24	2:00 p.m.	Thursday	Memorial Field	12	33
1961-11-23	2:00 p.m.	Thursday	Lyons Field	0	7
1962-11-22	2:00 p.m.	Thursday	Memorial Field	20	10
1963-11-28	2:00 p.m.	Thursday	Lyons Field	0	0
1964-11-26	2:00 p.m.	Thursday	Memorial Field	19	13
1965-11-25	2:00 p.m.	Thursday	Lyons Field	9	0
1966-11-24	2:00 p.m.	Thursday	Memorial Field	7	19
1967-11-23	2:00 p.m.	Thursday	Lyons Field	12	33
1968-11-28	2:00 p.m.	Thursday	Memorial Field	27	0
1969-11-27	2:00 p.m.	Thursday	Lyons Field	6	0
1970-11-26	12:00 p.m.	Thursday	Francis Field	22	8
1971-11-25	12:00 p.m.	Thursday	Francis Field	23	8
1972-11-23	12:00 p.m.	Thursday	Memorial Field	12	8
1973-11-22	12:00 p.m.	Thursday	Lyons Field	6	7
1974-11-28	1:00 p.m.	Thursday	Memorial Field	14	17
1975-11-29	12:00 p.m.	Saturday	Lyons Field	15	14
1976-11-25	12:00 p.m.	Thursday	Moss Field	6	24
1977-11-24	12:00 p.m.	Thursday	Lyons Field	28	7
1978-11-23	12:00 p.m.	Thursday	Moss Field	48	0
1979-11-22	12:00 p.m.	Thursday	Lyons Field	28	6
1980-11-29	12:00 p.m.	Saturday	Moss Field	14	28
1981-11-26	12:00 p.m.	Thursday	Lyons Field	0	7
1982-11-25	12:00 p.m.	Thursday	Moss Field	7	14
1983-11-14	7:00 p.m.	Monday	Busch Stadium	0	14
1983-11-24	12:00 p.m.	Thursday	Lyons Field	12	17
1984-11-22	12:00 p.m.	Thursday	Moss Field	27	14
1985-11-29	9:00 a.m.	Friday	Busch Stadium	28	11
1986-11-27	12:00 p.m.	Thursday	Moss Field	16	19
1987-11-26	12:00 p.m.	Thursday	Lyons Field	0	2

DATE	TIME	DAY	FIELD	WG	KW
1988-11-24					
1989-11-23	**12:00 p.m.**	**Thursday**	**Lyons Field**	14	16
1990-11-22	**12:00 p.m.**	**Thursday**	**Moss Field**	9	0
1991-11-28	**12:00 p.m.**	**Thursday**	**Lyons Field**	3	21
1992-11-26	**12:00 p.m.**	**Thursday**	**Moss Field**	8	6
1993-11-25	**12:00 p.m.**	**Thursday**	**Lyons Field**	12	24
1994-11-24	**12:00 p.m.**	**Thursday**	**Moss Field**	13	17
1995-11-23	**12:00 p.m.**	**Thursday**	**Lyons Field**	36	35
1996-11-28	**12:00 p.m.**	**Thursday**	**Moss Field**	33	12
1997-11-27	**12:00 p.m.**	**Thursday**	**Lyons Field**	0	35
1998-11-26	**12:00 p.m.**	**Thursday**	**Moss Field**	14	43
1999-11-25	**12:00 p.m.**	**Thursday**	**Lyons Field**	6	14
2000-11-23	**12:00 p.m.**	**Thursday**	**Moss Field**	31	9
2001-11-29	**12:00 p.m.**	**Thursday**	**Lyons Field**	14	10
2002-11-28	**12:00 p.m.**	**Thursday**	**Moss Field**	14	28
2003-11-27	**12:00 p.m.**	**Thursday**	**Lyons Field**	0	14
2004-11-25	**12:00 p.m.**	**Thursday**	**Moss Field**	23	24
2005-11-24	**12:00 p.m.**	**Thursday**	**Lyons Field**	20	19
2006-11-23	**12:00 p.m.**	**Thursday**	**Moss Field**	28	12
2007-11-22	**12:00 p.m.**	**Thursday**	**Lyons Field**		

TURKEY DAY HEAD COACH BIOGRAPHICAL INFORMATION

Webster

Clifford Wayne Ice	1964-09-16	Thomas, OK
Kenneth Wayne Manwarring	1959-05-02	Bonne Terre, MO
Jack Merle Jones	1938-11-22	Saint Louis, MO
Raymond Woodson Moss	1913-09-02	Hallsville, MO
John Trusten McArtor	1908-05-06	Saint Louis, MO
Frank Froebel Gaines	1899-07-25	Sidell Township, IL
Charles Arthur Roberts	1880-11-13	Revere, MO
A. W. McCollough		
Tom L. Gibson	1882-10-20	Webster Groves, MO

Kirkwood

Lawrence Paul Frost	1951-01-28	Saint Louis, MO
Michael David Wade	1960-08-18	Duluth, MN
Dale L. Collier	1941-09-23	Saint Louis, MO
Ronald Lowell Marler	1935-09-10	Flat River, MO
William T. Lenich	1917-12-02	Joliet, IL
Ernest Lee Lyons	1898-09-11	Oletha, IL
Albert "Hap" Bernard		
Edward H. Beumer		
W. C. Ashley		
J. F. Engerson		
Donnell Kirk		
Robert G. Kinkead		
James Hard		

WEBSTER-KIRKWOOD COACHING TENURES

WEBSTER GROVES

Cliff Ice	1999 – 2006
Ken Manwarring	1990 – 1998
Jack Jones	1965 – 1989
Ray Moss	1941 – 1964
John McArtor	1935 – 1940
Froebel Gaines	1932 – 1934
Charley Roberts	1907 – 1931
A. W. McCollough	1905 – 1906
Unknown	1904 – 1904
Tom Gibson	1903 – 1903

KIRKWOOD

Larry Frost	2004 – 2006
Mike Wade	1994 – 2003
Dale Collier	1980 – 1993
Ron Marler	1973 – 1979
Bill Lenich	1949 – 1972
Ernie Lyons	1928 – 1948
unknown	1923 – 1927
Hap Bernard	1919 – 1922
Ed Beumer	1916 – 1918
W. C. Ashley	1913 – 1915
J. F. Engerson	?1912 – 1912
Donnell Kirk	?1908 – 1908?
Robert Kinkead	1902 – 1905?
James Hard	?1901 – 1901

LARGEST POINT DIFFERENCES

1917	76-0	76 points	WG	Coach Charley Roberts
1978	48-0	48 points	WG	Coach Jack Jones
1954	46-7	39 points	WG	Coach Ray Moss
1950	37-0	37 points	WG	Coach Ray Moss
1997	35-0	35 points	KW	Coach Mike Wade
1951	33-0	33 points	KW	Coach Bill Lenich
1998	43-14	29 points	KW	Coach Mike Wade
1937	28-0	28 points	WG	Coach John McArtor
1968	27-0	27 points	WG	Coach Jack Jones
1909	23-0	23 points	WG	Coach Charley Roberts

ONE-POINT CLUB (CLOSEST GAMES)

1912	13-12	1 point	WG	Coach Charley Roberts
1921	7-6	1 point	WG	Coach Charley Roberts
1922	7-6	1 point	WG	Coach Charley Roberts
1946	7-6	1 point	WG	Coach Ray Moss
1959	14-13	1 point	KW	Coach Bill Lenich
1973	7-6	1 point	KW	Coach Ron Marler
1975	15-14	1 point	WG	Coach Jack Jones
1995	36-35	1 point	WG	Coach Ken Manwarring
2004	24-23	1 point	KW	Coach Larry Frost
2005	20-19	1 point	WG	Coach Cliff Ice

TIED GAMES

1931	0-0	Coach Charley Roberts & Coach Ernie Lyons
1942	12-12	Coach Ray Moss & Coach Ernie Lyons
1944	0-0	Coach Ray Moss & Coach Ernie Lyons
1952	0-0	Coach Ray Moss & Coach Bill Lenich
1963	0-0	Coach Ray Moss & Coach Bill Lenich
1986	13-13	(OT 19-16 KW) Coach Jack Jones & Coach Dale Collier

RIVALRY COACHING RECORDS

Gibson	1-0	1.0	1 season
McCollough			2 seasons
Roberts	14-7-1	.67	25 seasons
Gaines	1-2	.33	3 seasons
McArtor	4-2	.67	6 seasons
Moss	11-9-4	.55	24 seasons
Jones	12-13	.48	25 seasons
Manwarring	3-6	.33	9 seasons
Ice	4-4	.50	8 seasons
Hard			
Kinkead			
Kirk			
Engerson			
Ashley	1-1	.50	3 seasons
Beumer	0-3	.00	3 seasons
Bernard	0-4	.00	4 seasons
Lyons	9-11-3	.45	23 seasons
Lenich	8-14-2	.36	24 seasons
Marler	3-4	.43	7 seasons
Collier	10-4	.71	14 seasons
Wade	7-3	.70	10 seasons
Frost	1-2	.33	3 seasons

Photo, Art and Story Credits

Collections or archived sources:
Alton High School www.Alton.Madison.k12.il.us
Clayton High School www.Clayton.k12.mo.us
Beaumont High School www.SLPS.org
Kirkwood High School www.Kirkwood.k12.mo.us
Kirkwood Historical Society www.KirkwoodArea.com
Kirkwood Public Library kpl.lib.mo.us
Kirkwood School District R-7 www.Kirkwood.k12.mo.us
Saint Louis University www.SLU.edu
Truman State University www.Truman.edu
Webster Groves High School www.Webster.k12.mo.us
Webster Groves Historical Society www.HistoricWebster.org
Webster Groves Public Library wgpl.lib.mo.us
Webster Groves School District www.Webster.k12.mo.us
Webster-Kirkwood Times www.TimesNewspapers.com

Professional photographic sources:
Photography www.KriewallPhotography.com
Nordmann Photography, www.NordmannPhoto.com
Nordmann Sports Photography, www.NordmannSports.com

Other groups and individual sources:
Carole Lintzenich Buck
Charter Communications www.CharterCom.com
Dale Collier

Cindy Jones Coombs
Erv Dunkel
Greg Filley
Sean Funcik
Don Gaines
Shawn Buchanan Greene
Dave Jones, Jr.
Bob Krone
Ima Lincoln
Audrey Lyons Marti
Ray Pepin
Tom Poshak
Charles A. Schneider
Penny Stein

Professional artistic sources:
Mark Arnold www.AndArnold.com
Marilynne Bradley www.MGBrad.com

Additional story credits:
Webster Groves Historical Society
    A Word From ...Our Coach, page 30
    Foot Ball, page 32
    The Kirkwood-Webster Contest, page 33
    Webster Defeats Kirkwood, 6-0, page 36

Photo Courtesy of Nordmann Photography

Turkey Day Game Book Committee
Candice Gwin, Shawn Greene, Charles Schneider, Erin Schafers, Mike Kearney